The Christian Idea of Education

THE CHRISTIAN IDEA
OF EDUCATION

PAPERS AND DISCUSSIONS BY

WILLIAM G. POLLARD

E. HARRIS HARBISON

ALAN PATON

MASSEY H. SHEPHERD, JR.

JOHN COURTNEY MURRAY, S.J.

JACQUES MARITAIN

GEORGES FLOROVSKY

REINHOLD NIEBUHR

STEPHEN F. BAYNE, JR.

EDITED BY EDMUND FULLER

A Seminar at Kent School

ARCHON BOOKS   1975

© 1957 by the Kent School Corporation
First published 1957 by Yale University Press.
Reprinted 1975 with permission in an unabridged
edition as an Archon Book, an imprint of
The Shoe String Press, Inc.,
Hamden, Connecticut 06514

Printed in the United States of America

Library of Congress Cataloging in Publication Data

Fuller, Edmund, 1914-   ed.
    The Christian idea of education. *Archon Books, 1975.*

~~Includes bibliographical references.~~
    1. Education—Philosophy—Addresses, essays, lec-
tures. 2. Church and education—Addresses, essays,
lectures. I. Pollard, William Grosvenor, 1911-   II.
Kent School, Kent, Conn.   III. Title.
[LB7.F8   1975]   370.1   74-19178

ISBN 0-208-01470-5

265p.
22cm.

LB
7
F8
1975

To the memory of Edward T. Gushee,
whose energy and vision set the pattern for
Kent's Fiftieth Year celebration.

Preface

THE PAPERS and transcripts of discussions in this volume are the products of the major one of a series of events by which Kent School commemorated the fiftieth anniversary of its founding.

In November, 1955, there was held at Kent a seminar on the Christian Idea of Education. The Rev. Dr. William G. Pollard, Executive Director, Oak Ridge Institute of Nuclear Studies, was Chairman. A series of papers was presented by eight distinguished leaders. The more than 500 participating guests met in smaller group discussions, each headed by an able chairman, often with one of the chief speakers present, for conversations on the themes of the main addresses. Some 200 schools and colleges were represented.

The eight formal papers are presented here in the sequence in which they were delivered. Because the many small group meetings were so stimulating it was hoped that at least some of the high points of these might be preserved also. This was a difficult undertaking.

The excerpts from the group discussions which are inserted between the papers have been edited from some 853 pages of stenotype transcripts. They are the best, though by no means all, of the worthwhile material, and it was possible to make such transcripts at only a limited number of the meetings. No group sessions occurred after the last two addresses, hence no transcript material touches upon Father Florovsky's or Dr. Niebuhr's papers.

It is important to remember, in reading these edited transcripts, that they represent the spoken word. If, therefore, they lack something of the smoothness and clarity of the written word, they offer instead much of the excitement, immediacy, and occasional happy spontaneity of conversation.

Apart from the intrinsic value of the ideas in these excerpts, they disclose the vital quality of this seminar as a continuing dialogue. Ideas are not simply stated here—they are questioned, tested, probed, challenged. Total agreement was not achieved, nor was it expected or sought.

The Rev. John O. Patterson, Rector and Headmaster of Kent School, said, "It is our hope that this meeting may be a means of regaining and restating something of the vision of what general education could be within a Christ-centered culture."

Dr. Pollard, the Chairman, added: "The purpose of this seminar is to examine and identify in a fundamental fashion the peculiar characteristics of the educational processes and objectives which constitute the Christian idea of education. The emphasis will not be on religious perspectives in teaching, nor on the problems of the Christian teacher, but will rather be concerned with education in its entirety from a Christian viewpoint."

Accordingly the emphasis throughout is not upon method but upon concept. Definitions of existing conditions, of purposes, and of need were sought. The points of view represented among the speakers are those of educator, scientist, historian, novelist, theologian, and philosopher, from Christian roots in Anglicanism, Roman Catholicism, Eastern Orthodoxy, and Protestantism.

The interweaving of themes is one of the fascinations in this material. Dr. Pollard opens with the idea of a two-root origin of our culture—the Judaeo-Christian and Hellenic. Dr. Niebuhr closes with a pursuit of the same thought from different aspects. In a transcript, Father Murray questions this concept of twin roots.

We find Father Murray and Father Florovsky analyzing the whole problem of synthesis between Christianity and non-Christian culture from strikingly different premises. Dr. Niebuhr touches the matter of synthesis, also.

Inevitably, Professor Harbison, too, discusses synthesis, in the context of an address driving to the heart of the inescapable question of the compatibility of positive religious commitment and liberal education. In so doing, he set off some of the most animated discussion of the seminar.

Father Florovsky and Dr. Niebuhr both remark the contrast between Hebraic and Hellenic concepts of time as these bear upon the significance of history.

It is interesting to see that Dr. Pollard's opening words in the first discussion transcript, and Professor Maritain's opening remarks in his address, are almost identical observations that the Christian idea of education is rooted in the Christian idea of man.

Alan Paton discusses the life of school in terms of the person in community, while Massey H. Shepherd, Jr., finds the epitome of this concept in the centering of the Christian school in the Holy Eucharist. In Alan Paton's words: "In a school . . . of Christian intention, I take part regularly in worship, prayer, and praise, so that I may remember who I am and whither I go. Above all, in the Eucharist I offer myself to Him to Whom I belong."

In keeping with its intentions, the seminar proposed no conclusions. Yet it could be said to have concurred in a conviction that before we can educate as Christians we require as a base a profound Christian insight into the nature of man and the social, natural, and supernatural orders in which he lives. Only such a grounding can bring into integration the bewildering diversity of subjects, objects, ideas, and materials involved in the process of education.

Appended to the seminar papers, by way of summation of Kent's Fiftieth Year program, is an address delivered on Prize Day by the Rt. Rev. Stephen F. Bayne, Jr., Bishop of Olympia. It was conceived as a part of this book—a drawing together of many of its threads.

The idea of the unity of truth permeated the seminar. Bishop

Bayne captured this vision of integrated knowledge and understanding vividly: "Brotherhood and the table of atomic weights and the Lord's Prayer and the history of the Hittites and the discovery of gunpowder and the Creed and the multiplication table and Heisenberg's Principle of Uncertainty and the Agnus Dei—all of this and all truth comes to us in one magnificent, tumbling hodgepodge, because it is all God's, and God is one."

It is impossible to thank adequately all those who contributed to this volume by their help in the planning and running of the seminar, and their participation in it. We are especially indebted to the President and Trustees of the Edward W. Hazen Foundation for a generous grant in aid of the publication of this book. Kent School has in preparation a number of volumes on aspects of education and study, both for student and faculty use. The present work, though arising from a different context, is a companion to these Kent text and study books.

Edmund Fuller

Kent School
Kent, Connecticut
August, 1956

Contents

Dark Age and Renaissance in the Twentieth Century

WILLIAM G. POLLARD

THE IDEA OF EDUCATION is intimately involved in culture. Indeed education is just the means by which culture transmits and reproduces itself. Thus the idea which any culture entertains about education is of necessity inextricably bound up with all the thought forms which characterize that culture and set it apart from all others.

We are creatures of mid-twentieth-century Western culture. That culture since the nineteenth century has become increasingly secular. It is dominated by scientific ways of thinking about the world and human experience, by visions of technical achievement and progress, and by deep-seated prejudices against past cultural bonds from which it has just succeeded in liberating itself after great struggle. We are immersed in that culture. We can only communicate with each other within it. Whatever we discuss must be spoken of in terms peculiar to that culture, and in thought forms rooted in its special criteria of validity and reality. This we cannot escape, however much we may long for a more genial environment in which to consider the theme of the Christian idea of education.

The decade since the end of World War II has seen an enormous ferment in the matter of religion in higher education. The extensive programs of the Hazen and Danforth Foundations; the numerous books which have been published in recent years; the growing number of periodicals such as *The Christian Scholar, Crosscurrents,* and the Faculty Papers of

1

the Episcopal Church; and the many conferences, seminars, summer institutes, and other meetings for college people being held on this theme all bear witness to the extraordinary growth of interest in it. Even the most antagonistic observers cannot fail to sense the significance and intensity of this general ferment and to acknowledge its growing importance and power.

Chiefly as a result of my taking Holy Orders I have found myself swept up into the stream of this movement and more and more heavily involved in it. It is certainly an exciting and thrilling thing of which to be a part. But at the same time I have found myself increasingly uneasy about the kinds of issues which arise, and increasingly frustrated by the framework of thought within which they are discussed. Often I have found myself overcome with a sense of impotence, as though the kinds of questions being asked and the terms in which it seemed necessary for me to answer them were alike incapable of leading to any real insight. As a result of such experiences I have become more and more convinced that the whole problem of trying to formulate deeply and meaningfully for ourselves the Christian idea of education is radically limited by the peculiarities of our contemporary cultural context. To transcend this context is like breaking out of a prison or extricating oneself from a net; it is an extraordinarily difficult undertaking, a tough business. Yet if we are really to be able to form an adequate idea of education from a truly Christian view of the nature of things, this is just what I am convinced we shall have to accomplish.

My thesis is that the most fruitful and significant category within which to consider this subject of the Christian idea of education is that of renaissance. The renaissance which began in the twelfth century consisted in the dawning recovery by the West of its lost capacity to respond meaningfully to the hidden treasures of its Graeco-Roman cultural heritage. In exactly the same way I would assert that there is beginning to dawn here in the middle of this twentieth century another renaissance in Western civilization. This time, however, it is not our Graeco-Roman heritage but rather our Judaeo-Christian cultural stem which has been lost and to whose hidden treasures Western culture is just beginning to recover the capacity to respond meaningfully. If it should be possible to maintain such a thesis, then it seems to me that it provides us with an analogy which is extremely fruitful of deep insights into the task which we of the mid-twentieth century have set ourselves in trying to formulate the Christian idea of education in our terms. Our situation would be analogous, for example, to that of a group of educators in the twelfth or thirteenth centuries gathered together for the purpose of trying to formulate the classical idea of education. We have only to try sympathetically to place ourselves in their cultural context to sense how drastically they would be limited by the bonds of that context and how inadequately equipped they would be for dealing meaningfully with their subject.

I

Let us begin then the development of this thesis. First I would point out that historically what we now designate as Western civilization was the product of the coalescence of two radically different cultural roots. One of these, the Graeco-Roman, has its origins in the Greek city states of the sixth century B.C., notably Athens, rising to the Golden Age of Periclean Athens with its later fruits in Plato and Aristotle, spreading after Alexander through the whole Mediterranean basin, and finally culminating in the magnificent flower of Roman civilization under Augustus. The other of these roots, the Judaeo-Christian, has its origin in a series of Bedouin invasions of Palestine during the fifteenth to thirteenth centuries B.C., rising to the golden age of Solomon's empire with its later fruits in the Hebrew prophets and the deuteronomic reformation, and spreading, at first during the Persian period through the Jewish dispersion, and then later, with tremendous power in the first and second centuries after Christ, throughout the whole Roman empire through the Christian Church.

These two strands of Western culture are distinctive and parallel cultures in their own right. Each has a long and full and varied history of its own. Each is a primary, distinctive, and bona fide element in the story of the ancient world. Each has its place in, and played a major role among, the nations of the Mediterranean basin. Each expressed itself through a great body of literature produced over many centuries. They are in every culturally significant way parallel in stature, importance, and duration of historic existence. When we look backward over the whole sweep of Western civilization, we cannot move continuously in a single line straight back to ancient Greece. Rather, when we come to the time of our Lord's incarnate life, we must make a distinct branching and thereafter follow independently two distinctive roads into the past: the one leading through Rome to Athens and before, and the other leading through Judah to Israel and before. Western civilization is historically a two-rooted affair.

These two cultural roots of our civilization represent radically contrasting frameworks of thought and ways of looking out upon the great central problems of life and history and destiny. One who has become thoroughly steeped in Judaean culture so that he can look out upon the world about him through the eyes of a man of Israel, is likely to find Greek letters and philosophy unintelligible, pointless, and quite unrewarding. The reverse is equally true. When, therefore, these two cultural streams became inextricably mingled as a result of the spread of Christianity through the Roman world, it was like the attempt to mix oil and water. The reaction was violent and the result was a period of great intellectual turmoil which required several centuries for its resolution. No more fascinating period in the history of human thought can be found than that between St. Irenaeus and St. Augustine in the West, or between Origen and St. John of Damascus in the East. This is Western civilization in formation. It is the record of the process by which the two radically contrasting strains of our cultural heritage were successfully brought into a delicate synthesis whose necessary complementarities gave to Western culture its unique dynamism and power.

It should not be necessary to point out such obvious central features of our history, and indeed it would not be if it were not for a remarkable bias against acknowledging even the existence of our Judaeo-Christian heritage, which has prevailed almost universally throughout our culture in the last half of the nineteenth century and the first half of this one. In my own college career in the late twenties and early thirties I had a full year's course in ancient history and another year in European history. In the former course Israel, as one of the nations of the ancient world, was completely ignored. So far as the classroom lectures and even the textbook (with the exception of two isolated paragraphs) were concerned, there was no way to tell that such a people ever had existed. We learned much about Egyptian, Babylonian, Assyrian, Persian, Greek, and Roman literature, art, thought, political history, and modes of life. But not a word was uttered about anything Hebraic from one end of the course to the other. When one considers the priceless treasure of the literature of Israel and the fact that this nation in the ninth and tenth centuries B.C. was the leading empire among all of the lands around the Mediterranean, this represents a well-nigh incredible bias.

Later in the course in European history the same bias reappeared in a different form. Here of course it did not consist in ignoring the existence of our Judaeo-Christian cultural heritage, since that would be clearly impossible. Rather, in the early stages of European history when the Roman empire was declining, Christianity was presented as if it had ap-

peared out of nowhere, very much like the several barbarian
hordes, with no cultural roots of its own. Moreover, there
was, throughout, the suggestion of a dark, almost malevolent,
and certainly acultural influence, again comparable to the
barbarians, which slowly broke down the fine flower of classical
culture and civilization and ultimately brought all Europe into
the cold night of the Dark Ages. Moving rapidly over this
period, the course, as I remember it, then entered into the
Middle Ages in which the Church during the secular power of
the papacy was presented more or less as a prison within
which Western culture was trapped. This prepared the way
for the presentation of the Renaissance as a slow and painful
extrication of Western civilization from this dark prison in
which Christianity had enslaved it, accompanied by a cor-
responding rediscovery and rebirth, to its true heritage in
which it could again derive its nourishment from its true roots
in Graeco-Roman culture.

I realize that I have painted here an extreme picture which
fails to do justice to the intricacies and subtleties of the total
situation. At the same time anyone who received a college
education twenty or more years ago will, I think, agree that
the net effect of it was to create some such general impression
as this. The cumulative effect of the whole process, developed
subtly in course after course in history, philosophy, economics,
sociology, classical languages, and the sciences, is to develop
just such a picture of the primary course of development of
the civilization of which we are a part.

This becomes especially clear when one examines the
various types of curricula in general education which a number
of colleges and universities have developed in recent years. One
of these which has been in use for some time by a midwestern
university is typical. It consists of four courses, each of which
is four semesters in duration, which are given during the fresh-
man and sophomore years in the humanities, the social
sciences, the natural sciences, and English composition and
electives. The humanities course begins in the first semester

with Greek and Roman culture. It then moves in the second semester to medieval and Renaissance culture, and is described as showing how the ancient culture was inherited, transmitted, and rediscovered. The third and fourth semesters are devoted respectively to European culture of the eighteenth and nineteenth centuries and to recent American culture. Parallel to this, the course in social studies begins with a semester called "Early Man and His Society" and is described as the rise of civilization, presented from an anthropological viewpoint, from the Stone Age to Greece. The second semester is entitled "The Transition to Industrial Society" and is described as a survey of the economic and social organization of Western Europe from late Roman times to the eighteenth century.

It is clear that any student will certainly emerge from such an educational experience as this with a one-root view of the culture of which he is a part. Everything which he holds to be real and true and of great value in Western civilization— our science and technology, our ideals for social and political structure, our literature and art—he will believe originated in our Graeco-Roman stem. Concerning our Judaeo-Christian stem he will know nothing of any real, historic, cultural root, but will be aware of it only through the fall of Rome and the seamy side of the medieval Church. With it he is likely to associate only a dogmatic, uninquiring frame of mind; the persecution of science and intellectual freedom; inquisitions, tyrannies, injustices, and indeed all forces which down through the ages have opposed and at times thwarted the progress of Western civilization. In short, he will emerge with a drastically one-sided, biased, and prejudiced view of his own history.

II

The professors who transmit this view to each oncoming generation are not consciously biased or prejudiced men. On the contrary the majority of them are dedicated to objectivity and truth. They believe the picture which they develop for their students and hold it to be true. They would be the last to assent consciously to a prejudiced or biased educational program. They all unquestionably are teaching reality as they see it.

The real problem is far more profound and basic than a mere question of intellectual dishonesty or even of a bias based on ignorance. Nor is it a difficulty which, as the preceding discussion may have implied, is peculiar to our institutions of higher learning. Rather it pervades every walk of life and every aspect of our culture from the most intellectual to the most mundane. Our basic difficulty is that we live in an age when our whole civilization has in effect lost the capacity to respond to its Judaeo-Christian heritage. Just as the dark age of a millennium ago was a period when Western culture had lost its capacity to respond meaningfully to its Graeco-Roman heritage, so the nineteenth and twentieth centuries are essentially another dark age in which the capacity of response to our other cultural root has now been just as thoroughly lost. To me the recognition of the truth of this quite sweeping assertion seems fundamental to a really meaningful grappling with the Christian idea of education.

In most universities the literary treasure of our Graeco-Roman heritage is offered by a department of classical languages and listed among the humanities, while that of our Judaeo-Christian heritage is offered as a course in Bible by a department of religion. There are in these days of science and technology few enough students who register in either, but for those who do there is a striking difference in the relationship of the courses they take to the rest of their university experience. From a reading course in the great Greek and Latin works, any student can move without strain or perturbation into any of the other courses of his university curriculum in history, science, philosophy, mathematics, business, or engineering. This he can do because the general ideas, framework of thought, and view of reality which he encounters in classical authors are entirely agreeable to those which he finds throughout all aspects of his own contemporary culture. Our Graeco-Roman heritage is very much alive today, and the capacity to respond to it meaningfully, sympathetically, and with spontaneous understanding comes naturally to us. But another student who enrolls in a class in Bible finds himself in a totally different situation. Whatever his reaction to the course may be, he cannot fail to feel the tension between the whole framework of thought which he encounters there and all the rest of his university experience. He may rebel against what he senses to be pressure toward incorporation into a traditional religious body, and so adopt a consciously unsympathetic attitude toward the course. Or he may enjoy the course and endeavor as best he can to incorporate it into his personal life as an island in the sea of his total educational experience. In either event he will be continually conscious of the tension, and this will be because the framework of thought and view of reality which he encounters in Biblical literature belong to a heritage now lost to his contemporary culture.

In recent years several universities have become conscious of the extent to which contemporary higher education ignores the Judaeo-Christian root of Western civilization, and a number of them have taken steps to reintroduce it forcibly into the curriculum. In one university which I have visited recently a basic course in the humanities required of a large number of students is called "The Greeks and the Bible." Ostensibly this seems a solution of the problem we have been considering. When, however, one examines more closely the content and manner of presentation of this course, one begins to appreciate the depth and magnitude of the problem we face. To begin with the course is taught by the English department, which, in order to handle the large number of students involved in it, has had to engage the services of large numbers of young instructors. The administration has established the content of what is to be taught through a syllabus and detailed schedule of lessons and assignments. But the teachers themselves who follow this schedule as best they can are creatures of our contemporary culture. They have earned a Ph.D. in some area of the humanities devoid of Biblical inspiration and outlook. They are at home and comfortable in Hellenic environment, but generally puzzled and uneasy in Hebraic thought forms.

This points up the futility of correcting the ills and deficiencies, the prejudices and inadequacies of contemporary culture by academic programs, curriculum revision, or administrative policy. I have said that the key to our problem is to be found in the idea of renaissance. Now a renaissance is a kind of major transformation of individual spirits which spreads mysteriously like an infection. Those who become infected by it have their eyes opened to behold a whole new range of reality whose very existence is hidden from their contemporaries. There is a heady sense of power and an exhilaration about it which cannot in any way be forced, or promoted, or planned. The rediscovery of the hidden treasure of our lost Judaeo-Christian heritage is a renaissance process, just as was the rediscovery of the hidden treasure of our lost Graeco-Roman heritage in the first Western renaissance. Only as really infected individuals find their way into the faculties of our educational institutions can anything significant happen. As Evelyn Underhill has expressed it, "If you would lead someone into the mountains, you must love the mountains."

On other occasions when I have expressed these ideas the objection has been raised that a much greater number of people in our age know about our Judaeo-Christian heritage than do about our Graeco-Roman. Many more people own Bibles than copies of Homer, Aeschylus, Cicero, or Virgil. This of course is true, but, if anything, it seems to me it only serves to give greater emphasis to the point I am trying to make. For it is truly remarkable to see how totally absent typically Biblical categories of judgment and response continue to be in the common life of people who set great store by the Bible in that isolated segment of their life which they designate and set apart as religious. In spite of the quite high percentage of affiliation with some Christian body which we have in America and the widespread dissemination of Bibles throughout the land, the effect on our basic cultural thought patterns is essentially negligible. Where, for example, in our newspapers or magazines, in radio or TV commentaries, in business and professional associations, or elsewhere in the manifold activities of contemporary Western civilization do you find evidences of the great Biblical themes of grace and providence, of sin and judgment, of the Lordship of Christ over history, of the contingency of all created things and moments on Him who stands above all creation? We simply do not think of our life and history in such terms. We would be by and large baffled and unresponsive to a newspaper editorial or radio commentator who pictured the current crises of our time within such a framework. We have really lost the capacity to look out upon our world and our history through the eyes of one standing fully within the Judaeo-Christian tradition.

There is a curious resistance from both the religious and secular elements of our contemporary life against any real or meaningful exposure to the hidden wealth of our Judaeo-Christian heritage. On the one hand, those who regard themselves as standing within the formal remnants of that heritage, the conscious representatives of Christianity or Judaism, have separated the literature by which that cultural heritage expressed its understandings and insights into its own historic experience so completely from its setting in a live human culture that it is no longer for them in any sense an expression of a cultural heritage at all. This literature has become a single, undifferentiated, and impregnable entity, the Bible. Thus removed from any relevant context in actual human history, it has by this process been effectively innoculated against acquiring the power to transport men into a sympathetic involvement in the life and outlook of the culture which produced it. On the other hand, for those who consciously stand outside the stream of the Judaeo-Christian heritage there is the constant necessity to stand guard against the claims made upon them by the institutional remnants of that heritage which hedge them about on every side. How, for example, could the ardently secular historian or student of the humanities engage in a serious study of Biblical literature and still find the strength to resist, as he must, the next religious-emphasis week which descends upon his university? So for both parties in our culture the Bible is, for different reasons, taboo, and the vast treasure of its literature by which a real people expressed a unique understanding of human destiny remains effectively locked within it. The title of the course about which we spoke earlier is interesting in this respect: "The Greeks and the Bible." The one a real culture to which we have access through literature, the other an undissociable book set apart on its own and isolated from culture. It is interesting to contemplate the reasons why course titles, such as "The Greeks and the Hebrews" or "Literature of Ancient Greece and Israel" would be quite unlikely to be chosen.

III

Nineteenth- and twentieth-century Western culture is of course a very different phenomenon from either the Hellenic or Latin cultures of classical civilization. When I say that we today are culturally nourished by our Graeco-Roman root and isolated from our Judaeo-Christian root I do not mean to imply that modern culture is patterned after or in any sense identical with classical culture. The point is rather that this stem of our cultural heritage is not at all alien to our modes of thought and understanding, whereas the other is. A college student of today who is introduced for the first time to Thucydides or Plato, to Cicero or Virgil, finds himself rather much at home in the ideas and outlooks which he encounters. He recognizes important differences, to be sure, between them and contemporary writing, but there is in them, nevertheless, very little which seems so alien that he cannot respond sympathetically from his own experience to the outlooks on life and history which he discovers there. The same student, on the other hand, even though formally associated with Christianity or Judaism and regarding himself as a committed and practicing member of a church or synagogue, nevertheless finds himself in alien territory when he comes to Biblical literature. He may read it regularly in word and proposition and even assent to it as authentic statement. But its inner life and power are quite likely to be inaccessible to him. The great Biblical themes of redemption and judgment in history, of freedom and grace and sin, of covenant and idolatry, seem strangely vague, far away, and unrelated to the ebb and flow of life and history as he understands it. It is in this sense that I mean that however much contemporary Western culture may differ from classical culture, it has retained to the full the capacity to respond to that heritage. In the same sense, however much it may have retained the institutions and outward forms of its Judaeo-Christian cultural stem, it has well-nigh completely lost the capacity to respond sympathetically and understandingly to that heritage.

If it is proper to define a dark age in Western history as a period in which the West has lost the capacity to respond to either one of its two cultural roots, then the nineteenth and twentieth centuries are just as much as the eighth and ninth a dark age. The periods when the West has been most truly itself, when its peculiar and unique dynamism and power have been most fully realized, are those during which it has achieved a synthesis in tension of its two cultural roots such that the people at large have possessed the capacity to respond meaningfully, without conscious strain or unease, to the richness and treasure of each heritage. This was first achieved at the time of St. Augustine of Hippo, and it came again in another great period beginning with St. Thomas Aquinas. These are the times when the greatness of the West has been manifest.

To many it seems strange to think of the nineteenth and twentieth centuries as a dark age. From the standpoint of the triumphs of science and medicine, of productivity and standard of living, of education and social welfare, it seems just the reverse. Yet underneath all our material prosperity and accomplishments there is a deep-seated malaise, a sense of meaninglessness and frustration, and a background of dark and foreboding suspicions about the feasibility of modern man's whole enterprise which have been widely noted in much recent commentary. A surprising proportion of contemporary thought is sufficiently dark to justify the use of such an adjective to describe the age in which we live. Moreover, no cultural epoch which in the perspective of history has been recognized as a dark age was considered such by those involved in it. Once a people really has lost the capacity of meaningful response to a whole heritage which constitutes an essential ingredient of those distinctive features that entered into their original constitution as a people, they thereby lose at the same time the very key which is indispensable for an understanding of the emptiness they feel within them. When one considers the extent to which Western culture today has lost the capacity to respond to the buried treasure of its Judaeo-Christian heritage, one is reminded of the dire prophesy of Amos:

> "Behold the days are coming," says the Lord God, "when I will send a famine on the land; not a famine of bread, nor a thirst for water, but of hearing the words of the Lord. They shall wander from sea to sea, and from north to east; they shall run to and fro, to seek the word of the Lord, but they shall not find it."   (Amos 8:11,12)

If it is true that we are in the midst of a dark age, it is equally true that there are at the same time loose among us the first stirrings of a renaissance. It is the recognition of the full scope and exciting implications of this fact which constitutes the heart of the matter I am trying to express here. For it seems to me that if this one idea could really penetrate among us and come to be recognized in the full range of its manifold implications, then our enterprise would be charged with power and spirit.

To be involved in a renaissance is a heady and thrilling thing. It means the possession of a vision which few can share, and along with it the certainty of the reality and destined realization of that vision. It is like seeing a new and lovely land from a mountain top or discovering a choice and precious jewel locked in a hidden cavern but not being able to share one's discovery with the great majority of one's associates. For how does renaissance man react to the uniqueness of his position? He sees himself as one who through the mystery of grace has had his eyes opened to perceive that which it has not been given to his contemporaries to see. And he sees the great body of those about him, of whom he himself was so recently a part, snared in an intellectual and spiritual prison from which, struggle as they will, they do not seem to be able to extricate themselves. He longs to share with them the insight and the vision which, he knows not how or why, has been given him. He knows for a certainty that those very insights are just what his brethren are searching for desperately, and indeed are destined to possess ultimately. Yet the thought forms of his time make a barrier to communication which he can find no way to penetrate.

IV

The Christian idea of education is something that can only be realized when the renaissance, which is just now emerging in the twentieth century, has run its course and come to its full flower. It is not an end which we can plan and bring about by skill and ingenuity. It cannot be approached through teaching methods, curriculum revision, or the injection of selected Christian interpretations into existing courses. Rather is it a germ with which an occasional teacher here or there, without ever quite knowing how, may become infected. Once infected, he becomes, whether he will or no, another center from which the infection spreads. He glimpses a vision of a new world and is captivated and thrilled by it.

On numerous occasions during the last few years I have met with faculty people for discussions of religious aspects of their educational task. As a general rule such discussions turn quickly to demands for practical ways of making day-by-day classroom activities contribute to Christian education. Often these persons have attended previous conferences on this subject. They have heard and assented to lectures devoted to a diagnosis of the ills of contemporary education, of its fragmentation into meaningless diversity, of its futility in the face of the dark and powerful forces of contemporary history, of the sickness of soul which its prevailing secularism and relativism have produced. They have heard, too, the Gospel proclaimed in words which are fresh and new to academic ears, and to this also they have assented as far as is possible within the limitations of the thought forms of the contemporary academic mind. Having listened to and been stirred by these broad and all-inclusive treatments of the subject, they naturally turn their view upon their own particular and special roles in the total educational task. With real and genuine concern they ask, What can we do in these specific roles to bring into actuality the Christian idea of education?

Here, for example, is a person whose task it is to teach Chemistry 202, Quantitative Analysis; or Economics 311, Money and Banking; or Mathematics 121, Analytic Geometry; or History 305, English History since 1688. This person now asks for specific practical suggestions for making the teaching of his particular subject more Christian. To what extent is he justified in introducing religious instruction or ideas into the content of his course? What is the difference between ordinary chemistry, economics, mathematics, or history, and Christian chemistry, Christian economics, Christian mathematics, or Christian history? How can he resolve the dilemmas which arise in the performance of his teaching task because of his department head's militant atheism and antagonism to the Christian Church? What new and more fruitful approach can he take with the two sections of engineering students who are required to take his course but are impervious to everything which is not immediately practical and utilitarian? What can we, who genuinely desire to find the means for making contemporary higher education really Christian, say to such questions?

It is in coping with such questions that the idea of dark age and renaissance in the twentieth century has seemed to me fruitful. The temptation is to provide answers to such questions, as if to imply that the difficulties and dilemmas which produced them really were capable of being solved in our time simply by adopting an appropriate policy and procedure. But a dark age is something given to those born in it as their special lot within which they are called to lead their lives. And a renaissance is something which comes by grace as a lovely and exciting gift, with its own natural period of gestation in the culture within which it germinates. It is not something which one plans and executes. It is not a subject for carefully elaborated strategy which the studied intervention and clever ingenuity of men can promote and carry out. To imply that the nature of the problem is such that an approach to its solution in terms of strategems is feasible is to obscure the true character of the situation.

I do believe that, within limits, some valid and adequate Christian answers can be given to practical questions involving the classroom. Often such answers are too stereotyped to do justice either to the range and complexity of the problem or to the fullness of the Gospel, but at times I have heard answers given which I had to acknowledge were true to the deepest realities and full range of the Christian faith. What then of this point about renaissance as opposed to strategy? To me its validity seems unaltered by limited answers. For then the questioner returns from the conference to the same situation from which he came. Into this situation he brings now a correct answer or an appropriate policy. He finds this helpful and constructive, to be sure, for now he can cope smoothly and confidently with at least some difficulties which previously caused him much distress. He is grateful to the conference for the practical help it has given him. But, however much this may happen, his situation still is basically the same. The total community within which it is his lot to perform his assigned tasks still is empowered and motivated by the same basic drives, dependencies, and goals. In the end he is likely to feel a sense of frustration as though he had somehow been cheated without quite understanding how.

Suppose now, as another example, we consider a small, originally church-founded, liberal arts college which in common with its sister institutions has come to see itself as infected with the prevailing secularism of our time. Into the presidency of this college is brought an active and devoted churchman who determines as the primary policy of his administration to make it again into the truly Christian institution which its founders intended it to be. What shall he do to accomplish this end? Will he not be confronted by a host of insoluble dilemmas? As soon as he begins he finds that his faculty is divided into those who wish to cooperate with him in his endeavor and those who view the whole policy as an intrusion into the sacred domain of academic freedom which must be resisted with every ounce of energy. Also there are scoffers who stand on the sidelines and employ their lack of involvement to uncover and cuttingly expose all that is self-righteous and artificially pious in the program. The students too become divided by the very fact of the existence of this policy. There are those who are too

tualized in our time. Let us be content to leave its actualiza-
n in the hand of Him Whom we adore and serve, Who has
ended on high and lives and reigns externally as Lord of all
tory. Let us leave it, in other words, where by nature it
eady resides, within the mystery of grace and the sureness of
stiny. In the meantime it will be enough for us only to
mpse the beauty and wonder of the Christian idea of educa-
n so that our spirits are gripped by the power of such a
ion and our hearts are suffused with the joy of it. Then re-
rdless of the immediate cogency of discussions in which we
y engage, or the immediate success of projects which we
y undertake in our schools, we shall still share the priceless
ivilege of being partakers of the renaissance in Western civi-
ation which first began to emerge out of the dark age of the
entieth century. What more could any of us ask than that!

easily and patently religious on the one hand, and on the other
those who sense that the institution has designs upon them to
force them into a mold to which they have no intention of con-
forming. And so it will be with every phase and aspect of the
program which he has determined to force somehow into reality. In the end, if he is wise, he will humbly acknowledge the
patent artificiality of any program which aspires by human
potency and ingenuity to make the contemporary school or
college other than what it is its lot to be, an institution of the
mid-twentieth-century dark age.

When I say such things I am generally vehemently accused
either of an unproductive fatalism or of an incurable pessimism. Yet those who know me best find me the very opposite
of the fatalist and the pessimist. In my own heart there is too
much of a real sense of mission and of the awful realization
of the reality of responsibility to make the appellation of fatalist at all applicable. Moreover there is a sense of adventure
and sheer joy and a feeling of confident expectation and hope
continually bubbling up within me which is the very opposite
of pessimism. Thus I am sure that my forebodings over much
that is done these days in the interest of making contemporary
education more Christian cannot be disposed of so easily.

Within the last six months I have been made aware of a
movement in Greece which comes closer to exemplifying the
renaissance which I envision than any other contemporary
movement I know of. It is the Christian Union of Professional
Men of Greece. I refer you to their Christmas Manifesto of
1946 and to the draft of their full statement of position in
a book entitled *Toward a Christian Civilization.*

Here is a group of leading university professors, scientists,
doctors, lawyers, and other professional men whose hearts have
been set on fire; who obviously have been seized by a great
passion, comparable only to the thrilling power of a renaissance in the midst of a dark age. Theirs is no mere project or
program to be planned and negotiated and put into effect by

strategy and promotion. Rather there, in this little land which is at once the seat of origin of the rich Hellenic heritage of Western man and the fertile soil within which the Apostolic Church first took root, the glory of Catholic Christianity is coming alive again with great power. There inside the great but long sleepy Orthodox Church the Holy Spirit is bringing something to life again which has been dormant; and this not within the established hierarchy and institutions of the Church itself, nor in any explicitly or formally religious way, but spontaneously out of the full Body of Christ itself. As they themselves put it, it is not more of the content of the Gospel, not just more words, that modern man needs to know, but it is the living power of the Gospel which must somehow come right down into the total life of the people and the nation as a whole. This is an excellent example of what I mean when I say that a true renaissance is now under way in our culture.

This is the primary challenge of our age, the challenge to become participants in the twentieth-century renaissance. In any dark age when a renaissance is just beginning, what a choice privilege it is to be one of those few who respond to it and are seized by its exhilarating power, so that they come to know surely that their lives have become one with the destiny of their age. It is tragic to be alive at such a time and yet never know or understand that which is emerging into being with great power out of the depths of one's own age.

If we can come to a realization of how integral and necessary the Judaeo-Christian root of Western culture is to the central integrity of its being, as well as the extent to which the West has lost the capacity to respond meaningfully to this heritage, we will be placing the Christian idea of education in the context of the whole broad sweep of the civilization of which we are a part. Unless we do this we are in danger of being victimized by the very prejudices and deficiencies that make the twentieth century a dark age in Western history, and as a result we might look upon Christianity as merely one of many

diverse elements in the brew of contempora[ry] tion. For it is characteristic of these prejudices that we divide life into religious and nonreligi[ous] think of religion as though it were a segment on the same footing as other segmentary subj[ects] up the whole spectrum of human knowledge

It is one of the symptoms of the disease w[hich] contemporary Western man that he thinks Christian heritage as "religious" while regar[ds] Roman heritage as "cultural." In Professor J[.] neat phrase, the nineteenth and twentieth ce[nturies] a "retreat from Christianity into religion." T[his] have seen, is really a total movement in the h[eart of] man which has carried him unsuspecting in[to the] shadows of a new dark age. For us who live for the formally religious and nonreligious al[ike] idea of education is, therefore, something m[ore won]dous than a carefully formulated statement project to be undertaken in any given con[text] or college. It is rather an idea which is d[eveloped] gradually in history over a long period bu[t] power and an inner exaltation of spirit which in our culture more and more as its power it is nothing less than the ultimate fruit of a we can recognize and respond to even th[ough our] contemporaries may remain blind to it.

If we see it in this light, we shall be quit[e] in the wonderful power of this renaissance e[ven] ably is not to be our lot to see it bear fruit i[n] not necessary to transport Petrarch in time the Italian Renaissance in order to tap the tion which lifted his spirit in its early phas[es] given him to see actualized in this life what and surely was destined to be. So let it be [we] not demand of history that the Christian id[ea]

DR. WILLIAM G. POLLARD FURTHER DISCUSSES, IN A
GROUP MEETING, THE THEMES OF HIS PAPER, "DARK
AGE AND RENAISSANCE IN THE TWENTIETH CEN-
TURY."

DR. POLLARD: The Christian idea of education is intimately related to the Christian idea of man, and of the nature
of human life and destiny. The Gospels interpret these subjects
for us. They reveal to us some profound insights into the nature
of man and of human history, not in the form of pat answers
to questions but by freshly illuminating the fundamental problems of human predicament and human life.

A view of man which sees history as under the Lordship of
Christ in a world brought into being by Him and destined for
some mysterious end under God gives to human life a different
flavor, a different context from that which dominates much of
our twentieth-century culture. One of our great difficulties today is that we have idealized Christianity, as if it could only
be realized apart from the actual stresses and strains of ordinary life, as if it were a way of escaping the contingencies and
terrors of existence.

In the Bible you enter a world in which you can understand
the relationship between God and creation in a unique manner
without denying the realities of creation as it is and of human
nature as it is. How does one respond to the vigor and power
of wrath and war and conflict in the Old Testament, or in the
New Testament, too? What are we to do with this wrathful
God Whom we encounter both in the Old and New Testaments, on Sinai, in Job, in the twenty-fifth chapter of Matthew,
in Revelation? What are we to do with these tremendous elements encountered throughout the Scriptures?

My answer is, glory in them. They mean that we are grappling now with something real, not something idealized in the
human imagination, some utopian vision remote from actual

existence. The great power of the Old Testament resides precisely in this, that undoubtedly this people, Israel, was formed from a group of wild Bedouin desert nomads by a transforming experience of the Storm God. All peoples have had the god of the storm and the volcano, of sheer destructiveness, absolutely independent of human desires, ambitions and hopes. The storm and the volcano destroy with a kind of numinous awesomeness that surely was the initial contact with God, the initial revelatory act between God and a group of wild desert Bedouins who made a response to this experience different from that of any other people in human history.

They were filled with a fierce exaltation, an almost frenzied exuberance, by the presence of Yahweh in the storm, in the volcano. They were not cast down in fear, but were lifted, exalted by the presence of enormous power. This certainly was the origin of their sense of selection as a people, as God's chosen people. This was choice not in an abstract proposition of being chosen but in the sense of being lifted with a truly remarkable power experienced in community. It was not an abstract thing at all.

Certainly throughout their early period this experience came upon them almost exclusively in warfare, as one notes from the fifth chapter of Judges, the Song of Deborah, and other ancient pieces of Hebrew literature. It was the great, overwhelming wrath, power, and magnificence of Yahweh that seized them, lifted them and gave them power to go into battle.

This Biblical history is so real; this is not an idealized portrayal of man, but a picture of humanity as it has been throughout all history and in all cultures; it is the reality of human existence. The unique thing about Christianity is its proclamation of the news of God's entry into history. No other religion has anything to compare with that. The Incarnation is an act of God on behalf of His people, on behalf of His creation and His creature.

With that comes the climax of a great drama of acts of God over a thousand years of the history of a real people. This is a reality, the fact that Christianity has the redeeming power that comes from the death and resurrection of the Incarnate Lord. This is unique.

We are still confronted by this majesty and power and wrath. There is wrath in human life. Anyone who does any pastoral work today sees the wrath that is there. St. Paul says, "And we were by nature children of wrath like the rest of mankind." This is the human status. Yet what we do in contemporary education is try to convince people that ultimately we are going to be wise enough and ingenious enough to eliminate war and wrath and terror from existence. What many teachers of philosophy, history, economics, and sociology do today is convey a sense of enthusiasm and vigor and power about what men are going to be able to accomplish in human progress, how we are going to eliminate war, greed, poverty, and human sin by taking hold of these things scientifically.

Well, we can't. They may still teach it, but this vision has lost all its power. At least, students don't respond to it any more. They don't really believe that human history and humanity actually are made that way, that man's self-perfection is at all a feasible undertaking. But through the Christian view of man you can introduce them to something that is full of the realities of existence, that isn't blind to the fullness of the human state.

What is its great symbol? The cross. There is no more vivid, gripping picture of the power of human evil than can be seen in that scene around Calvary with the shouts, "Crucify Him; crucify Him," and this is the way mobs will be in the twentieth century and in the fortieth century, if there is one. This is not something you cure by human ingenuity and progress.

This is something you approach through death and resurrection and through transformation. It is the reality of the Gospels. This is what so excites me about the Christian Union of Professional Men of Greece.[1] They are opposed to this business of presenting Christianity as a goody-goody idealism and code of ethics, the notion that bad people aren't Christian and good pec͵le are, and so on.

The power of the Gospels in history has been the power to go right down into all the dirtiness and reality of human life and history as we find it; the power to go down into it, lift it, and transform it. The men of the Christian Union long to be vehicles to restore in Greece not anything unreal but something that has the power to reveal and acknowledge the total reality of the human estate.

The Christian must face every bit of tragedy and evil and terror and wrath in the human condition. Closing one's eyes to the existence of these elements isn't going to solve anything. This is where the Christian idea of education could be applied. We haven't realized it, though there are small islands of it. It awaits the renaissance. Yet it is felt already in groups like this, here and elsewhere. It ceases to be a dispassionate idea, a detached discussion of policy and procedure, as more and more people become aware that in Christianity is a tremendous power that could come right down into modern man and modern society, and could lift, transform, and redeem life without denying the undesirable, distasteful realities of human existence.

That is where Christianity is something quite different from the Socratic vision of virtue. Yet Christianity, as fully as the Socratic idea, has wonderful visions of what human life can be and is meant to be. It doesn't dispense with ideals, but it does bring an answer to the terrible illusion that men in all cultures throughout history have had, that somehow it ought to be possible to make life into this ideal thing by man's own ingenuity.

Christianity and the cross are there. You will experience the

1. See p. 19.

reality they express. You won't escape, you won't rebuild the world so that it will no longer have any crosses in it.

VOICE: Then the Christian idea of education would have to involve the total nature of man, good and bad?

DR. POLLARD: Yes.

VOICE: And it would involve the reality of God as revealed to man through the Incarnation?

DR. POLLARD: Yes. This revelation and the nature of man would be a central framework from which one views everything. There are a lot of auxiliary things that go along with this, too. I think one of the most important ones is the Christian idea of history. An academic community in which a truly Christian educational process was going on would feel itself to be the object of grace and providence at every step, it would sense the Lordship of Christ over all history, not only its own history but the history of the whole world, Christian and non-Christian. He is the Lord of Russian and Japanese history as much as He is of American history.

VOICE: It would have to include the sense of judgment, too.

DR. POLLARD: Whenever there is providence in history, it is the interplay of judgment and redemption. That is what the historic process is, that is what our lives are in this world. The academic community of today simply doesn't think of history that way. It thinks of history as a sort of determined product of impersonal economic and sociological forces which is so complex that we don't understand it. Therefore the surprises and bafflements of history are merely a result of the limitations of human understanding, but basically they are the product of a vast network of impersonal forces. This is one point where the issue becomes critical. If an academic community, or an educational process, really feels that history is this kind of thing, then it isn't exemplifying the Christian idea.

VOICE: Then, Dr. Pollard, wouldn't it be necessary for more people to become familiar with theology?

DR. POLLARD: It would, yes. Not theology as an abstract

thing. You know, theology is a subtle sort of thing. I suppose it is a lot like theoretical physics. Theoretical physics is a creature of a live, operative community of inquiry, of physicists, and out of that community it can begin to synthesize and share understandings and meanings. But if ever this community becomes dead, then theoretical physics will just be parroting, it will be more and more meaningless. I think it is that way with theology. Generally in our day theological discussions are devoted to trying to answer questions that haven't even arisen in the minds of many people, and when it is doing that it is as fruitless an activity as you can have.

But suppose that out of the life of a community there arises a tremendous concern with just how Christ could have been both very man of very man and very God of very God. How could the Almighty God of all creation become incarnate in a single individual? Suppose this becomes a burning question with people at large, in a context in which they know it is the truth, and they long to try to understand it, to explore it in the caverns of their experience? Then theologians arise in their midst as part of them, as part of the community sharing the same longing to understand something intensely and vividly real, whose reality is so intense and so vivid that it cannot possibly be questioned. They have got to grapple with it and attempt to solve it. Then theology is alive. Then it becomes a bona fide area of rational inquiry, but its necessary concommitant is a real Christian community that is alive.

VOICE: I admire your statement, sir, and I agree with you that we would not find these things in Socrates, but I do think we would find them in Aeschylus or in Sophocles, that view of man's place and the terror and wrath of God.

DR. POLLARD: Yes, but would you find the solution of the Cross and the Resurrection and the Ascension in Sophocles? You only find the tragic.

VOICE: I still do not think that we can find the uniqueness of Christianity anywhere other than in the person of Jesus, not in any view of history, any view of philosophy, any view of ethics, but only in this person.

DR. POLLARD: I am saying it is the person of Jesus.

VOICE: With all the implications.

DR. POLLARD: With all the implications of the person of Jesus, as the Incarnate Son of God who was crucified by the wicked son of man, was resurrected on the third day and ascended to heaven.

The discussion turns to the subject of academic communities.

DR. POLLARD: We are members of communities, and these academic communities, with all our secular colleagues, many of them much better men than we, are a powerful thing. It is grand to be part of an academic community, and certainly we must never break that real community by setting ourselves up as superior in the sense of passing judgment on our fellows, or anything like that. That is not the way to treat the involvement in the particular role in which God has placed us. On the other hand, I wouldn't simply say, "Join forces with them."

The real trouble with the academic community, as I sense it, is that it hasn't any resources with which to carry on.

VOICE: Why do you find on some campuses that it is the secular ones who are the first to come out in defense of certain individual human rights where the Christians ought to be standing for those, from a Christian point of view, yet are silent?

DR. POLLARD: This is a judgment on us.

VOICE: How can you say the secular people have no resources?

VOICE: Think of T. H. Huxley, for example, he had tremendous resources.

VOICE: And I don't think Socrates was strictly—

DR. POLLARD: Individuals do have resources. But I don't think the academic community does have resources to cope with what it faces today. There is a sort of sense of despair, of fragmentation, of not knowing where to go or what to do that tends to pervade the academic communities that I see.

I don't know what will happen to the university of today. I am not presumptuous enough to think that I am going to play any great role in it, but I have discovered something wonderful and tremendous, and the only thing I can do is to tell faculty people about it because I believe they would find it so, too. Most of those I have talked with started Bible study groups, and not on the basis of religious commitment but with anybody welcome who wants to find out about the Bible and to study it in its historic context, as it is now possible to do.

There is something unique about the twentieth century with respect to the Bible, because Christians and Jews of previous centuries have not had some of our really remarkable ways of viewing it. Now we can read the early source of Samuel in its historic context, and it is a wonderful, epic thing. I have found that this kind of study is something that does catch on here and there—not with too many—and it does not represent a program.

I cannot force people to become interested in physics. In the past when I had to teach physics, I wondered, "What can I do as a physicist, if I love physics?" Well, I came to realize that this love for it now and then excites a kindred spark here and there. This is sufficient, really, for us. It had better be sufficient, because I do not think that we have the potentialities to do much more than that.

I think this is my meaning about a renaissance or rediscovery going on here and there, and I think it is a sufficient objective to long to share this treasure with others. There is so much power in it that I believe it is going to accelerate. It is a kind of infection; it is spreading, and this is going to catch hold of the hearts of people, and other people will be enormously excited by these same discoveries. Well, goodness knows what will happen then. I think this will radically transform our present-day churches and synagogues, and everything else.

VOICE: I wondered why you chose the word renaissance rather than reformation?

DR. POLLARD: Because I really think it is a process of rediscovering something lost, not reforming something degraded.

I think one can excite interest and enthusiasm in this realm of Biblical literature in exactly the same way that, at times, people have been enormously attracted to the classical heritage. It is a tremendous thing to discover the Biblical literature for oneself and feel its power. This is wholly apart from any specifically religious conversion or approach. I believe the fruits of this discovery, once it happens, would be to lead men into the power of the Gospel, but I don't feel I can control these ultimate fruits.

VOICE: We would undercut our insistence on the total nature of man as being both pretty good and also fallible if we went around pretending that we alone have the truth.

DR. POLLARD: Yes, as though grace were not required.

I suppose a good many of you have read *Cry, the Beloved Country*. It just occurs to me that all our movements and discussion groups say we must do this, or we must do that, to solve various problems. Somehow one realizes the magnificence of *Cry, the Beloved Country* is the way in which one sees clearly how the only things that happened that really dealt with the tragedy of that story came definitely by grace and prayer, were unexpected. The very tragedies resulted in putting it into the hearts of people who otherwise never would have taken an interest, to throw themselves into a situation. And by a miracle, really, something that no kind of project could have brought about began to work.

DEAN GIFFORD: [2] Dr. Pollard, as dean of a theological

2. Frank D. Gifford, Philadelphia Divinity School.

school, I have noticed that I have a great many men of science, chemical engineers, physicists, pharmacists, now desiring to go into the ministry. I wonder why?

DR. POLLARD: I do, too.

DEAN GIFFORD: Could you say a word on that?

DR. POLLARD: I just don't know. But I am convinced that it is true.

DEAN GIFFORD: I have had five times as many chemical engineers as lawyers, for example.

DR. POLLARD: I know. The Bishop recently assigned a professor of mathematics at the University to me to prepare for orders.

VOICE: Possibly an explanation of Dean Gifford's point is that scientists, having advanced more rapidly than some of those in the other disciplines, have begun to come more readily and more quickly than others to the realization that science is incapable of answering the ultimate question or dealing with the ultimate matter.

DR. POLLARD: This tends to be the situation with physical scientists today. The realization of the vastness of the field of scientific inquiry, in that type of understanding it provides, never changes, no matter how far you go, and one wakes up to the fact that it is only this kind of understanding that science is capable of giving.

But all these other questions, no matter how far science goes, no matter how it keeps proliferating, it never touches, never approaches. I think physical scientists are waking up to the fact that there is a whole realm of reality lying outside their methods of inquiry.

THE REVEREND JOHN COURTNEY MURRAY, S.J.,
PURSUES A WIDE-RANGING DISCUSSION OF CERTAIN
QUESTIONS RAISED BY DR. POLLARD'S PAPER.

FATHER MURRAY: Listening to Dr. Pollard, I was struck
by these questions: In what sense could you say that Judaism
has been creative of a culture? That is a historical point. Secondly, to what extent could you say that the Jewish community
of America today is creative of something that would be called
the American culture? It is indeed present in the United States
as a religious community. The synagogue is part of the American way of life, if you will. But what I am getting at is, I suppose, Werner Jaeger's idea that there is only one culture, at
least in the world to which we belong, usually referred to as
the "West," and that culture is Greek in its origin, not Jewish;
it does not emerge as Judaism; it only becomes a culture by
reason of its Greek substratum. People might dispute Jaeger's
view, but nevertheless it is a view.

Hence, this very difficult problem with which we are faced
today. Our pluralist society puts us under severe difficulties
in the discussion of it, because words do not mean the same
thing to everyone, and even the word "Christian" as applied
to America, its culture and education, is not sufficiently inclusive. Because you have not only the Jewish community but
the ethical humanists, and you have quite a lot of other people,
the contemporary philosophical naturalists, and all the rest
of them.

Now, do we not have to determine what is the wellspring
of culture, as such, before we can discuss the question of what
is the Christian culture? It is like the question of a Christian
history. You cannot decide what a Christian history is or might
be before you answer the question, "What is history?" And,
of course, as we all know, that is an extremely difficult question.

Therefore, I don't know but what the angle of approach should be rather from the standpoint of culture and education, and that then we should take the adjective "Christian" in the second place on rather much the grounds that Professor Harbison emphasizes [1]—that is, the function of the Christian faith to illuminate a culture or an education.

DR. FINCH: [2] Father Murray's question of whether Judaism is a culture is relevant here. Obviously, it makes quite a difference to our problem if all we mean by culture is our Graeco-Roman heritage, or if we also regard Judaism and the Judaeo-Christian stream as a culture, too. In short, we have Jaeger's view against Father Pollard's. I would like to hear Father Murray speak a little more on why he would or would not feel that the Judaic strain is not actually to be regarded in the same way as the Graeco-Roman strain.

FATHER MURRAY: I think I would say—and this I think was an interesting point brought up by Dr. Pollard's very splendid paper and the two-root theory that he proposed—I think I would be inclined to say that that which was culturally creative in the Jewish tradition has been absorbed into the Christian tradition. Just as I would also say that that which was culturally creative in the Greek tradition was later also absorbed into the Christian tradition, so that, properly speaking, historically, our culture at the moment has only one root, a root that is an organic, integrated synthesis of elements. One of these elements would be Germanic as well as Jewish, Greek, and Roman, of course taking the two pagan antiquities together. The Germanic idea of law was tremendously powerful in the medieval synthesis.

So, indeed, you can go back and say that the one root from which our culture at the moment flowers, if indeed it is flowering, has itself several roots. That is, it was integrated from a number of pre-existent traditions. Nevertheless, as we view it

1. See Professor Harbison's paper, following.
2. Henry L. Finch, Jr., Sarah Lawrence College.

from our present perspective today, our culture has just this one root, because all these previous syntheses have already been accomplished. Maybe they have indeed disintegrated, but the present fact of their disintegration does not obliterate the historical fact of their integration.

Hence, if I seek the roots of our culture, I must indeed go back to the Bible, as Father Pollard suggested, but I go back to it not as it existed—certainly not in the days of its composition, which would be a bit of a feat except for a technical Biblical scholar—I go back to it as situated within the totality of this one stream of tradition to which at the moment we are tributary.

This was my difficulty on that two-root theory. First of all, in the sense of origin, there are more than two. And I think I would be inclined to say that in the historical context there is now just the one complex root.

DR. FINCH: If this synthesis has disintegrated, it might seem that, in looking for a reintegration, we might have to go back quite far. That is, it might be the occasion for examining the elements which went into the synthesis. I suppose that is what Father Pollard was doing; he was saying that we need to reintegrate. Therefore, we must examine what made up the Christian synthesis which in some way or other did not continue.

FATHER MURRAY: I expect he was proposing some such thing as that, and that is why I don't think I would put myself, as it were, in opposition to him in any way. Perhaps I picked up unfairly that notion of two roots. It could be possibly a bit misleading.

VOICE: Are we trying to have a renaissance, or say a sort of new society as in the Renaissance in the twelfth and thirteenth centuries; or are we trying to get back to the original Christian idea of the first two centuries, or even of the Augustinian age? If we are in the dark age now and are looking forward to the renaissance and are trying to act in a way as an early beacon light, do we want this renaissance to be just a rehash of the first Renaissance, or are we trying to get something different out of it?

FATHER MURRAY: I would expect that Father Pollard was using the term "renaissance" as I would use it. It does not mean a return to the past, much less does it mean your good word "rehash" of what we have had. It did not have that meaning historically. It meant really the return of the past to the present, rather than the opposite notion. It was the discovery, in turn, of ancient grammar, in the Carolingian Renaissance, and then philosophy, logic and philosophy, in the twelfth and thirteenth centuries, and then the plastic arts and literature in the quattrocento.

But they did not go back to pagan antiquity except in the third renaissance, and that was where the synthesis failed. They were trying, having come upon this ancient body of truth and human achievement—in Pollard's words—to make it meaningful in the present and organize it into a synthesis that would be valid for the present, and which would, by definition, mean a transcendence of any former synthesis.

The thing that has to be coped with today is the great contemporary fact of science which, of course, in the medieval synthesis or even in the quattrocento, was not very much of a consideration at all. Science then was in the Ionian stage, almost, and only just beginning its tremendous rise. That is, I suppose, the most striking "cultural" fact that we confront at the present moment, and that I suppose educators are everywhere terribly exercised about. What do you do about science?

VOICE: Isn't it the scientific attitude that science—or perhaps the better word is "humanism," rather than "science"—isn't it the feeling that man has within his powers the ability to get what he wants without any vertical reference? Isn't that what the educational institutions have done—fostered that attitude, or at least not discouraged it?

VOICE: The self-sufficiency of man?

VOICE: Self-sufficiency, optimism.

VOICE: Is that in balance now, or is that at an extreme?

VOICE: It is still prevalent. Isn't that one of the reasons for this seminar? That still is pretty much the case in the educational institutions.

VOICE: What are the bad features of that?

VOICE: It is an illusion, for one thing.

DR. WARREN: [3] In a sense, it is a kind of religion, too. It is a kind of idolatry that has beguiled—nothing else is offered—and this seems to be offered, and it looks so good and it does such wonderful things, and so on, that the poor guy who has not had much offered him looks to it as a hopeful possibility. You can't blame him for doing that, particularly when the rest of us haven't done our job very well. One of the things beguiling about science is that it has been very comfortable for a lot of people. In this pragmatic "it-doesn't-pay-off" culture we are living in, science seems to be a profitable thing for people to give themselves to. It is amazing how many parents want their child to have a "scientific education." They are not thinking about his education but about the kind of income he will be able to earn when he is finished with this rather expensive and elaborate process of school and college.

Maybe this is an injustice—and I guess it is—but often it doesn't seem to have been given much more thought than that. "We bring him here, and we feel he will make a nice salary when he gets through here." It isn't quite that crude, but there is a lot of that at work. A lot of institutions are certainly given to it. Some of them advertise themselves as big places where "If you come to us you will be able to do these wonderful things." Why fool around with a liberal arts program when you will not be able to make a living out of it?

VOICE: Is that not why this problem is very important at the secondary school level? Because at that point you do not tend to spend nearly as much time on science as you seem to

3. Matthew M. Warren, Headmaster, St. Paul's School.

in the university. Even the great liberal arts universities now are more than half science, let alone the technical schools. It is in the secondary schools that you can reach the boys with some idea of the values of life rather than just the techniques and skills in which you are trying to train them.

FATHER MURRAY: Isn't that one of the challenges to Christian education, that somehow at the end of schooling, whether it be secondary or college or university, the student would emerge not only with a knowledge of science but also, say, with a knowledge of the value of science in the total human and Christian scheme of affairs, and an awareness of its relation to all other disciplines of the human spirit, all other areas of human activity? He would have not only this body of techniques and skills and accumulated information but also a genuine understanding of where this comes into the whole human enterprise.

Above all, there is the rather crucial question, how do you go about being a scientist and a Christian and still one man living some manner of interiorly unified life instead of the lopsided one that I am afraid is too frequent a phenomenon today? We see the scientist to whom religious belief is meaningless, and the man of religious belief to whom science is a complete enigma. The latter tends to be rather antagonistic and to become declamatory about the destructive influence of science on contemporary civilization, and so on. The scientist, who usually is a man of great intellectual integrity, doesn't, any more than the rest of us, like to have someone stand there and throw rocks at him. At the same time he would be open to some intelligent discussion of this question of whether science has some manner of human premises, philosophical and religious, or is the autonomous thing that some happier age than ours used to think it was.

This is one of the great challenges put to the Christian educator by the fact of contemporary science. He has to cope with it; and he copes with it not by merely introducing into the curriculum "X" number of courses in this or that scientific discipline: sociology, microbiology, and even nowadays psychiatry. He copes with it by putting the student in the way of organizing in his own mind scientific knowledge, humanistic achievements, and also religious faith.

DR. ZILBOORG: [4] This raises a question involving actual forces of our present-day manner of living. Being a psychiatrist, I think the greatest number of characteristic traits develop within the family. The greatest number of families in our community are Christian, and it is the Christian families that produce the greatest number of pragmatically thinking youngsters who regard a school as a place where they are going to get training. When you give them a subject which at first does not show what they are going to get out of it, they say, "What will it get me?"

Therefore, the role of the Christian educator today seems to be a triple one. He first wants to overcome within himself the idea of merely stuffing in a certain amount of information to pass exams. Second, he must overcome—and this is a much more difficult problem that requires a great deal of tact—he must overcome the malicious influence even of the so-called Christian family which looks at a school as a training center where the boy is going to be trained to get a bigger and better living. Third, he must train himself, because he himself was not fully trained, either by life's circumstances or by his family, to teach human values and the concept of the unity of man. Whether you study mathematics or philosophy, physics or art, you are studying something that human beings produced through their creative aspirations, and something that we happen to be privileged to inherit, and have to carry with us, and to carry on.

The problem then, today, as I see it, for an educator—and I see it from my medical consulting room—is how to convert the parent to a situation where he will not interfere with the

4. Dr. Gregory Zilboorg, psychiatrist, New York State Medical College.

educator, who has to be a Christian educator, and then produce a Christian education—in other words, we rely on the family all the time. We have to rely on the family.

At the same time we must struggle against the utilitarian tradition that has been established in the past half-century within the family. At least this is true of the United States, and to a great extent it is true in England—but not to the same extent. It is not true so much in France. It is very true in Germany, despite the fact that they still preserve some sort of philosophic vocabulary. It is true, of course, in Russia.

VOICE: The parents of the next generation are the ones in school now. What should be done in school now with regard to the relationship of these future parents to future educators?

DR. ZILBOORG: That is the serious question and problem. What should be done now? The cardinal point is that the school, in order to do its work of inculcating into the minds of people the idea of the unity of man and the Christian tradition, must in some way either re-educate the parents or break with the parents. In either case it is not going to be very popular. That is a serious practical question.

DR. WARREN: Of course, both the school and the parents are uncertain about their roles. The parent is putting phenomenal pressure on the child to excel in the school; but actually this is the school's role, and the school, in order to give this child some place to run from the undue pressure of the parent, begins to protect and support and help the child, so that you have these two roles reversed: the school, which normally should put the pressure on the child to perform his tasks and perform them as well as he is able, and the parent, who should support the child and help him enter into himself and to accept the disciplines of school and life in general. This reverse I think is very critical. Sometimes it is a matter of just pointing out to the parents that the pressure is doing more harm than good. They should tell the little boy they love him, and take whatever he gives them. They give him almost the impression that they might expel him from the family if he doesn't perform according to their ideas about him. So that it seems to me that the family needs as much help here as the boy does.

DR. ZILBOORG: Aren't we falling into the trap of our present-day civilization? We are constantly preoccupied with the means, techniques, and skills which we will bring out and start working on in order to produce some sort of change. Would it not be more correct to examine our consciences and see clearly that we live in a period where pragmatic action and pragmatic behavior and an acquisitive type of life have become the fundamental ideal? We can fight Communism as much as we want to, but as long as we speak of economic determinism, as long as we speak of the enlightened economic self-interest of the average man, we are accepting a sort of Marxian idea and a business idea of life as opposed to a religious idea of life.

Is it not then the job of the educator to be a sort of self-sacrificing individual who does the best he can? I think in this respect Dr. Pollard's paper is most poignant. It is not a question of which schools and which educators will invent a special method by means of which they will put over Christian education. It is a question of the general trend in our postwar civilization, postwar after the first World War. I am a child of the first World War. I remember it very well. Since that time we have become what is called very practical.

It is a type of missionary work which is before the present-day educator. For the present-day psychiatrist, since Father Murray mentioned it in a moment of laxity, this is our job, and I doubt whether there is any great answer as to how to do it. We can only become cognizant of it, and fully aware of it, and be low-spirited at times about it, and harp on it with any parent we can get hold of who is not going to talk to the headmaster and ask for our resignation, because this is a type of missionary work.

I remember when I was in my second medical school in the very beginning of the twenties, in this country, there was not a member of the class of 120 who didn't think that it was absolutely silly to occupy oneself with reading a book outside medicine because you had to study and think already about six years hence when you would hang out a shingle.

This is true of engineers in M.I.T., and this is true of lawyers in the best law schools, and this is true of all the schools, because our schools now become not centers of education but centers of training. They are all specializing, even in high school. When you graduate from high school, what do you take up? Typing and accounting. We have got to throw these things out of high school. Neither the public in general nor parents in particular will permit us to throw them out at present.

I think that the only salvation lies in seminars like this where a great many of us will be put to thinking on the subject and go home and spend a couple of sleepless nights, or more. Only that way—there is no technique of how to do it.

VOICE: Thank you for a very pragmatic answer.

DR. ZILBOORG: Yes, it is historically pragmatic. I recall.

FATHER MURRAY: Moreover, I would like to contradict it.

DR. ZILBOORG: That is very pragmatic, Father Murray.

FATHER MURRAY: I mean contradict it in this sense, because it seems to me that we run across a strange paradox in this particular area—that is, that what sounds like a pragmatic question is a highly theoretical one. The question is, how is education to be made religious or Christian?

Usually when you use the word "how," as Gregory points out, you are inquiring into techniques and mechanisms, and into some sort of routines, and what not, whereby you do in certain ways the things that you know you want to do. Whereas the question How is education to be made religious? was the great theoretical question to which, of course, Newman de-

voted his *Idea of a University*—at least a large portion of it
—those discourses that deal with religion and literature,
religion and all the other disciplines.

It is a question of how these disciplines are somehow to be
—and here I willingly accept Professor Harbison's metaphor
—"illumined by your Christian faith." [5] How do you illuminate? That is a lovely word, a lovely concept. I think
we all have some sort of intuitive grasp of what it means.
But what does it mean? How do you illuminate history, how
do you illuminate science, how do you illuminate literature
by the Christian faith?

When you say "How?" it means that you have in your mind
a real theory, a theory of the relationships between your religious faith, between all its propositional and doctrinal enun-
ciations, and the particular discipline in question. It isn't a
question of technique; it is a question of understanding profoundly both the nature of your faith and the nature of the
discipline under discussion, and in terms of this profound
understanding of both, understanding the manner of integration that is possible and desirable between them—because it
varies in different disciplines. It is not a question of technique,
Gregory, really. Do you agree?

DR. ZILBOORG: Father Murray didn't contradict me. He
merely elucidated my confused statement.

FATHER MURRAY: If I had been more courteous, I would
have said I was elucidating instead of using the rude word
"contradict."

DR. FINCH: Perhaps this brings us back to Dr. Pollard's
question of where this gets a foothold in the curriculum.
Actually, as the situation exists now, you have a great many
courses and a great many subjects which contain implicitly
antireligious points of view. As I gathered from what Father
Pollard said, his view was that this is because we have lost
some of the tradition. That is obvious in the case of history.

5. See Professor Harbison's paper, following.

for example, where the whole Judaeo-Christian tradition is overlooked or treated with a kind of animus, or something of that sort.

Is it part of our approach here to try to reintegrate into the specific subject matters of the curricula some of the lost tradition or lost point of view, or are we taking the attitude that I suppose Jaeger would, that this sort of thing is somehow irrelevant to logic and science, and should be treated as a kind of separate phenomenon in the religious department, or as a separate course in Bible, or something of that sort?

FATHER MURRAY: I take it your implicit objection is to the notion of religion being just another subject?

DR. FINCH: Yes.

FATHER MURRAY: Added to all the other subjects that are part of the curriculum, but pretty much on all fours with all the rest of them, and unrelated to any of them; is that what you have in mind?

DR. FINCH: I must confess that I rather agreed with Father Pollard's view. I think that it serves to bring out something else, too. It serves to bring out the fact that you actually do have a positive onslaught against religion which exists in the field of psychology, sociology, economics, philosophy, and so on. That is, that the subjects implicitly attack religion and at a great many points, and the students understand that religion has been demolished, so to speak, that we no longer need it, that it is simply a lost phase of our culture. If you merely create another subject, you are trying in one very small part of the curriculum to combat something which may be widespread throughout the rest of it; and this would not work.

DR. CROCKER: [6] I teach biology. I don't feel the subject matter itself is against religion. It is the teacher of the subject. Chad Walsh, in a recent article in a religious journal, said you can pray and meditate all you will, but you cannot

6. Denton W. Crocker, Colby College.

change the periodic table. It stays as it is. It is neither for nor against religion. It is the teacher of physics or chemistry, or what have you, who is for or against, or even worse, somewhere in the middle.

So, I suppose, really, our objective would be to bring into the classroom something of this inspiration, of this insight, to add to the hind- and foresight, as the teacher can bring this in. Although Walsh also goes on to point out, in an area with which he is more familiar, how in English you can actually work the religious viewpoint in very, very well.

DR. FINCH: I don't think it depends entirely on the teacher. I agree with Father Pollard that there is an objective subject matter which is there regardless of who teaches it, and that is the fact that there has existed, after all, this tremendous body of cultural phenomena, namely, the whole Judaeo-Christian tradition. And those elements are objectively present. For example, in Marxism there is a tremendous amount of the Jewish-Christian point of view. I think that is fairly clear. I think it is in Freud. It is true that it has not been brought out, and that is due to the teacher, to some extent, but the thing is there objectively.

DR. ZILBOORG: Aren't you a bit too hard on a couple of disciplines which came in *ex post facto,* let us say—that is, psychology and cultural anthropology, which in recent years claimed that you can get along without religion? The antireligious trend in our civilization had begun much earlier. I am rather inclined to believe that there were some psychologists, cultural anthropologists, and anthropologists who were antireligious because they caught on to this spirit of anti-religion.

I personally am a psychiatrist, a psychoanalyst, and a Freudian—all three things—very bad. I don't feel badly about it at all, and I didn't exclude God either from my thought or from my aspirations. I may exclude him from my behavior and then I am beyond myself—but twenty-five years ago—and I don't remember the name of the man—a teacher in Bryn Mawr [James H. Leuba] had made an interesting study of the attitudes toward religion on the part of scientists. It must be thirty years ago. Later on it was published in *Harper's Magazine.*

He found the following rather extraordinary thing, that the scientists proper—mathematicians, physicists, and biologists —are more religious, and the closer you come to the humanities—history, literature, sociology, psychology—the more and more you become nonreligious. He resumed that study about ten years later and found again corroboration of his data. The percentage is staggering. The closer you come to the humanities the more you find total antireligious attitudes, while in the scientist, even thirty years ago, you find religious attitudes.

You know that Darwin excluded the name of God in the first edition of *The Origin of Species,* in 1859, but in the second edition, in the preface, the name of God does come in. It slipped in somehow; this despite the fact that it was excluded from the first edition.

I still believe that the teacher himself must be the key. There is no specialty of religion. There is a specialty of history of religion. There is a specialty of the history of the history of the Judaeo-Christian religion, but there is no specialty of religion. There is no special subject. And those who make it a subject unmake religion and call it "Religion."

I would feel that every teacher, from a medical teacher to the teacher in various schools, whatever he teaches, if he approached his subject from the historical perspective, if he gave his pupils the feeling that it didn't begin yesterday—if he himself did not exclude Anaximander, who had ideas in 700 B.C. which are close to the ideas of Darwin in the 'sixties, if he approached the whole subject historically, would give the pupil the feeling that it is not all something created by us—hurray!

We treat the process like a big football game and call it

education, and he who gets the most points wins. We have lost the historical perspective. I am sure what Dr. Pollard meant is the need to recapture our past and relink ourselves with our past. If you teach philosophy or if you teach history, and teach the history of history before you teach history proper, and teach history of philosophy before you teach philosophy proper, people will not miss Aquinas, they will not fail to notice the historians of the past; they will not fail to notice what Aristotle had to say. Naturally, they will not miss the Judaeo-Christian tradition at all.

I am not one of those who is afraid that if you stress the Judaeo-Christian tradition a great many people of other denominations might object or might not feel at home. They would not feel at home anyhow if you bring up a religious attitude. If they do feel religious—a Hindu would feel extremely interested in a very excellent presentation of the Judaeo-Christian tradition in a curriculum of three to five years, I am sure, and so would the Chinese.

FATHER MURRAY: I think we had hold of a real subject in this science-and-Christianity kind of thing, and it is terribly relevant to what the schools and colleges should do. Maybe we ought to pursue that a little bit more.

I think I would be inclined to agree with our scientist here that the conflict is not between the different disciplines but between their adherents. I would rather think that the terribly important thing for a Christian educator to do today would be very precisely to locate the reasons for this pseudo conflict, because the war between religion and science is one of those "ignorant armies clash by night" kind of propositions. One army doesn't know where the other army is, usually. It is not a fight at all, even though it seems to be.

There was a book written recently by a man named Culler, called *The Imperial Intellect*.[7] It is a study—and a profound and brilliant one—of Newman's educational theory. The first

7. A. Dwight Culler, *The Imperial Intellect. A Study of Newman's Educational Ideal*, New Haven, Yale University Press, 1955.

part is an interesting biography of Newman that brings out quite a number of new things, especially the place that the four great illnesses of his youth had both in his intellectual and religious development, and the second part of the book is devoted to an analysis of his educational theory; critical and at the same time sympathetic, a model of criticism in many ways. But he gets on to this problem and he brings out what Newman thought about it.

Why is it that the scientist today feels this conflict in his own mind? It isn't an affair of reason, but of his whole consciousness, and especially his imagination, which is, of course, as we know, the author of all error. Reason itself does not err, it errs in consequence of the pressures brought to bear upon it by imagination and by the whole affective life of the individual.

There is a thesis in Scholastic theology which many students find impossible to swallow, that the human intelligence is, per se, infallible. Reason itself does not err except under the influence of the imagination and passions, the whole emotional side of imagination which influences thinking in such wise that one's thinking goes wrong. If we could think in some sort of emotional and social vacuum, we would always think correctly.

It is true more in our own day than in Newman's that the pursuit of science (and the growing branch of science is nuclear physics) requires such intense concentration and absorption that everything else is at the moment disregarded, and the very fact of the disregard creates a vacuum which is intolerable to the scientist, and he builds up the vacuum with his own thoughts, which are scientific thoughts, in such wise that his own intellectual universe is scientific. And no other universe, be it philosophical or religious, can make any sense to him at all.

Doubtless many of you in this room, like myself, have had that experience in dealing with scientists. I could name you offhand half a dozen very close personal friends of mine who are scientists and are men who never had a religion, or if they had, have lost it. In each case it is the same pattern that is repeated.

Isn't that something that the school ought to face? We have got in front of us these young boys, say, in secondary school. Even more importantly, we have the older students in the college and the university. Shouldn't it be possible to make an impact upon their imaginations with the humanities and with Christian doctrine in such wise that we would, as it were, immunize them from the impact of the scientific experience? Their literary, artistic, philosophical, and historical experience and, above all, their Christian experience ought to be made so vivid, so solid intellectually and so captivating emotionally and imaginatively, that they will be immune from what you may call this intellectual disease which affects the scientist, to which he falls victim.

I know one man, for instance, with whom I have had many dealings, whose constant plea is, "Why can't I believe? I would love to believe. I would love to have a religious faith." There is no antagonism there at all. It is only that his whole mental life, his whole emotional and imaginative life has been captivated by the single enterprise to which he has devoted himself with an intensity before which we religious people ought, of course, to be very humble, and which renders him incapable of belief.

That is the modern predicament, a very different predicament in this whole problem of religion and science from what it was in the days of Thomas Huxley, when the question was, "Can this proposition which religion teaches be reconciled with that proposition which is taught by science?" Religion, for instance, gives you the account in Genesis of the origin of the first human pair. That is an origin in religion. Can that be squared with all that we know in evolutionism? Or some old fundamentalist idea of the age of the world. Can that be squared with what science teaches?

That can all be washed up. Nobody carries on that argument any more nowadays. The argument is much more subtle, much more difficult, and it is an argument of which the Christian educator must be aware because in the conduct of his school and in the carrying out of all his disciplines he can prevent the conflict, prevent it from rising in terms of, I say, this vividness of emotional impact. And I am not speaking now of oratory or even the Greek protreptic, the thing they addressed to the young men trying to draw them to philosophical studies, a little exhortation. No exhortation. The substance has to be highly intellectual, but it has to be so warm, so living, so impregnated with possibilities, and all that, that the young man will make it a part of himself, and then when the scientific experience becomes part of him, it is just a part, and it fits into the whole and it does not become the whole.

Of course, the same thing works—this is a two-way street —with the scientific experience. That should be a real experience in school. The religious experience should not be communicated in such a way that science somehow becomes suspect. Do you see at all what I am driving at? This isn't a curriculum problem. I agree with the one who said it is a teaching problem.

DR. FINCH: As I understood Father Pollard, he was saying that something has been left out of the subject matter, and that it is due to the attitude of the teacher that it is left out. But the fact remains that in the field of history, as he was saying, objectively there exists a Judaeo-Christian heritage which is part of the subject matter which, because of the attitude of the teacher, we have tended to minimize or ignore.

The same thing applies to English literature. An English teacher selects from a certain range of subject matter and may tend to select certain things which are, for example, in the line of contemporary fashion, rather than other things, which may raise embarrassing religious problems. Particularly he may overlook the Christian-Jewish writers in a given period.

So this is where the subject matter really has to be changed.

FATHER MURRAY: You are altogether right in that, and I think nowhere does it show up so clearly as in what is certainly too frequently the philosophy department's curriculum in the run-of-the-mill university today. There are one or two exceptions, but they are exceptions. I can remember a university at which I happened to teach once. I had the privilege of being there for a year as visiting professor, and we had a meeting of the faculty at which one of the points on the agenda was the review of the reading lists for what they called intensive philosophy majors.

It was pretty much the pattern: Plato, Aristotle, Descartes. So I said, "Just one moment. You know, really, after all, you can hardly skip 2,200 years in such a blithe fashion. You do have a few things of some historical importance—not least, of course, the impact of Christianity on the philosophical intelligence."

How in the world could you know anything about philosophy unless you had somehow studied, and quite seriously studied, that tremendous historical fact, and then all the monuments, the documents from Justin Martyr onward, that revealed this impact, and then the great systematization and so on, and so on? So you are altogether right in saying some curriculum changes are imperative.

DR. FINCH: In regard to philosophy there is a special problem, and that is the word "philosophy," which is, after all, a Greek invention, and does not include in its narrow sense Hebraic thought, and tends to exclude the religious element as not being, so to speak, philosophy.

It may be that what we need to do is make even a more radical extension of the content of philosophy, which would make it possible to include Hebraic thought on the same footing with Plato and Aristotle. It would perhaps even involve a kind of new terminology, because the terminology of our philosophy is so Greek.

If one took Father Pollard's suggestion absolutely seriously and literally, what we would do is not begin with Thales, but begin jointly with Thales and the Hebraic thinkers on the same footing, and then trace these as the two sources of philosophy in this extended sense. I don't propose that this can be done, but I merely say that is one of the implications of what I think he was saying earlier.

DR. ZILBOORG: May I follow the example of Father Murray and say that I raise an objection by way of extension? I listened to Dr. Pollard, and my impression was that the examples he cited from the curricula, giving examples of total absence of various periods in Judaeo-Christian thought in philosophy, were only examples to demonstrate to what extent we exclude from our education and thinking these particular areas. I do not think he believes that by inclusion of these particular things in the teaching of history and the teaching of philosophy you would raise the Christian standards of our education. I think he pointed out merely that this is a cultural phenomenon. We drop it all out and we make it a specialty called "religion."

I am inclined—seriously inclined—to believe that if we psychiatrists, psychologists, philosophers, biologists have a certain attitude, a Christian one, that attitude will convey itself directly, intuitively, to our students, independently of how well we teach the experiments. It will inevitably come over. I think practically this is by far, at the present juncture, the easiest way of doing it.

I find, in my practice, a pretty good cross section of what you might call the well-educated person, the well-educated American who comes from the prep school and a good university, and who is totally devoid of any religious preoccupations unless he is especially brought up with religious attitudes.

To an enormous extent, without my taking part in it at all, toward the end of the treatment a number of people begin to be interested in ethical religious ideas (not that I transformed their neuroses from pragmatic to religious-hallucinatory— I assure you I avoid it as best I can), they begin to be interested in these things and seek information.

I cannot tell you how I convey to them my attitude, but there are millions and millions of ways of conveying this attitude without being censorious and didactic at all. The moment you become censorious and didactic, and you include it in a curriculum, our practical civilization will say to you, "What am I going to do with it?" and will drop it aside. If you instill in a person a sense that this is not an old story, then the person begins to think—you kindle the flames, and the person begins to develop in many ways in him or herself.

I find time and again, after thirty years of seeing sick people, who are in no way different from healthy people except that they are more sensitive or responsive, that this is the way to do it. I am afraid that if you begin to change the curriculum in order to get there, we will not get there. But the curriculum will gradually change as we get there. There is no doubt about that. The curriculum will naturally change as it has naturally changed in the past seventy-five or one hundred years.

DR. FINCH: Could I ask you a question, just following that up? Would you be in favor of changing the curriculum to this extent: that we would introduce, as a fundamental subject in the curriculum, material which has to do with the Judaeo-Christian tradition, where that has been left out, let us say, in the realm of historical study or philosophical study, on the same footing with material that has to do with the Graeco-Roman tradition?

DR. ZILBOORG: I wouldn't object, but I wouldn't insist upon putting it in, because the modern mind, the little boy, a boy two years old says, "Will you turn on the radio?" He already knows about the radio today as soon as he begins to talk. About the time he reaches prep school at the age of fourteen, he knows everything about the instrumentalities of having fun today and never mind tomorrow.

If you begin to introduce something new deliberately into the curriculum, then you will give the boy the impression that you are doing a little practical preaching and spending your time that way instead of training. I would rather have the curriculum develop naturally through the upheaval of a demand from below—that includes your parents who are so "practical"—then the curriculum will change. The historical ebb and flow of life will produce a change in the curriculum.

DR. WARREN: Isn't there a distortion here in the field of history? For example, if you are teaching Elizabethan literature, you distort it by leaving out the upheavals of religion in that period. Yet, it seems to me that very few people who teach in these areas are very sensitive to the significance of the religious upheaval at the time, the time which produced this literature.

This is what troubles me. I wouldn't want to see us start doing this, introducing a great many eccentric things into the curriculum, but I would like to see us, with the present curriculum, give the students an orientation with reference to the fact that there was a violent manifestation at certain periods in our history, in which religion had a very major part. At times it was deplorable, at times it was quite pure and refined, but this had an organic relationship to all the learning which is there.

DR. ZILBOORG: I could not agree more with what you said, and at the risk of appearing importunate, I could share with you very briefly an experience that I had as a teacher.

When I started teaching medical students some years ago, I taught them the way they are taught, namely "You do this," and "You do that," and then a neurosis is not cured, and then you try again, and then it is still not cured, but you try, and you do your best. I never reached the point of teaching them success, because success I don't think is taught. But some years ago I began to be interested in the history of psychiatry, and I devoted a great deal of time to the study of it. I now don't give one single course, whatever it is, without the history of the particular psychological discipline that I happen to teach. As a result, now we have in at least three universities in the United States a course in the history of psychiatry as an accepted course. It gradually slipped in at the University of California, on the Berkeley campus, in the New York State Medical College in New York City, a course of many lectures—as many as thirty a year. But there we find the difficulty that you pointed out in the beginning.

"When will we have time?" people object.

Well, there comes the necessity of the teacher being inspired. The history of psychiatry, the first two years, was given at eight o'clock in the morning. And you will admit it is a very ungodly time, if the college is an hour and a quarter from your home. Now it is given at the regular time as a recognized subject, and they are already preparing somebody to give that course if and when I drop out.

This is very important, and you cannot teach psychiatry without teaching a great deal about religious strife and the various problems of relationship of soul to psychological apparatus and to human functioning in society. It is fantastic to what extent medical students—the hardest guys in education—to what extent they respond. It depends on the teacher, and he gradually slips in a change of the curriculum. Just as the chemist will teach, and give the story of how Robert Boyle spoke about the pressure of gasses, and also introduce Boyle's theological views, because Boyle was a very religious man; and so was Newton, and Newton considered his physics inseparable from his religious views. We separated them; not Newton.

FATHER MURRAY: Just as a footnote to that, in this whole thing of change, whether it would be even curriculum change, there is another matter which has to be pointed out. It is not so much the question of the vocation of the Christian educator, but I should think rather the vocation of the Christian scholar; there are the changes introduced by the progress of scholarship itself.

All of us know, you see, that the field of scholarship in various disciplines tends to be overshadowed by certain myths that masquerade as scholarly hypotheses or discovery. So many of them have been exploded. You take the work of a man like Crane Brinton on the Jacobins, who used to be heroes in America. Consider all the work that has been done since 1920 on the French Revolution, the picture of the French Revolution that is given in the up-to-date, sophisticated course today, to use the canonizing adjective that prevails on our university campuses (the worst thing in the world to be is naïve, and to be sophisticated, of course, is the accolade). Take the work done by prominent medievalists with regard to the importance of the Middle Ages, and the obliteration of the concept of the Dark Ages.

So many of the myths still linger, like the division of history into ancient, medieval, and modern, a division which, as you know, came in from a study of Latinity, and then somehow got over to the other field. Now everybody is very unhappy about it. I wouldn't doubt that a generation or so from now we will not have courses in Ancient History, Medieval History, or Modern History. Everybody will know it is perfectly silly.

Take the work of a man like Butterfield about what he called "the Protestant Whig myth of history" that arose in the nineteenth century, under the influence chiefly of social Darwinism, that the history of mankind is a history of progress constantly. And the Protestant idea coming in, that you have the birth of human freedom at the Reformation and everything before that was simply slavery. No intelligent man today holds that. Take the theory of the single Renaissance of Wolcott. Now everybody holds the triple Renaissance. Take, for instance, the contemporary argument about democracy. It used to be held and taught that democracy began in 1789. Now everybody knows, who knows anything in political history, that it didn't, that the roots of the democratic concept are importantly medieval. The whole medieval concept of law, the whole medieval concept of the position of the ruler with reference to the community, the concept, the whole history of constitutionalism, which of course is of the essence of democracy, all these things progress.

I think that this religious revival today will not really eventuate in anything solid until it touches intelligence and galvanizes intelligence to genuine scholarship in all that pertains to religion: history, doctrine, and everything else. Therefore, the Christian scholar has a terribly important vocation here, and this is related both to the theme and the problem of the teacher.

If the teacher really is a scholar and knows these things, then he will not be getting off a lot of this half-baked stuff which usually used to be pretty much the stock in trade of the antireligious teacher in the classroom of the university of, say, not more than ten or fifteen years ago. It is the scholarly task that needs to be done here.

DR. FINCH: Part of the problem in the middle is that you have prepared no previous material, so that it introduces a lot of new ideas without the same background that the students have for the Greek strain.

FATHER MURRAY: Which is why I say you cannot understand medieval philosophy in any way until you realize the impact of the Christian experience on human intelligence.

DR. FINCH: Wouldn't you say Hebraic, too?

FATHER MURRAY: No, because I don't think the Hebraic intelligence was philosophical. But I was going to mention that before, that if you really want to get into the Hebrew tradition, then you are condemned to do what no one at the moment, as far as I know, has successfully done (I happen to be professionally a theologian—that is what I am supposed to be, at any rate), that is to say, you would have to introduce the student to Biblical theology. But it just happens that, at the moment, there is not on the Catholic or Protestant or Anglican or any other religious market an acceptable Biblical theology, curious as it may be. It is not curious; it is very explicable.

DR. WARREN: I was going to say, it is frightfully hard to do.

FATHER MURRAY: Yes, it is not only frightfully hard to do, but the doing of it was blocked for a century, at least, by the so-called Higher Criticism; it shunted all Old Testament studies and, to some extent, New Testament studies down the wrong alley completely, and only recently have they said, "No, that isn't what we are supposed to be doing."

Moreover, most of the stuff they did was perfectly silly. All their supposedly scholarly results are in reverse, the dating of the Gospels of the New Testament, or the authorship of the Pentateuch, the theories of one hundred years, the German schools, all today are completely washed up. Nonetheless, as of the last five years, I would say, for the first time has come the realization that this historical, logical approach to the Scriptures is valid and important; but that this is the word of God, and what we need is a Biblical theology; not a dissection of the Old and New Testaments, but an integrated synthetic presentation of the Bible in its own categories which, of course, is the inherently difficult thing.

When you start importing modern ideas or Greek ideas into the Hebraic tradition, then you are really succeeding.

DR. WARREN: You also have the problem of language. I don't know why I didn't think of this before—perhaps it is my own ignorance and stupidity—but if you are going to do this sort of thing, along with offering Greek and Latin at the secondary school level, in all honesty you should offer a course in Hebrew.

FATHER MURRAY: Quite.

DR. FINCH: That would be quite logical.

DR. WARREN: It is never done. We pushed the Latin and Greek to the limit.

DR. FINCH: That is an inheritance from the Renaissance, and that is what I think Father Pollard was speaking about when he said that we had a one-root instead of a two-root education developing.

DR. ZILBOORG: You can go too far. As one who was taught Hebrew very early and until the age of eighteen read everything in the Scriptures that was written in Hebrew and Aramaic, I want to tell you that it is a very, very tough job.

I would like to restate what I call the megalomanic approach, that man can do everything, that he can take care of himself, that man has declared his independence, and that all our education is now oriented in the direction of man being able to do everything. I think the exclusion of Christianity or any religion is due primarily to man taking the place of God in the present-day concept of the creation of the universe.

Liberal Education and Christian Education

E. HARRIS HARBISON

MY CONCERN in what follows is to state and try to answer a question of considerable importance to educators and Christians: Can a liberal education be a Christian education—and (vice versa) can a Christian education be a liberal education? The question is centuries old, and I have no new answers. But it has become a live question on many of our school and college campuses in recent years, and because we have become confused about it, it seems worth while to review the main historical outlines of the problem and some of the most durable answers to it.

The relation of Christian faith to *liberal* education is still the crucial question, I believe, in spite of the steady decline during the last two generations in the relative number of American students devoting themselves mainly to the liberal arts in higher education. If we cannot come to some agreement about what bearing Christianity has upon that traditional education of all men for citizenship and enlightened living that we call "liberal," we will never agree on what bearing it has upon the technical and vocational training which is mushrooming in such spectacular fashion in our society. The problem cuts across the line that divides secondary from higher education, and in this discussion I will largely ignore that line, although I am well aware that there are significant differences between the school and college settings of the question.

Let us consider first the idea of a liberal education. It is well to recall at the start that liberal education originated independently of Christianity, that it later developed in response to historical forces (such as the revival of the classics and the birth of modern science) which had nothing directly to do with Christianity, and that its main objectives have often appeared to be opposed to Christian ideals. Graeco-Roman society gradually came to agree on those "arts" which were peculiarly appropriate to the education of its ruling classes—that is, those who were legally freemen and did not have to work for a living with their hands. These were the "liberal arts": grammar, rhetoric, and dialectic; music, arithmetic, geometry, astronomy; the ancestors, in short, of what we call the "arts and sciences." The classic definition of them comes to us from the early Renaissance, from Peter Paul Vergerius: "We call those studies liberal which are worthy of a free man; those studies by which we attain and practise virtue and wisdom; that education which calls forth, trains and develops those highest gifts of body and of mind which ennoble men, and which are rightly judged to rank next in dignity to virtue only." Note the key words in this description: "liberal," "virtue," "wisdom," "ennoble." I think that on the surface of it we can say three things of this idea of a liberal education: It is on the whole, *secular,* deep-rooted in this-worldly concerns and aims. It is *aristocratic,* redolent of the ideals and standards of a ruling class. It is *uncommitted* to anything beyond an amorphous humanism as an explanation of the meaning of existence.

This is not the whole story, however. Like all great ideas, this idea managed to transcend its historical origins in a particular stratum of a particular society. Our dictionaries still preserve a significant ambiguity in the meaning of the word "liberal." Its aristocratic parentage is still evident in one group of synonyms: not servile or mean, unrestricted by pecuniary or utilitarian considerations, generous or bountiful. But out of this has grown another broad set of meanings, more culturally creative and more widely applicable: free, broad-minded, catholic, sensitive to new facts and open to new truths. Only at their very best have aristocracies actually incarnated these latter attitudes, but it is upon these broader meanings of the word that the best in the ideal of a liberal education has been founded.

The history of the Christian attitude toward the liberal arts is part of the larger history of the Christian attitude toward antique culture in general. Early Roman Christians were deeply suspicious of the secular schools to which they had to send their children to learn the three R's because they had no schools of their own. Virtue, wisdom, ennoblement of the mind—these were not characteristic Christian concepts —and the writings from which their children learned the rules of grammar were not Christian writings. Tertullian denied that Christianity had anything whatever to learn from classical culture, and even Jerome, humanist that he was and always remained, once dreamt that he was scourged before the Judgment Seat for being a Ciceronian rather than a Christian. It is important to remember that for the first thousand years of its existence Christianity developed no culture distinctly its own. Christians simply adopted classical culture—the liberal arts included—with various degrees of misgiving and enthusiasm. For a few brief centuries in the High Middle Ages, Christians tried to create a Christian civilization—and failed. Some twentieth-century Christians nostalgically bemoan that failure, but the present Pope is more realistic. In addressing an international congress of historians at Rome during the summer of 1955 he remarked: "One must not characterize the culture of the Middle Ages as *the* Catholic culture. . . . The Catholic Church does not identify itself with any culture; its essence forbids this." Even more outspokenly, the leading spokesmen of Protestanism have refused to identify Christianity with any form of culture, whether classical humanism or medieval ecclesiasticism or modern scientism. And so the liberal arts, although the basis of the curriculum in secondary and higher education from the Dark

Ages to our own day, have never been considered bone of their bone and flesh of their flesh by Christians. And properly so. Except perhaps for one brief historical moment in the Middle Ages, there never has been a truly "Christian" culture.

The plain fact is, however, that Christianity and the liberal arts have grown up together. They have interpenetrated each other in ways too numerous to mention. Christians from Jerome and Augustine to Paul Tillich and Jacques Maritain have held aloft the ideal of a Christian scholarship based upon the liberal arts and applied to the Christian tradition itself. Augustine's *De Doctrina Christiana,* the classic text of Christian Humanism, established the argument that for the committed Christian the liberal arts could be a means to deeper understanding of his faith, a steppingstone to profounder comprehension of Christian belief. Since Jerome and Augustine, there have always been powerful voices to proclaim that there is nothing inherently incompatible between Christianity and the liberal arts. Some Christian Humanists have gone further and maintained that they stand and fall together.

The Middle Ages domesticated the liberal arts in Christian society. At the medieval University of Paris theology was queen of the sciences, but theology was firmly based upon preliminary study of the liberal arts and the liberal arts faculty always far outnumbered the theological. The medieval Schoolmen were the first to work out a whole Christian theology and *speculum mundi* on the basis of the seven liberal arts, particularly logic. It was the Renaissance, however, that bequeathed to us the ideal of a *docta pietas* or *pietas literata,* a cultured devotion, compounded of the best in classical and Christian ideals. Perhaps it was best incarnated in the remarkable school that Víttorino da Feltre set up in Mantua early in the fifteenth century for children of the aristocracy and of his fellow intellectuals, but also of the poor and obscure as well. Vittorino believed that education should be a balance between three things: bodily exercise and athletic competition; rigorous training of the mind, particularly through study of the Greek and Latin classics; and instruction in Christian piety. He never saw any conflict between his enthusiasm for pagan literature and his devotion to Christianity. He set his students the example of regular confession, accompanied them to mass, and always took a personal part in their daily religious instruction. This, says a modern student, was "no nominal reconciliation between the new and the old. Christianity and Humanism were [to him] the two coordinate factors necessary to the development of complete manhood." [1]

Vittorino was not alone. In the next century Christian Humanism came to full flower in the north of Europe. Pietas literata, a Christian liberal education, was the ideal of Protestants and Catholics alike. "What profits all our learning, if our character be not correspondingly noble, all our industry without piety, all our knowing without love of our neighbor . . . ?" wrote Jacob Wimpfeling of Alsace.[2] There was wide agreement that a balance between knowledge and devotion must somehow be worked out. "A wise and persuasive piety should be the aim of our studies," wrote Johann Sturm of Strasbourg. "But were all pious, then the student should be distinguished from him who is unlettered by scientific culture and the art of speaking." [3] John Colet founded St. Paul's School in London on these same principles, and tried unsuccessfully to persuade Erasmus, the prince of Christian Humanists, to head it. Erasmus devoted his life to proving that Christianity needed the cleansing influence of liberal learning if it were ever to be restored to its primitive purity, and that the learning of his day needed to be Christianized if it were not to become dangerous. To those who asked what

1. W. H. Woodward, *Vittorino da Feltre and Other Humanist Educators* (Cambridge, 1905), p. 67.
2. In F. P. Graves, *A History of Education* (3 vols. New York, Macmillan, 1909–13), 2, 149.
3. *Ibid.,* p. 159.

Biblical scholarship had to do with salvation, he asked whether ignorance was any proof of holiness.

Luther disagreed sharply with Erasmus on a great many things, but on one thing they were agreed: the value to Christianity of liberal learning and honest scholarship. Luther knew that a preacher could not wait until the scholars reached agreement on the meaning of a text before he ventured to preach from it, but he maintained strongly that there must always be scholars in the Church who knew the three languages of Scripture, Hebrew, Greek, and Latin. "A saintly life and correct doctrine are not enough," he added. In urging the officials of German cities to establish schools, he incidentally expressed his regret that he had not had more of the liberal arts (particularly the ancient poets and historians) and less of theological sophistry in his own education.[4] Calvin helped establish the tradition of a learned ministry in the Reformed churches by basing the curriculum of his Academy at Geneva firmly upon the liberal arts. Jesuit higher education was no less clearly founded on the liberal arts and sciences. To Comenius, the great seventeenth-century Christian educator, education had three main tasks: "Erudition which aims at man's reason, moral education which aims at man's character and independence, and piety which aims at his understanding of God." [5]

And so Christians down to the seventeenth century came to terms with the more literary and philosophical elements in the traditional liberal arts and accepted them as reconcilable with Christian belief—nay, even as aids to Christian self-understanding. In somewhat the same way Christians from the seventeenth century down to our own day have slowly come to accept the natural and social sciences, which have

4. *Works of Martin Luther* (Philadelphia, Holman, 1931), *4*, 117, 123.
5. Robert Ulich, *History of Educational Thought* (New York, American Book Co., 1945), p. 192.

undergone such spectacular development during the last three centuries and now form two of the usual three "divisions" of liberal learning (natural sciences, social sciences, humanities). We sometimes forget that science is just as integral a part of a liberal education as art and literature, history and philosophy. The enormous quantitative expansion of scientific knowledge in modern times, together with the qualitative refinement of its methods, has tended to re-emphasize the contradictions between liberal learning and Christian belief. But it seems to me that we of the twentieth century are on the verge of a working reconciliation between science and Christianity not unlike that reconciliation between the humanities and Christianity which was the work of Christian Humanism in Erasmus' day. At least the conviction is spreading that "science is not enough," much as the conviction spread among Erasmus' followers that the revival of classical learning by itself was not enough, no matter what its early enthusiasts claimed. And this may prove to be the beginning of a more intimate relation between Christianity and liberal education, of which science is now an integral if not a dominant element.

Perhaps one reason why liberal education and Christianity have never finally split apart in the West is that they have always shared one central belief and concern: belief in the dignity of personality and concern for its integrity. Christians of course cannot claim exclusive parentage of this belief for Christianity. It owes almost as much to Hellenic thought as to the Gospels. In other words, it is our joint heritage from Athens and from Jerusalem, a fusion of Graeco-Roman respect for man as something more than the beast and Judaeo-Christian respect for man as made in the image of God. Quintillian, for instance, was just as concerned as any Christian educator that the teacher should treat each pupil with respect as a person, each as capable of his own measure of growth. When Erasmus preached patience and understanding in the teacher and inveighed against the "hangman type" which "crushes into indifference many earnest, studious natures," he owed his inspiration as much to Quintillian as to Jesus. Perhaps you have heard of the dear old schoolmarm's advice to young teachers: "Whenever you uncover the spark of genius in a pupil—water it, water it!" Her intent, if not her actual program, is typical of the best in both classical and Christian pedagogy.

What is the answer then to the first half of our question: Can a liberal education be a Christian education? I believe the answer is a qualified yes. A liberal education can be, and often has been, illumined by Christian faith. Augustine was the spiritual father of a host of educated Christians who have believed that Christian insight casts a flood of light upon the knowledge that man has gained about himself and his world from other sources. To the Christian, no genuine learning can be really alien. In oft-quoted words Augustine said, "Let every good and true Christian understand that *wherever truth may be found, it belongs to his Master.*" [6] Erasmus found Christ in Plato, and could even imagine saying "St. Socrates, pray for me." An important qualification is suggested by this case, however. Christians have often been too possessive about the truth discovered by the arts and sciences. Over and over they have been tempted to "Christianize" the liberal arts, to manipulate their data into Christian shape, to transform the liberal arts into Christian arts. Erasmus, it could be maintained, distorted Plato and misunderstood Christ in reading one into the other.

There is a certain integrity in the methods and results of the liberal arts which cannot be compromised with impunity by religious faith. This is why I believe that Christians should always be suspicious of attempts to devise a specifically "Christian curriculum," that is, presumably to develop a "Christian

6. *Ibid.*, p. 79.

history," a "Christian sociology," a "Christian mathematics," and so on. I believe the historical experience suggests that a liberal education may be *illumined* by Christian belief and insight without affecting its "liberal" quality, but that the moment one tries to *transform* it into a "Christian curriculum" trouble begins. Then too often the classics must be cut and expurgated, indexes of prohibited books must be drafted, logic must be chopped to fit theology, and the dimensions of the universe must be remeasured to conform with Genesis.

With some misgivings I may suggest a modern analogy, that of radiation. A certain amount of radiation is beneficial to organic life on this planet; it fosters growth and may even check malignancies. Larger amounts of radiation are disintegrative and destructive of organisms. In somewhat the same way, a humble, inquiring, and penetrating Christianity may irradiate the liberal arts in a signally beneficial way. A possessive and imperialistic Christian ideology may destroy the integrity of liberal learning by the intensity of its radiation. I suppose the chief danger today is that the liberal arts are disintegrating into intellectual anarchy through the lack of beneficial irradiation of *any* sort, Christian or otherwise. Departmental provincialism, the isolation of scholars from each other and from society, intellectual irresponsibility —*these* are the most obvious dangers today in academic communities devoted to the liberal arts—not the imminent end of freedom of inquiry and research as the result of the resurgence of Christian belief, as some would maintain. But there is always the opposite danger, that Christians who are concerned about the plight of liberal education may try to repeat the mistakes of the Roman Church with respect to Galileo and the boners of Protestants with respect to Darwin—that is, to demand that liberal learning be made to fit the Procrustean bed of dogmatic Christianity. The cure for the divorce of liberal learning from Christianity is not "Christianization" of the content of the curriculum but more learned and committed

Christians in liberal education shedding what light they can, in humility and devotion to truth, on the wider meaning of the subjects they teach.

This leads us to the second half of our question: Can a Christian education be a liberal education? Here, of course, I am using the word "liberal" in the second broad meaning mentioned a short while ago: open-minded, above provincialism, receptive to new truth, eager for fresh perspectives. How can a *Christian* education, an education presumably beginning and ending in religious commitment, possibly be a *liberal* education in this sense?

The answer to this question of a great many Christians down through the centuries has been that it cannot. Open-mindedness and commitment, they point out, are logically incompatible. Genuine receptivity to new truth implies weakness of faith. The "liberal" belongs not among Christians but in the limbo Dante reserved for those who refused to take sides.

There is of course much historical and religious justification for this point of view. To the cultured, liberally educated Roman of the first few centuries after Christ, Christian belief was, in Paul's words, scandalous and absurd. The natural reaction of many early Christians was to insist upon a firmness and precision of belief which would resist all erosion by secular philosophy and the natural reason. From the early Church down to Presbyterians and Jesuits in the age of the Reformation, Christians who took their faith seriously saw to it that no one was admitted to their company without careful instruction in the faith and strict examination to determine the results. *Catechesis* or religious instruction was recognized by the early Church as one of its major obligations, and the Church Fathers devoted much time and energy to discussing how to teach the rudiments of Christian belief to children and other candidates for baptism.

About the time of the Reformation, this instruction regularly took on the form of question and answer, and "cate-

chisms" in the modern sense began to pour from the new print-
ing presses of Europe. To one carefully nurtured on this catechetical instruction, with neat answers to all major questions
about his faith firmly implanted in his memory during childhood, it was—and still is—inconceivable that Christian education could be "liberal" in the sense we have suggested. A mind
formed by the constant iteration and reiteration of set phrases
is restless and disturbed in the presence of new truth. The idea
that there is moral and spiritual value in openness to new truth
can only appear subversive to such a mentality. At this distance
it is difficult to say whether Protestants or Catholics were the
worse offenders in the development of this authoritarian, catechetical Christianity. In the *Ratio Studiorum* of the Jesuit
Order the authoritarian note is predominant: "Also in things
which contain no danger for creed and faith, nobody shall
introduce new questions on any important topic, nor an opinion, without sufficient authority or without permission of his
superiors; nor shall any one teach anything against the doctrines of the Church Fathers and the commonly accepted system of school doctrines; but everybody shall follow the ap-
proved teachers and the doctrines accepted and taught in Catholic academies." [7] Such a statement could easily be matched
by equally dogmatic expressions on the Protestant side of the
fence.

It is apparent, I think, that catechetical teaching of this sort
is inevitably dogmatic, domineering, and divisive. There is still
too much of it around. It is a narrow sort of instruction-in-the-
faith aimed mainly at perpetuating the particular beliefs of a
particular community of Christians. It is not Christian *education* in any broad sense of the word. It pounds in, it does not
draw out; it demands conformity, not free response; it is instruction, but not education. It will not carry the present generation of students very far, it seems to me, in this confused
and tragic world of the twentieth century. Jesus seems to have
had this kind of instruction in mind when he lashed out at the

7. In Graves, *A History of Education*, pp. 219–20.

religious teachers of his day who made up heavy loads and laid them on men's shoulders but would not stir a finger to remove them, who shut the Realm of Heaven in men's faces and neither entered themselves nor let those enter who were on the point of entering, who filtered away the gnat and swallowed the camel.[8]

Not all Christian instruction has been of this sort, of course. Christianity would not be a living religion today if it had not been for the efforts of generations of selfless and devoted parents and teachers in transmitting the faith in all its breadth and depth. To take but one notable example, the Brethren of the Common Life in their schools of the fifteenth century developed an amazingly effective way of inspiring a simple, undogmatic, and practical Christian piety in pupils learning their three R's. More than any other group, they were responsible for changing the meaning of *religio* from its medieval sense of denoting the particular devotion of a monk to its modern sense of describing the devotion of layman and cleric alike. Until the Jesuits, the Brethren's primary and secondary schools were the best in Europe. Out of them came no single type or sect, but rather a generation of Christian leaders who grew to spiritual maturity each in his own way. It is a striking fact that Erasmus, Luther, Loyola, and Calvin were all influenced more or less directly at critical points in their development by schools founded by the Brethren. Through the tragic fury of the religious upheaval of the sixteenth century, the influence of Thomas à Kempis' *Imitation of Christ*—the finest product of the Brethren's mystical piety—worked like leaven. Jansenist instruction and Quaker instruction had something of this same quality of religious warmth combined with ethical seriousness, and other examples could be cited.

Do we have any examples, however, of Christian educational theory and practice which we could say were clearly and consciously "liberal," that is, based upon some explicit theory of Christian liberty? The question immediately recalls

8. Matt. 23 (after Moffatt).

figures like Erasmus and Comenius, Milton and Dostoievsky. Erasmus hated the little actual schoolteaching he had to do, but he wrote much on education and he probably had as much influence in the end on Christian education as either Luther or Loyola. Two things strike us at this distance about his attitude toward education: his insistence that a student's mind be treated with the respect due to a God-created thing, and his willingness to see any question of real human significance debated in the classroom, however controversial it might be. His *Colloquies,* begun as exercises for students learning their Latin, touched on most of the sensitive questions of his day in an effort to make the reader think. If Erasmus were a textbook writer today, I fear he would soon be out of a job and starving, thanks to the efforts of irate church groups, PTA's, and veterans' organizations.

Comenius was even more articulate than Erasmus about two ends of Christian education: that it must begin in individual freedom, and end in ecumenical-mindedness. Comenius was the first great ecumenical leader after the religious split of the sixteenth century, an apostle of a united Church and a league of nations as well. Through all his hazy idealism and his concern with the minutiae of pedagogy, there runs his dual faith in the unity of mankind and the freedom of individuals. "We must all have one and the same goal," he wrote, "the salvation of the human race." " . . . there is inborn in human nature a love of liberty—for liberty man's mind is convinced that it was made—and this love can by no means be driven out: so that, wherever and by whatever means it feels that it is being hemmed in and impeded, it cannot but seek a way out and declare its own liberty." Characteristically, it was the goal of his educational theory "to seek and find a method by which the teachers teach less and the learners learn more." [9]

9. Robert Ulich, ed., *Three Thousand Years of Educational Wisdom. Selections from Great Documents* (Cambridge, Harvard University Press, 1947), pp. 340, 346. Cf. Ulich, *History of Educational Thought,* p. 198.

The two classic statements of this kind of Christian liberty, however, were Milton's ringing appeal for freedom of thought in *Areopagitica* and the lofty irony of Dostoievsky's legend of the Grand Inquisitor. Both writers thought that God really meant man to be free in his response to truth and goodness. God, says Milton, takes no more delight in an unchallenged belief than in a cloistered and untested virtue. God deliberately refuses to compel man's response to his love, Dostoievsky seems to say through the various levels of meaning in the legend. Christ did not come down from the Cross when they shouted at him. "Thou didst not come down, for again Thou wouldst not enslave man by a miracle, and didst crave faith given freely, not based on miracle. Thou didst crave for free love and not the base raptures of the slave . . ." In the Temptations, Christ rejected "miracle, mystery, and authority" as means to compel men's assent to divine truth. "Thou didst desire man's free love, that he should follow Thee freely, enticed and taken captive by Thee. In place of the rigid ancient law, man must hereafter with free heart decide for himself what is good and what is evil, having only Thy image before him as his guide." [10] Echoes of Milton and Dostoievsky still rang in "A Letter to the Christian People of America," adopted by the General Assembly of the National Council of Churches in December 1952: "In all education, and in culture as a whole, the interests of truth are dependent upon freedom of thought. . . . It is, in fact, good for truth to have to struggle with error. . . . Error must be met by truth in free and open encounter. The conscientious expression of ideas must not be dealt with by a dungeon, a boycott or an *Index,* nor by arbitrary governmental action, character assassination, nor by the application of unjust economic and social pressures."

Enough has been said, I think, to suggest that the history of Christian education is not merely the story of endless cate-

10. *The Brothers Karamazov,* tr. Constance Garnett (Macmillan), Bk. V, ch. 5.

chizing by authoritarian sects determined to preserve their own identity through all future time. A distressing amount of it has been just this, but the liberal note has never been utterly extinguished. Thus the answer to the second half of our question is again a qualified affirmative: A Christian education, under certain conditions and in certain times and places, *can* be a liberal education.

And now what conclusions can be drawn from this hasty historical survey? You will gather that I have chosen to be more interested in *what sort* of Christian education we are to have in our day than in *whether* or *why* we should have Christian education at all. The latter are perhaps prior questions, but the other, I think, is more proper to a historian. The *quality* of what we have and its relation to the liberal arts have been my theme. And my central thesis is that *a liberal education can be illumined by Christianity provided that the Christian education which complements it is liberal.* There can be no fruitful discussion of any significant relation between a thoroughly positivistic liberal arts curriculum and a narrow, highly dogmatic Christian instruction. But between a truly liberal education and a truly liberal Christianity there can be a relationship of unlimited creative possibilities.

It is the genius of Christianity that it sees the eternal significance in concrete events. From the turning points of Hebrew history to the Incarnation itself, God (to a Christian) has been manifesting Himself in the actual, concrete events of history. The event is not absorbed and engulfed in the significance as it is in more mystical religions; it remains an event, to be accepted in all its materiality. But it is not merely an occurrence without meaning. It is a manifestation of a divine Will working in events, a Will which both reveals and conceals itself in the events of nature and of history. Our knowledge of the events of astronomy and physics as of human history need be no less precise and objective for being illumined by faith in the God who works through these events. The goal of the liberal arts is to provide *hindsight* and *foresight* of varying degrees of exactness in this universe of things and events; the part of Christian belief is to provide *insight*. Since our hindsight is never complete and our foresight is never infallible, insight is of crucial significance for living. Religion, writes Mark Van Doren, "acknowledges objectivity, yet on such a scale that the nature of things becomes infinitely less wonderful than their existence. Science and philosophy must rest in nature; their inquiry is confined to what things are and how they are connected, in number, place, and time. Religion goes on into the darkness where intellect must grapple with the original fact that things are at all. This is an overwhelming fact, for it measures our ignorance. Religion is the art that ⤴ teaches us what to do with our ignorance." [11]

But religious insight teaches us also what to do with our knowledge. Every fragment of man's hard-won knowledge of himself and his universe can take on deeper significance when considered in the mood of humble and childlike faith. This does not mean rejecting the sophistications of scientific method and returning to a Franciscan naïveté in understanding the world about us. Pascal is more helpful here to a twentieth-century Christian than St. Francis. Pascal saw that there are three levels or orders of existence. A drop of water, he might have said, at the level of ordinary, everyday, commonsense experience, is a clear, globular bit of liquid matter, useful for many things from washing and cooking to cooling one's brow and slaking one's thirst. At the level of science, it is H_2O, a formula which implies a considerable amount of exact observation, sophisticated experiment, and mathematical analysis. At the level of religion, if it is something given in love to a thirsty human being, it may become a symbol of that love of neighbor which grows out of love of God. Pascal insisted that the three orders of body, mind, and spirit are incommensurable

11. Mark Van Doren, *Liberal Education* (New York, Holt, 1943), pp. 141–2.

but related, and so they are. To view water as a symbol of
baptism need not affect a single step of the reasoning that results in the conception of water as H_2O. It may nonetheless
enrich the meaning of the material in question. In his *Varieties
of Religious Experience* William James remarked upon "the
difference between looking on a person without love, or upon
the same person with love. . . . When we see all things in
God, and refer all things to him, we read in common matters
superior expressions of meaning." [12] And so in the case of
events, their significance in the order of spirit should enhance,
not annul, their significance in the order of intellect. ". . . that
religion will conquer," Whitehead once wrote, "which can
render clear to popular understanding some eternal greatness
incarnate in the passage of temporal fact." [13]

Here is the essence of the relationship of Christian insight
to the data of liberal education. In every concrete fact and
temporal event there is potential meaning that beggars the
imagination. A liberal education does not reach its *own* goal
unless a student senses something of this meaning. Nor can a
Christian education worthy of the name be satisfied to stop
with general principles or intuitions and not push on to examine their incarnation in persons and events. Jesus never taught
his listeners fishing or agriculture or housebuilding or "positive
thinking," although he obviously knew quite a bit about each.
Nor, on the other hand, did he ever teach his hearers systematic theology. His teaching was never purely practical—nor
purely theoretical. Significantly he taught the people in para-
bles whenever he had something particularly profound to say
—and once he told his disciples why. He quoted Isaiah's bitterly ironic meditation on the frustration of prophets: "For
this people has become coarse within; they have ears that are

12. New York, Longmans, Green, 1902, p. 474.
13. Alfred North Whitehead, *Adventures of Ideas* (New York, Macmillan,
1933), p. 41.

hard of hearing, and they have shut their eyes, lest one day they see with their eyes, hear with their ears, understand in their hearts and be converted." [14] And he went on to explain what anyone might *see* in the humble, ordinary business of scattering seed on good ground and bad, if only he had eyes to see.

In the most poignant moment of Thornton Wilder's play, *Our Town,* Emily is allowed to return from the grave for one brief moment, to relive her twelfth birthday. The experience is too devastating to last for more than a few short minutes. Emily can see her mother from the perspective of all that has been and is to be; but her mother is too busy about the kitchen to stop and look and try to see Emily in the same perspective, as Emily pathetically asks. "It goes so fast," she says. "We don't have time to look at one another. . . . Do any human beings ever realize life while they live it—every, every minute?" [15] The answer is of course no. If we did, we would see with our eyes, hear with our ears, and be converted. And to pursue Isaiah's irony, this would be a very unsettling thing on any school or college campus. An Oxford don remarks, "On the face of it, religion is a nuisance in a university, though not, of course, anything like such a nuisance as cricket." [16]

Rather than suggest that Christianity should be a sort of divine nuisance on the campus, however, I think I shall stick by my earlier figures of illumination and insight. The right kind of Christian faith can flood a liberal education with meaning as light floods a Flemish painting and gives the scene coherence and significance. This right kind of faith will be an adventurous and inquiring faith, committed not so much to a particular church, a particular creed, or a particular ceremonial as to the person of Christ and to the Kingdom he

14. Matt. 13:15, in *The Four Gospels,* tr. E. V. Rieu, Baltimore, Penguin Books, 1953.
15. New York, Coward McCann, 1938, pp. 124–5.
16. Austin Farrar, in *The Twentieth Century, 157* (June 1955), 490.

proclaimed. It seems fair to say that the world is in too par-
lous a state, and this generation of students too dissatisfied with
ready-made answers and half-measures, for anything less
searching and demanding, anything less comprehensive and
universal, to suffice.

PROFESSOR E. HARRIS HARBISON DISCUSSES FURTHER THE THEMES OF LIBERAL AND CHRISTIAN EDUCATION

FATHER WEED:[1] Professor Harbison pointed out how Christian faith permeates scientific theory, in other words, throws light on scientific achievement, but the fact is that science is still science. How is it changed? What effect does this light of Christianity have upon scientific theory? Is it really made any different?

PROFESSOR HARBISON: I tried to make it clear that there certainly is no change. If there is, it goes against everything I was trying to say about the integrity of the subject, and about a way of getting at truth that has been developed sometimes by very hard-won steps and a particular discipline, and often at the cost of rather obstructionist experience—I am speaking historically—from theologians.

Now, let's grant that and go on. What is the alternative? If what these particular disciplines have turned up in the way of what you call fact has no relation to Christian perspective, then we are dealing with two utterly watertight compartments. I just cannot believe that.

I am not a scientist. I would feel more at home if you asked me what does our knowledge of historical fact involve for a Christian, and there, of course, you are immediately faced with the obvious truth that Christianity is an extremely historically minded religion which simply cannot avoid dealing with historical facts in some way or other, and with the meaning of historical facts. Conversely, what a secular historian turns up in the way of knowledge of the past inevitably is going to be important to the Christian in the broadest sense.

Where you get into difficulties is if you say, "Yes, but why should the Christian give himself any airs?" The answer is, of

1. Paul C. Weed, Jr., St. Luke's School, New York City.

course, that he should not. Does a Christian, for instance, think more scientifically than a non-Christian? I don't think we can claim that we do. On the other hand, as Christians, the data must have for us dimensions, profundity, implications that they don't have for a nonbeliever. I think that is obvious.

FATHER WEED: Would an application of what you mean be found in the discovery of the atomic bomb and the problem of a moral direction being given to the use of the thing?

PROFESSOR HARBISON: That particular example, I suppose, has a very long history. Man's power to control his environment always involved possibilities of good or of evil. I suppose from the first discovery of fire, men discovered that they could either cook their food with it or burn down the huts of their enemies.

The atomic bomb, it seems to me, is nothing new in that sense at all. It may be that at the profounder level the equivalence of mass and energy have implications for Christian theology that I certainly would not be capable of working out. I think there are possibilities in that range and that the Christian intellectual may find them very fruitful to work out.

For instance, the concept of efficiency in conservation of energy and engineering sometimes fascinates me as being an utterly non-Christian, if not anti-Christian, concept; and yet our whole material world depends on it—I mean, our whole technological society depends on it.

It may be that Christians have to come to terms with problems like that rather than with the more obvious and more ancient problems of the use of technology for good or for evil, for peace or for war. These have been with us for a long time.

VOICE: Would it be fair to say that in the world of today, scientists—I am thinking of people like those working on the Manhattan Project—having more social consciousness than those of us in the nonscientific world, know the implications of it? I am thinking of Dr. Compton, Dr. Urey, and so on. All those were closer to it. I don't think necessarily on a Christian level, but surely on an ethical and moral basis, they were more aware of the need for reconciling all the responsibility of the conservation of energy, if you please, on the Christian side.

PROFESSOR HARBISON: Yes, I think that is true, and I think maybe there are some reasons for it. One is that these men, at a certain stage in the discussion after 1945, were the only ones of us who knew the dimensions of the destructive power of atomic energy.

The second reason I think is that they came new to the social problem. I have often heard social scientists talk rather disparagingly about this sense of social conscience recently acquired by the atomic scientists, when perhaps the social scientist has been working all his life in a fairly long and steady tradition to understand how individuals and groups get into these tragic dilemmas that lead to war; whereas men like Urey, and Einstein himself, came to this kind of interest very late in their careers and in their collective history as scientists. This may not be entirely fair, but I think there is something in it, that the passion of the conviction of a man like Einstein is partly the result of horror and fear at suddenly being faced with destructive power that goes beyond the imagination.

VOICE: You mentioned a while ago that a historian, as a committed Christian, does not necessarily present the facts of history any differently than if he were not a committed Christian. How about the themes of judgment, providence, redemption, and so forth? If he is committed to the notion that the providence of God, the judgment of God, the love of God are all operative in history, does he write his history in such a way as to show how these themes are actually illustrated in history, or how these particular meanings are expressed through history?

PROFESSOR HARBISON: Do you know Butterfield's little book on *Christianity and History?* [2] I would follow him pretty closely, I would think, in answer to that. You see, granted that

2. Herbert Butterfield, *Christianity and History,* New York, Scribner, 1950.

you have a historian who is also a Christian—let's start with a hypothetical case—there are two extremes possible. One is the extreme of the medieval chronicler who sees judgment all over the place: everything that happens is a kind of inscrutable judgment of God. If the enemy wins, well, that is chastisement of God on the "good guys," as our children call them, and if the "good guys" win, why, that is a vindication by God over the enemies.

At its most elementary, this is the Old Testament view before it becomes conscious of the complicated, individual profundities of the problem. That is a rather naïve view, we'd say today. It assumes that God's will is directly manifest in events which take place in history, that God reveals himself quite clearly.

The opposite view, and it is still a Christian view, is a kind of Christian agnosticism which might say that God's will is in history but no human being can possibly discern it. This is pretty close to Karl Barth's position. Nazism is apparently a very evil movement, but Barth's first position was that we don't know whether it is good or ill, and that this is none of our business; God is working his will out inscrutably in history. We cannot, as human beings, either condemn it or approve it. Of course, he changed that under the stress of the war years, but he still clung pretty closely to the position that God's will is inscrutable.

Between these two views—and I think they are both nicely balanced in Luther—between these two views, something like a Christian solution could be found. That is, that God both conceals himself and reveals himself in historical events; and both sides of that statement have to be emphasized, because if God completely revealed his will in historical events, there would be no place for faith. Luther says it would all be obvious. If God completely concealed his will in historical events we might as well take the position of anyone who says that this is chaos. We can't see any meaning in it whatever. Somewhere between those two the Christian has to find his own balance between concealment and revelation.

I would take another step here. I would say that we are talking in technical terms about a professional historian who is a writer and teacher, and I would say some things operate on the level of his own belief that need not operate and probably should not operate in everything that he writes as a professional historian and everything that he says day after day, week after week in the classroom.

By this I mean that, as all of you know, what you say in perhaps one sentence which is forgotten by you immediately will be remembered by a student long after a half-hour lecture you have given on some point of judgment in history is forgotten. It may be that what you have worked out yourself and merely hint at in teaching or writing is more important than a very elaborate and documented and worked out defense of providence in history.

I sometimes think that to use the older theological terms like "providence," with students will cause more trouble than it is worth. With your conservatively brought up students it starts certain channels of thinking along older lines. With others it immediately sets up an antagonism. If you can say, "Is there meaning in this process to you?" and work from there, it is sometimes sounder teaching technique than if you start with providence.

Butterfield had a very interesting description of judgment. Of course, you remember that description of Nazism and judgment on Nazism. That is very ingenious, and I think it is pretty close to a good answer.

DR. PELL: [3] Your comments on dogma interested me very much. I think you said that education can be illuminated by Christianity if Christian education is liberal, that is, undogmatic. I wonder if you could expand that. Some of us have

3. Walden Pell, II, Headmaster, St. Andrew's School, Delaware.

been thinking we see more dogma, not of the wrong kind, coming into Christianity, and a little stiffening up of doctrine and definiteness.

PROFESSOR HARBISON: Well, I saw a certain stiffening of the clergy as I went through that passage, and I expected it. I suppose we have to say what we think—what we believe.

Dogma to me is, in its real definition, the officially sanctioned teaching. This is not doctrine I am talking about; it is dogma. Once you are talking about dogma, you are talking about propositions—about Christianity, what Christianity is—which are promulgated by authority; and that means, of course, human authority.

I come of a tradition, the Presbyterian, which said in the sixteenth century in so many words, "You can have dogma that is not promulgated by any human authority; it comes directly from the Bible." That is what Calvin insisted; what John Knox insisted. In other words, both of them, all of the early Puritan tradition, insisted that this is not the work of man; this is drawn directly from Scripture, and Scripture is intelligible to the person whom God inspires. I think to a person of the twentieth century that is unsatisfactory. Immediately the question arises who is the interpreter of Scripture, who says that this is dogma. This was fought out between Calvin and Servetus, whom he burned.

In the case of a church like the Roman, which is quite clear in its definition of what is dogma and what is not dogma, you have a clean-cut choice. Then I should say to a Roman Catholic that dogmatic Christianity is something very important to defend. I respect that position, but I think that for me I have to confess that wherever a human authority—and that means a church in its this-worldly aspects—is your source of dogma, I am suspicious of it as a historian and as a Christian. I think that the tendency to reduce Christianity to a set of propositions, which is the dogmatic tendency, has generally been limiting of creation, growth, and profundity, rather than fostering them.

VOICE: It seems to me that some of the problems stem from the tendency in education today to emphasize the liberal spirit in all things, and this means that we praise broad-mindedness instead of narrow-mindedness; we praise tolerance instead of praising a dogmatic position; and we assume that effective teaching almost perforce calls upon us to commit ourselves to the position of the liberal. It appears to some of us that it is a contradiction to be a liberal and to be a conservative in religion, to commit oneself to a single political party or a single denomination and still be free to be teaching objectivity to our students. This, to me, poses the central problem. Is the ideal that Professor Harbison set up representative of Christianity or of liberal Protestant Christianity?

PROFESSOR HARBISON: The answer to that is clear, isn't it? I can't claim to represent Christianity.

VOICE: Then automatically those Christians who have committed themselves to an inflexible denominationalism might have trouble agreeing with—

PROFESSOR HARBISON: Why, of course they would. Don't we disagree with each other? I disagree with them, but, my goodness, they have a right to their beliefs. Everything that I said this morning, I should think, would deny my right as a human being to say that I know they are wrong. Of course, I represent a liberal Protestant point of view. Let's say it is the one to which I am committed.

VOICE: That is why you were asked to be here.

PROFESSOR HARBISON: I presume so. We have all kinds of people represented on this program. We say what we believe.

VOICE: Would you like to comment on your notion of the relationship between liberal arts, liberal education, and liberalism as philosophy?

PROFESSOR HARBISON: I carefully avoided the word

"liberalism." If you could be more specific about what liberalism means to you and what I am being asked to relate it to, I would know better. As a historian, I am uneasily aware that liberalism has changed its meaning radically in the last hundred years, that what a mid-nineteenth-century person meant by it is not what a mid-twentieth-century person means by it. It means one thing in politics, another thing in economics, another thing in education.

As close as I can get to it, the word has been associated, and I think rightly so, with the search for truth wherever it leads. I am willing to grant immediately that the search for truth depends upon certain presuppositions; there are certain commitments that all of us as human beings have to start with. But I still think, as a person in an academic profession, that the commitment to truth wherever it leads is an important ideal; and I think if we all right here in this room got down to our basic beliefs we would say that this is one of them, that it is possible, if you devote yourself to it wholeheartedly, to attain a certain measure of truth by devoting yourselves to it above all other things. This is very close to the meaning of liberalism in education, if you put the "ism" in.

That is why I deliberately used the much-quoted statement from St. Augustine. Afterward Dean Rose of General Seminary suggested two or three other very apt quotations he had run across recently all the way from Hugo to Simone Weil, all along the same idea, that truth wherever it is found cannot be alien to the Christian. Your hard-boiled positivist on the college faculty will not admit the right of a Christian to even the title of being liberal or objective. I think it is fundamentally a fruitless kind of controversy.

Commitment doesn't necessarily destroy freedom. The commitment may be the beginning of a fruitful and open-minded search for truth. The idea that the truth you find will somehow destroy your commitment is the thing I am terribly afraid of, and that is what I find over and over and over again when this argument about dogma comes up. It is the fear on the part of people that something they find out is going to destroy the dogma.

Now Simone Weil and others are close to the heart of this thing when they say that the truly committed Christian cannot be committed to any proposition that is not subject to analysis, to testing, to trial in the heat of experience; because we are only human beings. We can't get hold of this absolute truth and put it down in a set of propositions and say, "This is it."

VOICE: You would set liberal education in some context other than positivistic liberalism?

PROFESSOR HARBISON: I think the people who translate liberalism into positivism are abusing words. They haven't thought through the kind of words they use. Liberalism and positivism are not the same thing historically or philosophically.

The word "liberalism" has deteriorated in Christian circles. The reaction against liberal theology, against liberal Protestantism, has run very strongly indeed, and "liberal" has generally been the label put on anything we don't like if we are moving back in a neo-orthodox direction, or in a neoclassical direction. We have two kinds of fundamentalism: one a kind of scriptural fundamentalism and the other a kind of creedal fundamentalism. I have run into both on occasion with the people in college, but I think there is something in this current that is valuable.

FATHER WEED: You spoke in your paper of being aware of the difference between the elementary level and the college level and secondary level schools. Certainly that is true, and mostly my experience in teaching has been with the elementary level. I have used the catechetic method a great deal, and I think if used in the right way it need not be the hard and rigid type. I don't see how you can get away from something of the catechetic method. You have got to teach some facts, but if you do enough of them, one fact will offset another so that the child or the person learning is able out of the whole series to make his own free choice as to what this thing is. I don't see how you can get away from some type of catechetic method when you are teaching. Otherwise, you cannot convey anything.

PROFESSOR HARBISON: Yes, I wouldn't pretend to argue that at all. I have enormous respect for the people who have experience at the primary, elementary level and who have, through experience, worked out what can be done with that age level to sensitize children to religious values while not closing off their own search for what is to be theirs some day.

The thing I am afraid of, as you could probably gather, is the kind of pattern-making that I think goes on in some education in this country which is primarily concerned with duplicating the particular Christian community in perpetuity, with drawing the lines very early when it is ready to draw them, with imprinting a particular interpretation of Christianity.

MR. PERRY: [4] May I take just one minute on a thing which we have experimented with at Milton Academy—this is the second year now—which, in terms of a search for truth on the part of individual students seems to us to have been rewarding.

I got this idea from the headmaster of Millbrook School who said that some of his seniors used to come up to him and say, "We think we have exceptionally fine preachers in chapel here, but they come at us with everything from so many different angles that we are rather confused as to what the basic tenets of Christianity may be. Might we have one very good man and have him take four or five consecutive chapel services and then give us a chance to talk it over with him?"

I did that with Graham Baldwin of Andover a couple of years ago. We called it "the basis of Christianity," and then we made it an entirely optional affair. We said the man will take the subject of God or Christ or prayer or immortality—some

4. Arthur B. Perry, Milton Academy.

large topic within the framework of Christian experience—and will preach on it in chapel for the customary fifteen to twenty minutes and then go to the library. What goes on after that I am not sure because we permit no adults, but because no adults are permitted, apparently the discussions are very lively and, I gather, rather fruitful. By starting with three or four major concepts, perhaps they manufacture for themselves, out of their own pursuit of truth at their age level, something that may be very rewarding to them. At least, they seem to have said so some years later.

PROFESSOR HARBISON: I think we have to remember one thing in this talk about dogma and education, and that is that an approach or an attitude which is appropriate in one kind of situation of human communication may not be appropriate in another. I suppose very few people who were arguing bitterly at lunch would think that I could believe in anything described as dogma. Actually, I do. I have had to sign a pretty mouth-filling statement as a trustee of Princeton Theological Seminary which certainly is classified as dogma. But the problem I was speaking about this morning is education.

There is a very important distinction, it seems to me. If you are preaching from a Christian pulpit, I don't think you can avoid certain dogmatic foundations in most of the major Christian denominational traditions; but preaching is not teaching. Teaching is something else, and I have respect for this aspect of the word "education," as I was trying to bring out this morning: that is, the aspect of it which is different from instruction. Instruction in the faith as it has traditionally been interpreted by the Christian church is one thing, but I think some people tend to confuse instruction in the faith with education in the broadest sense, and most of us are in the business of education. We are educating people who are Christians, Jews, and sometimes of other faiths, or militant agnostics. I think that the problem I was talking about this morning is something which, whether we like it or not, we have to face, and something we have to puzzle out. My only concern is to make it more self-conscious with most of us, because I think perhaps the best that we can do, and what a great many of us are doing in the classroom, in the teaching situation, is to prepare the ground, so to speak, for Christian faith, to suggest the Christian faith, to hint at implications of a subject in the perspective of the Christian.

If you try to turn the classroom, so to speak, into a place for dogmatic instruction, I should say you are wrong in most institutions of higher education in this country that I know of. You are not going to accomplish your end, and you are going to destroy many of the values you are trying to save.

You know the wonderful phrase from Montaigne, where he quotes somebody—I don't know who it is—from the Greek period who said, "Just give me that philosopher's conclusions. I can supply my own reasons." There is too much of this going on: supplying the conclusions and not the reasons. I would rather supply a student with the reasons.

DR. PELL: I think you are lost in a classroom if you just lay it down in a dogmatic way, and yet it interests me to find that boys of secondary school age are a little more susceptible to a dogmatic approach. They seem to ask for it a little more than they did, say, twenty years ago; or when I started to teach sacred studies and religion. Certainly when I was being taught it myself, we were great skeptics. Everything had to be proved, explained away, or gotten out in some roundabout way; but the boys I get now rather want you to tell them something definite.

PROFESSOR HARBISON: Are you pleased by that?

DR. PELL: No, I am not particularly pleased. I was surprised by it, and it caught me off balance a little bit at first. But it's interesting that they seem more eager for something definite, almost dogmatic, than they used to be, say, twenty-five years ago.

FATHER WEED: Professor Harbison, you said that we

should be suspicious of a specifically Christian curriculum of any kind. I don't know just exactly what you had in mind.

PROFESSOR HARBISON: Let's take the extreme example that I mentioned. Is there a Christian mathematics?

FATHER WEED: Obviously not.

PROFESSOR HARBISON: There was a Nazi mathematics, you remember. I mean that quite seriously. That was maintained by Nazi philosophers. There was a decadent Western mathematics. There is right now a Communist biology, as you know. The inheritance of acquired characteristics has been "proved" by Lysenko and the boys that were there. We haven't gone along with the evidence, but this is the kind of thing that has happened quite often in Christian history. That is what I am worried about.

Christian curriculum is an ambiguous term, and I am not sure that it has its place in a talk like this, because I find everyone has his own idea of what a Christian curriculum could be and what it means to him, and quite often it means what I was trying to commend and not trying to condemn. A Christian curriculum—well, if you take that in its literal sense, I am suspicious of it; but I suppose it could be interpreted to mean what all of you might be trying to build.

VOICE: I would like to ask: What is the scope of the expression "secular education"? Is it the absence of emphasis on teaching from a Christian viewpoint? That expression is used quite a bit by Dr. Pollard as though in all education today the emphasis were on the secular side.

PROFESSOR HARBISON: That is a big question. I think the development of the idea of what is secular, and what is secularism, is an immensely complicated thing. I would be prepared to maintain as a starter that Christianity is one of the most secular-minded religions in the world. Why? Because it has always insisted that its beliefs be carried out and rooted in this world. In the parable of the Last Judgment, we are judged by what we have done in this life, whether we have given a cup of water to a thirsty man, and so forth, and in almost concrete material terms.

This is quite strikingly different from Buddhism and Hinduism, so that when you say we live in a secularized world, a secularized society, it is, of course, literally true. A great deal of the Christian core has gone out of it; but at the same time I don't feel that this is as hopeless or as illogical historically as some people might feel.

I discern a feeling of hopeless resentment that back somewhere in Western history there was a Christian civilization, a Christian age. If we could only get back to that, we would be all right. Well, I know a little bit about that civilization, and I can see certain great advantages to it, and I can see certain great disadvantages to it, such as the arrogance of an institution which took unto itself to represent Christianity—not only to represent it but to build society, build culture around it. In some ways it is a magnificent, exciting ideal, and I would tell my students, and believe, that this came closer than any attempt ever to build a Christian culture.

This is the starting point for any talk about secularization; but you know, in many ways the work of a man like Latourette at Yale, in those great five volumes on the nineteenth century and the expansion of missions, is an eye-opener. It is a maintaining of the thesis that the nineteenth century, not the thirteenth century, is the great age of Christianity. Christianity spread further, faster, acquired more people as members, and brought more people in touch with itself than at any age of its previous history.

You can call the nineteenth century, if you like, the peak of secularization, but it was also a period in which the conscience of Europe was sensitized by Negro slavery, and about wage slavery, in ways pretty closely connected with Christian roots.

Yet secularized education, as the words are used by a great many clerical deplorers and viewers-with-alarm, is an authentic problem. Public education in this country is pretty thoroughly nonreligious, and since it is nonreligious, it naturally takes on aspects, in the minds of the students, of being antireligious. This, I believe passionately, has got to be changed.

You may have noticed recently in the *New York Times* a teachers' manual that is being presented, suggesting moral and religious values which might well be a kind of code of ethics of the teacher. It has been backed now by Protestant and Catholic groups, interestingly enough. There has been a long history, a long battle, but Protestants have come to feel they can join the Catholics on this, though the Jews are holding back. They have had a long experience of the danger of any kind of religion in the classroom. They feel that they will suffer by it in the long run, and therefore they are fighting it; but I think until you get some kind of mention in our public schools of the fact that religion is important, a thing to be studied, a thing to be taken account of, a thing to be looked at exactly as other important human activities are, we are going to have an awful battle in our sabbath schools and right down to our seminaries to restore the religious view of life. I think it can be restored. I think religion can be taught in our public schools and is increasingly being taught. It is being taught in a cool, inquiring way that need not ruffle things.

DR. PELL: I have been reading quite a bit on the English religious training in the state schools there, and I am wading through one of those books now. It certainly is interesting how far they have gone and what very thorough outlines of Christian history and doctrine and the Bible they have, and what a thorough course it seems to be. They have worked it out, and are going along now doing it in all parts of England.

PROFESSOR HARBISON: The more thorough it is, the safer it is, on the whole. I mean, the more scholarly it is, the more substance there is, the safer it is for the teacher to handle.

FATHER WEED: A year ago I had to appear in court in the case of the custody of a child who had gone to the Higgins

School, and the judge asked me why I thought that St. Luke's School was a good school to send this child to. I said, quite simply, "Because we teach Scripture there." He said, "Sir, do you mean to imply any criticism of our public school system? Don't you know that it is the foundation of American democracy, and democracy is the fruit of Christianity?"

PROFESSOR HARBISON: That is a good definition of secularism: teaching democracy and assuming you are teaching Christianity.

THE REVEREND GEORGES FLOROVSKY DISCUSSES
POINTS ARISING FROM PROFESSOR HARBISON'S
PAPER.

VOICE: I would like to know this: Whether a Christian, a committed Christian teaching religion, should let it be known that he is a committed Christian or whether he should try to conceal his position and even be the devil's advocate on occasion in discussing religious questions?

PROFESSOR THOMAS:[1] I wonder if this question of whether we should make an open avowal of our own religious bias at the beginning of a course is not just a part of a much larger question which would shift the emphasis a good deal if we saw it as a whole, and that is, namely, the question of what ought to be the attitude of the teacher toward those who do not accept his particular bias, not only at the beginning but throughout the course.

I may be wrong but what seems to me perhaps more important is the *way* one makes an avowal of one's own biases rather than the time when one makes it, and the way one treats people who don't have the same bias. For example, I refer to a Jew or a member of another of the Christian branches rather different from one's own. If one makes it perfectly clear that he thinks he has all the truth on his side and that these other positions are to be at best tolerated, perhaps even penalized if expressed too freely, then it seems to me that one does freeze the discussion.

On the other hand if one quite naturally makes an avowal with an attempt to show the people who would make other avowals that he not only tolerates but genuinely respects their positions, and that it isn't all a closed issue, and he is not going to penalize the position of the pupils, then I think the whole spirit of the classroom becomes very different.

1. George F. Thomas, Princeton University.

FATHER FLOROVSKY: The general question to me is this: To what extent should the personality of a teacher tell in his teaching? It should not be forgotten that both in secondary schools and in colleges students are very much interested to know who their teacher is. They want to have some personal contact, and dislike to be taught by any teacher incognito, as it were. They want to detect what is behind the teacher, and therefore they will not get any value out of the course if you conceal your position. If they cannot defy you then they usually are disappointed and probably are not so much concerned with what you are telling them.

PROFESSOR THOMAS: They are likely to be bored.

FATHER FLOROVSKY: They don't like to be taught by a teacher. They want to be taught by Mr. So-and-so, and I don't believe it is wise to fool them or to try to pretend that you are not what you are.

I would like to take up the question of bias next. Biases exist not only in religion but everywhere; it is hardly possible to be impartial, even in mathematics, and of course absolute impartiality is not possible in English literature. Would you conceal from your class that you regard Milton as a great poet and a man of generally great imagination? No, you would not do that. You would not treat him as a superstitious man who was indulging in some mythology influenced by some cabalistic traditions, and so on and so on. Well, that is bias.

Whether you regard Byron as a great man or an immoral person, and you are bound to do one or the other, that is bias. You cannot conceal that sort of thing. It would be the same in great literature as to whether you emphasized Euripides or someone else, and it would be the same in mathematics when you emphasize Euclid over some other great mathematician. That would be bias.

Further, whether you are a nationalist or an internationalist in your treatment of history, whether you think that the formation of national states was progress or a regression, that would be a bias. Again, referring to mathematics, you might be a partisan of the strict method and require strict proof or logical argument for everything. Therefore, as did a great German mathematician, you would refuse to use any argument *au contraire* because it never could be strict and therefore you would refuse, as many mathematicians do, to use irrational numbers and complex numbers and substitute something else. That is a biased approach.

So you are bound to have your position in this field because it belongs to your competence. You cannot be indifferent and treat genius and nonentity in literature on the same level. In short, it is very difficult to conceal your identity. The way in which you reveal it depends upon the situation and upon the size of your class. If you are teaching eight hundred or lecturing to a large group your personality tends to be broader. If you are dealing with a group of twenty, and you meet with them regularly, you must appear as a living person, and if you are trying to conceal anything you become artificial and insincere.

PROFESSOR THOMAS: What you are saying, it seems to me, is not merely that the student is going to be interested in the personal opinion and attitude of his teacher as well as in the subject he teaches, but also that it is right and proper that the personal opinion and the attitude of the teacher should enter into his teaching in an integral fashion because he cannot divest himself of all presuppositions.

FATHER FLOROVSKY: I would just give examples of why certain people with very definite and probably exclusive convictions are favorite teachers. Why are students so very much interested in a teacher like Niebuhr? He is definitely a very biased person and everyone knows that he has a bias; not only in theology, he teaches philosophy also. Is it possible to find an effective teacher of philosophy who has no stand? It would be very dull teaching if a professor of philosophy did not belong to any trend, including his own. It is inevitable that the

teacher will be Kantian or anti-Hegelian. One has to be pro or
anti. Is it a bias? It is just a fact. You cannot dissociate that
from teaching.

PROFESSOR THOMAS: I'm inclined to think that it is entirely possible for a person both to have his own position and
to hold it strongly and to avow it at some point, and at the
same time to be objective, leaving his own views out while he
is expounding and while he is trying to enter into another position and make it live for the student. I think we want to do
that. I think only a rather poor teacher lacks that combination.
That needs to be done. If a teacher is called upon to make
some sort of a critical evaluation of someone's position, he
should be able to do it, and of course a teacher should be able
to clarify his own position as well.

I don't think there is a necessity for being either purely objective in some sort of superhuman way, a complete detachment, or being so subjective that one would use a classroom
always just to propagate his own view. It seems as if we have
to do both these things. We should follow where the argument
leads and state the position as objectively as we can, and then
at some other point our subjectivity would enter into the position. If you didn't teach *Paradise Lost* in such a way that the
student understood the modified Calvinistic position behind it
and the Humanism that also influenced Milton and all those
other factors, you would not be doing your job well as a
teacher of English literature.

FATHER FLOROVSKY: The first question is about the trust
of the class in the teacher, whether the class should know that
the teacher is biased. Does this mean biased in the sense that
he has a definite stand and has a definite conviction? This is
the question; and it is a fact that certain boys and girls, if they
are told that the teacher of history is an Episcopalian or a
Roman Catholic, are immediately prejudiced, whether the
teacher shows his views or not. That is, again, not only true in
religion. If you go to a biology class in some noncommitted

universities and the students know that you are anti-Darwinian, and you are completely free to be anti-Darwinian, and you may be a very good specialist, they are already, maybe, prejudiced because Darwin is canonized in certain schools and excommunicated in others.

Then there is the political question. Certain boys, if they know that you are a Republican, will distrust you from the start. Others would distrust you because you were a Democrat. The important element is how you establish their confidence in you.

What about impartiality in philosophy? Every teacher of philosophy, for instance, must interpret Hume objectively and not attribute to Hume some nonsense to which he never committed himself. But is it possible, you see, for a man who knows all the shortcomings of Kant to interpret Kant or even expound him in the same way as a committed Kantian? He simply cannot do it—because your presentation depends upon your own position.

As a simple example let's take a lecture on the history of art. You regard Gothic art as something absolutely antiquated. You try to be impartial, but if you regard Gothic art as something perverse are you really able to present it in the same way, to describe monuments in the same way, as a man who regards it as the highest achievement? It is not the bias which you want to impose but it is your own personality. You cannot transcend it. It is quite obvious that we may try to be as objective as we can, but your presentation would differ from mine very much and another's would be different too, not because we deliberately misinterpret but because we can only look from our point of view. We cannot look from another point of view.

VOICE: I would like to have clarified this idea of dogmatic teaching. The kind of thing I am concerned about is whether we should say, when teaching noncommitted people, "Gentlemen, Christians say that Jesus is the Son of God," rather than saying, "Gentlemen, Jesus is the Son of God." I would take the latter to be dogmatic teaching and the other undogmatic, and in that sense I will say that I think the teacher should always take the former position and say that "This is what the Christian says and this is what he means when he says it," rather than saying, "This is what is true."

FATHER FLOROVSKY: I suggest that whether we assert authority or restrict it, in both cases we are being dogmatic. If we assert or restrict authority we cannot escape this. Even if we say, or rather refuse to say, "Christ is the Son of God," and put it in the form, "Others say this—the Christian Church or the Pope," we already assert something dogmatically. We can instill doubt dogmatically, also. My feeling is that when you proclaim the dogma of your convictions or the teaching of the Church, or if you say that "In the year 451 certain bishops proclaimed the dogma," in both cases you are being dogmatical, because you are deliberately avoiding saying, "It is the true teaching." You say, "Well, certain people have said it," and you instill a certain doubt. You present the statement as just a factual statement without any reference to the actual truth. You are saying that you cannot show that it is truth and you cannot show that it is not truth. If you tell the truth, or avoid it by saying, "Certain people say it is the truth," in both cases you are being dogmatical, and I don't see any way you can escape it. If, to avoid saying something is beautiful, you say, "Well, somebody says it's beautiful," your intention is quite clear, and you can't avoid being dogmatic.

PROFESSOR THOMAS: You mean that negations can be as dogmatic as affirmations?

FATHER FLOROVSKY: If I say, "There is only one God Almighty," and somebody says, "I don't believe in any God," well, the latter is mistaken for an undogmatical statement but it is dogmatic.

The Person in Community

ALAN PATON

FOR HALF OF MY LIFE I have been a teacher; by that I mean that for half of my life I earned my living by teaching. And for more than half of that time I was the Principal of the Diepkloof Reformatory, a reform school for African boys, that is to say, Negro boys. Of the six hundred boys there, many had never been to school and many had hardly been at all; it was clear that there would be little of the kind of teaching to which I had been accustomed. Here indeed I was to be compelled to teach a boy by letting him live; or to put it in another way, the community was to be his teacher. And it was to be mine too.

I was sent as Principal to Diepkloof Reformatory because our Parliament had passed a new Children's Act transferring all such institutions from the Department of Prisons to the Department of Education. At that time Diepkloof was a place of barbed-wire fences, walls, bolts, and bars; its very buildings turned barred and shuttered windows like blind eyes and deaf ears to the outer world; it was a community turned in upon itself, of unquestioned authority and unquestioning obedience. Was it safe to be so obedient? Would it be any safer to be free? Can one really be obedient without being free? Can one really be free without being obedient? These were the questions that were in my mind; these are the questions that are in my mind now.

To the principal of such a reformatory Parliament gives tremendous authority and power. No community can live without authority and power, yet nothing can destroy community more easily. What a sweet taste is power, how habit-forming, how corrupting, so that to gain it many men will sell themselves, and indeed any other person. Because it can so corrupt, we must know whence it comes.

Why is this community here? Who is this boy for whom this community exists? We all know what he is. He is an offender; perhaps he stole or robbed or murdered. But for his sake money is poured out like water, buildings are erected, principals, priests, psychologists, teachers, counselors, are all assembled together. Though he is the least of all, yet all this is done for his sake. Is he in secret the child of someone great, maybe, that it would be a matter of such moment for him to be saved? Who is he indeed? This question is the most important of them all.

It is not only this boy who is the person in community, it is you, it is myself. We are born into the community, and as we grow up we must enter more and more actively into its life. Perhaps when we are thirty, forty, fifty years old, we may decide to become hermits and to live alone. But we cannot do that while we are young. If we were shut off in childhood from the life of community we would never become persons at all. It would be like shutting off a sapling from the life of the forest; you could build a room about it and shelter it from the heat of the sun, the force of the wind, the cold of the snow, but what kind of tree would it be?

The community is our forest. There is no other place we can ever be. We must understand it as well as we are able, for it is our inevitable home. We must at all costs understand it, so that its inevitability will be the thing about it that we think about least. This is not primarily the place where we have to be, it is the place where we are; this is not our prison but our home. This is the road we must walk, and the walking of it is called life, and because we shall walk it only once, then how important it is that we should walk it with some purpose that we can call our own.

I, the child, cannot choose into what kind of home I shall be born, but I, the writer, can choose any kind of home I like. The home I shall choose is not an uncommon one. My parents are loving, but do not always know what love should do. They are Christians, but do not always know what a Christian should be. They are sinners, but do not care to be addressed as such. They want me to grow into a good man, and they send me to a school, like Kent perhaps, with that purpose as chief of all the purposes they have in mind. They know that when I leave the school there will not be much more that they can do. I shall be running my own affairs.

Into this home I am born quite helpless, but there are people to help me. I am nothing but I am everything. Knowing, myself, nothing about self-fulfillment, I help others toward it. I shall never again with so little effort be able to bring such joy. The first word I speak sends my community into transports. My mother looks down at me and says, "He is quite a person."

And she is right too. I am a person born into a world of persons. I am the person in community. My parents are Christians, and therefore I learn the Christian doctrine of what a person is. I do not learn this all at once; I am still learning to understand the Christian view of what a person is. Perhaps under the influence of humanism, or positivism or psychological determinism or the world's carelessness or plain arrogance, I throw the doctrine away, and with the doctrine I throw away many other things also. Perhaps later, needy and sick of soul, I return, conscious of the wasted years, saying as Eliot might have said, "I will not turn, I will not turn, I will not turn again." Suddenly, in a blinding light, I know who I am.

The Christian view of what a person is is both proud and humble. This Christian view can best be stated by using an old Jewish story. A certain rabbi used to say that all men should keep in their pockets two pieces of paper, one piece in each pocket. When a man was feeling complacent and self-satisfied, he should take out the piece of paper on which was to be written, "I am dust and ashes." But when he was dejected and dispirited he should take out the other, and on that was to be written, "For my sake was the world created."

I am made from the dust, but it is in God's image that I am made. I am God's creature, one of two thousand millions living upon the earth, yet even the hairs of my head are numbered. How magnificently the 139th Psalm conveys the paradox of this unimportance, this all-importance, of man.

> O Lord, thou hast searched me, and known me. Thou knowest my downsitting and mine uprising, thou understandest my thought afar off. Thou compassest my path and my lying down, and art acquainted with all my ways. For there is not a word in my tongue, but, lo, O Lord, thou knowest it altogether. Thou hast beset me behind and before, and laid thine hand upon me. Such knowledge is too wonderful for me; it is high, I cannot attain unto it. Whither shall I go from thy Spirit? or whither shall I flee from thy presence? If I ascend up into heaven, thou art there: if I make my bed in hell, behold, thou art there. If I take the wings of the morning, and dwell in the uttermost parts of the sea; even there shall thy hand lead me, and thy right hand shall hold me. If I say, Surely the darkness shall cover me; even the night shall be light about me. Yea, the darkness hideth not from thee; but the night shineth as the day: the darkness and the light are both alike to thee. For thou hast possessed my reins: thou hast covered me in my mother's womb. I will praise thee; for I am fearfully and wonderfully made: marvellous are thy works; and that my soul knoweth right well. My substance was not hid from thee, when I was made in secret, and curiously wrought in the lowest parts of the earth. Thine eyes did see my substance, yet being unperfect; and in thy book all my

members were written, which in continuance were fashioned, when as yet there was none of them. How precious also are thy thoughts unto me, O God! how great is the sum of them!

This uniqueness of myself is of the very essence of the Christian view, but it is a uniqueness of myself in the eyes of God. Away from him my uniqueness is lost. Read this famous passage from Thomas Wolfe:

> . . . a stone, a leaf, an unfound door; of a stone, a leaf, a door. And of all the forgotten faces.
>
> Naked and alone we came into exile. In her dark womb we did not know our mother's face; from the prison of her flesh have we come into the unspeakable and incommunicable prison of this earth.
>
> Which of us has known his brother? Which of us has looked into his father's heart? Which of us has not remained forever prison-pent? Which of us is not forever a stranger and alone?
>
> O waste of loss, in the hot mazes, lost, among bright stars on this most weary unbright cinder, lost! Remembering speechlessly we seek the great forgotten language, the lost lane-end into heaven, a stone, a leaf, an unfound door. Where? When?
>
> O lost, and by the wind grieved, ghost, come back again.[1]

This terrible and beautiful passage says to me more about man's lostness than any other. He is still a person, but he is lost. He is lost because he no longer knows who he is. He knows only that he came from the dust, and to the dust he will return. I am strongly reminded of a sentence from the final scene of *Death of a Salesman*, where the son says of his dead and pathetic father, "He never knew who he was."

We could not live our lives upon the earth if it were not

1. *Look Homeward Angel* (New York, Scribner's, 1929), p. 2.

for the heat of the sun. But suppose we were too proud to
have our earth dependent on the sun, suppose it were possible
for us to reject the sun and to declare our independence. Then
the light of the world would go out, all life and all warmth
would be gone; our freedom would be death.

But Christian doctrine teaches that man is more than a
body, and that his light is more than the sun. Not for nothing
do we sing the hymn, "Sun of my soul, thou Saviour dear."
For God is the Sun of the soul, and our being is in Him. The
world takes this for preaching but it is something far more
than preaching; it is the truth about who we are. When the
truth is lost we are lost also, in the darkness and terror of
Thomas Wolfe's world. And this truth is found not only by
saints but equally by sinners; and indeed it was sinner rather
than saint to whom it was granted to express it in unforgettable
words—Francis Thompson in "The Hound of Heaven."

> I fled Him, down the nights and down the days;
>   I fled Him, down the arches of the years;
> I fled Him, down the labyrinthine ways
>   Of my own mind; and in the mist of tears
> I hid from Him, and under running laughter.
>   Up vistaed hopes I sped;
>   And shot, precipitated,
> Adown titanic glooms of chasmèd fears,
>   From those strong Feet that followed, followed after.
>   But with unhurrying chase,
>   And unperturbèd pace,
> Deliberate speed, majestic instancy,
>   They beat—and a Voice beat
>   More instant than the Feet—
> "All things betray thee, who betrayest Me."
>
>   I pleaded, outlaw-wise,
> By many a hearted casement, curtained red,
>   Trellised with intertwining charities;

(For, though I knew His love Who followèd,
    Yet was I sore adread
Lest, having Him, I must have naught beside).
But, if one little casement parted wide,
    The gust of His approach would clash it to.
Fear wist not to evade, as Love wist to pursue.

But we must return closer to our theme of the person in community. Yet we have not really left it. This person in community is a unique being in the eyes of God, and when he forgets who he is his uniqueness becomes aloneness, and in terror of his aloneness he seeks security in the religion of collective man or in the religion of race and nation, or he shouts his defiance into the gathering dark, or he consoles himself that science, having split the atom and created life, will soon turn its attention to himself and bring him—chief joy of his desiring—quietness and peace of mind. Or, most terrible of all, he will, as in Budd Schulberg's well-known novel, *The Disenchanted,* shatter the image of God: life will mean benzedrene, and sleep will mean nembutal, and happiness will mean alcohol, and love will mean promiscuity. What other word is there than redemption? What other way, than to know who we are, persons unique in the eyes of God, with a freedom that can never be absolute, a freedom that can only be realized when we understand and obey the conditions of freedom?

But man in his arrogance will ask if this is really freedom. Does God really give freedom when it can only be realized under Himself? Can freedom really be obedience? (Here you must pardon me when I take some simple examples which I have already used in talking to the older boys of Kent School: the football hero, the carefree holiday, the music enthusiast.) The example of the music enthusiast is one that appeals especially to me; it applies to the whole world of the arts, including that of writing, which is of especial interest to me.

When we hear great music, we say we are spellbound; when we hear great speaking, we say of a fellow creature that he held us, even in the hollow of his hand; a great actress enthralls us: literally, holds us in thrall; a book grips us; a song captivates us; in American speech we say, "I am sold," presumably into some kind of captivity. But a common element of all these bondages is the experience of freedom; we give ourselves freely up to the experience of being bound. But they have something else in common also. We say of the boy that he has a love for football, of the holiday that we loved every minute of it. We call ourselves music-lovers, book-lovers, theater-lovers. In the experience of loving all sense of boundness disappears. We are glad to be what we are. No longer do we rebel against being what we are made.

Let us return for a minute to our simple community of the home. There too are the problems of freedom and obedience, of freedom and order, of self and society, of person and community. What kind of home is it where all are obedient and none are free; where all are free and none obedient? But there is a code of behavior to be followed, an authority to see that the code is observed, an authority to see that justice prevails. This is the external solution of the problem of freedom and order. But there is an internal resolution also. For where the authority is the authority of love, the conflict between freedom and order is resolved. If between my parents and myself there is a relationship of love, I move freely within this order. This community is literally my life.

But it is more than that. It is also the life of others whom I love. It is the guarantor not only of the kind of freedom that I enjoy in it but also of the freedom of those whom I love. I begin to learn that my freedom and the freedom of those whom I love is one and indivisible. You will remember John Donne's immortal statement of this truth: "No man is an Iland, intire of its selfe; every man is a peece of the Continent, a part of the maine; if a Clod bee washed away by the Sea,

Europe is the lesse, as well as if a Promontorie were, as well as if a Mannor of thy friends or of thine owne were; any mans death diminishes me, because I am involved in Mankinde; And therefore never send to know for whom the bell tolls; It tolls for thee."

How excited my father and mother would be if I stood up for the freedom of some member of the community not myself! And well might they be, for to stand up for the freedom of others is one of the marks of those who are free, just as to fail to do so is one of the marks of those who are ready to be enslaved. I am in truth learning the meaning of responsibility, and it has been taught to me by love.

No doubt many of you will remember the story of the small girl who was carrying a still smaller boy on her back; and on being told by a passing stranger, "My, what a burden you are carrying," she replied in innocence, "This isn't a burden, it's my brother."

In fact, I pause for a brief moment while I am writing this to reflect on the question, "Can responsibility be taught otherwise than by love?" And I reply to myself, "It cannot." Indeed many examples of irresponsibility and of indifference to the claims and needs of others are today seen by students of human behavior to have been due to deprivation of love in the very early years of childhood.

But childhood is over now. My parents prepare to take their hands away from me, and to send me away to school. My mother weeps a little in secret, partly because I am so small, partly because I am so big. With love, trust, hope, fear, they send me away. What they have done for me, they hope the school will continue to do. What they have failed to do, they hope the school will make good. Have they been too strict, or not strict enough? Have they been too this or too that? Well, they hope that the headmaster will have the eye of an eagle, the heart of an angel, the wisdom of Solomon.

This new community is different in many ways from the

home I have just left. Authority is more august, order more apparent, participation more complex; and love, if it is here —I assume it is, and I assume that it is unthinkable that it should not be—love wears a different habit, so that I do not always recognize it for what it is.

My participation in the life of this new community is more complex than anything I have known before. My academic education becomes more intensive. I am taught more about the world in which I am to live. I learn its history, its geography, its languages, especially my own, by which I communicate with others and they with me, not only others living but with some long since dead. I learn how man has learned to master nature; sometimes I learn in a few days what it has taken mankind centuries to discover; in a minute I am told a secret that a man has struggled a lifetime to wrest from the unknown; I learn in small measure to master nature myself. I learn how man has expressed himself, in art and music and words; I learn to express myself also. I discuss man's behavior and his achievements; ethics, morality, politics, religion. As my mind is fed, so is my body, not only in the dining hall but on the playing fields, and in sleep and rest. At a school such as this one, where there is a specifically Christian intention, I take part regularly in worship, prayer, and praise, so that I may remember who I am and whither I go. Above all in the Eucharist I offer myself to Him to Whom I belong.

I have had the privilege of spending some weeks in this particular community of Kent into which I have been so warmly brought. But I understand very clearly that it is a private and independent school, that it is not supported out of state funds, that it has a specifically Christian intention, and that it is, therefore, a school somewhat out of the common. Therefore, I shall not base my discussion of community on this school.

Furthermore, I know that there is a special American problem, namely, that the separation of Church and state makes the cherishing of Christian values a difficult matter, and that, in the words of the one-time president of the University of Chicago, freedom *of* religion has come to mean freedom *from* religion. There is another great problem which is related to this, and that is how far morality can be taught without the knowledge and practice of faith. All I know is that for myself, conduct and faith are locked together and that in me a period of faithlessness would inevitably lead to a change of conduct; and perhaps some of us have the sorrow of having a friend who is caught in the bondage of deterministic belief, and before our eyes goes into a melancholy decline. But although for me conduct and faith are locked together, it is still my duty to create a good community which will cherish these values, and which, in cherishing them, will teach them also to those who participate in its life.

In dealing with community in this fashion I am guilty of an abstraction, but I am sure we will all remember the many other factors and influences which make this community life.

Here is a school, and whatever other purpose it may have in view, its supreme purpose must be the personal good of each of its scholars. This school is a community in itself, but it is also a community that prepares for the still wider life that lies ahead. What a boy learns by living in this community must also serve him for the future. Is it possible to make some general propositions in regard to the life in community? This I have tried to do, aware and confessing that I am no master of systematic thought.

1. The first proposition is simplicity itself. *It is only in community that we realize ourselves as persons.* The very word "personal" implies community. It is only in community that our dignity as persons can be realized and that our needs as persons can be met. When we say "in community," we are not speaking in any spatial sense; it is only by *participation* that we realize ourselves as persons. One cannot be a Chris-

tian and not participate in the life of the Christian community; one cannot be an American and not participate in the life of the American community. One cannot, in other words, live in community without responsibility. To do it is to die, even as Manley Halliday, the chief actor in *The Disenchanted,* died long before his death. Than this, there is nothing more pitiable in all the earth.

This is relevant to the school community. As there cannot be life, neither can there be growth without responsibility. This responsibility must not be petty; it must be real, and must correspond to the powers and gifts and stage of growth. It must in some sense be responsibility for the whole community.

2. There is a personal good and a common good. They are both valid ends but are always in tension. *The common good is the common good of human persons.* The common good may mean a curtailment of personal freedom, but never an impoverishment of the personal good. I think that it was Lord Acton who said that the supreme task of the state was to enable men to lead good lives. And another great thinker has said that although a person is a part of the community he must be treated as a whole in himself. The common good is served, and indeed it is only then a good, when the community, and the authority of the community, have the profoundest reverence for the dignity of the person. The school is for the boy. The reformatory is for the boy, even though his life has so far been unsatisfactory by the standards of the community. He may be known as a thief and a liar, he may be the child of idle and dissolute parents, he may know almost nothing of books and music and almost everything of dirt and degradation, he may be one of the most contemptible of human beings, but for his sake was the world created. There is no thought more compelling, more restraining, more liberating, for those into whose hands he has been entrusted.

It is not his conduct, it is himself, that is our main concern. Insofar as the community can be good, this is the very stuff of its foundation.

3. *This common good is an ethical good.* It reverences personality, truth, and beauty as being of God and, therefore, of an order beyond and above itself. If it does not, it destroys itself.

Therefore, a person can give himself freely to the service of the common good. In this giving are both freedom and obedience. This giving is not a subjection of the person to the collective life; it is indeed the service which is perfect freedom. Happy the man who finds the cause to which he can give himself.

It is significant to note that arrogant and sinful man, who is bedeviled with the doctrine of man's self-sufficiency, can be deeply moved by the spectacle of a child in complete and happy absorption. And of course he is moved, for the last thing that the self-sufficient man can do is to give himself. Not for nothing was it said, "Ye must receive the kingdom of heaven as a little child."

The good school will seize every opportunity it can make or get to show its reverence of personality, truth, and beauty. Even the most august authority of the school will, with humbler persons, humble itself before that which is above all authority.

This subordination of ourselves, however important we may be, to something above us all, is made most deeply personal in worship, for here we subordinate ourselves to a Person above all persons. It is interesting to observe that it is this subordination of the person to that which is above persons which itself offers the greatest protection of the person. No community should be safer, surer, for the person than the Christian community. In no other community should a person be more able to realize himself.

It follows as corollary that the good school will not demand conformity beyond the limits in which conformity is necessary for the common good.

4. *The common good requires recognition of certain funda-mental rights of human beings, and especially those of dignity and privacy.* It is an outstanding achievement of American democracy that it has recognized and guaranteed these rights. I wish the same could be said about my own country.

It is sometimes said that men today suffer from an obsession with rights. I do not doubt that it is possible to be obsessed with rights and to forget about duties. But I cannot help noting in my country that those who protest against the obsession with rights are always those who already have them.

5. *When the community denies fundamental rights, it be-comes a tyranny.* It is the duty of all to resist any denial of fundamental rights. It is the duty of all to uphold them ac-tively. It is the duty of all to *use* their rights. I would note here that in any school community where the student body has some kind of authority, this duty and the opportunity to do this duty should be safeguarded beyond all danger.

Seeking freedom for ourselves and others is what keeps us free, and by our act the community is kept free also.

6. *When a person denies the common good, and seeks rights beyond it, or threatens the rights of others, he is an offender, but his own danger is greater—that of losing his personhood, his personality. The community is not put beyond danger by his correction; his restoration is also demanded.*

This is one of the most difficult tasks that can be undertaken, for it is the whole community that should restore him.

When a person neither uses nor cherishes his rights, he, too, is a danger to himself and to the community; great attention should be given to him, for no one slips more easily out of sight.

7. *The solution of the problems of such persons is in love.*

But the persons are not so different from ourselves. It is in loving and in being loved that we all are saved.

This love for persons should be shown not only by persons but by the community also. Therefore, authority should by no means concern itself too greatly with corrections; it should also concern itself with recognitions. By authority I do not mean only the headmaster: I mean also the student authority, if there is such, as such there should be. I mention in passing that I have noticed that in some schools corrections are kept entirely for misconduct, and recognitions entirely for bodily and mental prowess. Something is out of balance here.

A solemn thought occurs to me here—that it is recognition by love that is redemption.

8. *Authority is necessary in community, so that the code of behavior may be laid down, the common good may be maintained, and justice be done.* Authority is not an end but a means; it is a means to the common good; it exists for the common good and for the person.

Authority must not take away responsibility, for responsibility is the person's participation in community life.

9. *Authority and power are safe only in the hands of love.* Any boy with authority should be taught this. Because of our weakness, let authority and power be distributed as widely as possible. And let every person limit power and authority by actively upholding the rights of all. This is the true meaning of Christian democracy, which is our imperfect way of obeying the commandments of God.

Every boy with authority is in need of an education in the use of it. And a way of ensuring that authority is properly used is to invest it and all its exercise at all times with dignity (is this perhaps more a European than an American viewpoint?). There is no room for the barked word, the humiliation of any person, for then authority has forgotten what it is and whence it came. It has degenerated into power.

10. Finally and ultimately, while the duty of the community is to pursue the common good and to uphold the good of all its persons, it does not give them their value, which comes only and solely from God. *Our health and strength, and the health and strength of our community, depend on our knowing and our being what we are.*

I do not suppose for one moment, ladies and gentlemen, that I have done very much. In a moment I shall tell you what I think I can do, but let me first tell for what reasons—apart from personal incapacities—I cannot do more. Dr. Pollard is right that we are living in a dark age. Each man can give his own reasons for believing that to be so. But the speaker on "The Person in Community" should have reasons of his own. Of the depersonalization of human life we are all painfully aware; of the failure to create community, even of the dislike to be in community at all; of the loss of freedom and the growth of authority and power; of the curtailment of responsibility, of the fear of responsibility, even the sense of the futility of feeling and responsibility at all; of the personal lostness, the loss of purpose, most of all the decline of our power, our willingness to love.

It is a dark age, and I, too, believe that the Holy Spirit only can bring us out of it, if we are to be brought out. And I believe that Christian education may be one of the instruments of that salvation.

But in the meantime, there is something that I can do if I am responsible for a community that is not specifically Christian. In a depersonalized world I can try to restore these personal values; I can try to create that community in which all have one responsibility and therefore are free; I can try to create that community which, in cherishing these values, will teach them also to those who participate in its life.

ALAN PATON DISCUSSES THE THEMES OF FAITH, MORALITY, AND COMMUNITY.

VOICE: You indicated in your address, Mr. Paton, that when man is estranged from God he feels lost. Would you discuss that?

MR. PATON: When I said that, I was thinking of my own particular experience. I remember when I went to college. I took a course in physics and mathematics, and I was supposedly exposed to all the scientific thought of the world, and for a period of some six years I accepted the view which is largely current in our college circles, that if there was a divine being, he wasn't particularly concerned with us as persons. When I lost the belief that my Creator was particularly concerned with me as a person I found that it began to affect my relationship also with other persons.

I was married and we had children and I would still look back to that time as a lost period in my particular life and experience. I only hope and trust that it will not also be a lost experience for our children, the fact that in these years we ourselves were lost, just at the time when we had children.

One of those children is today married. I made up my mind that when they are expecting their children, I shall feel it my duty to go and say certain things to them, or rather to make some kind of confession to them, that these are things I wish I had done "when you were children," that they ought to do them and try to make them good in later years.

VOICE: I don't mean to probe here into something quite personal for you, but I wonder more specifically what you had in mind in terms of preparing these grandchildren more adequately for the experiences of community.

MR. PATON: I just thought I would raise very briefly earlier the problem that Dr. Shepherd has continued,[1] I think, when he also raised the question as to whether one could

1. See Dr. Shepherd's paper, following.

really teach or maintain a morality unless one had achieved a faith. I would say that in the particular period I was telling you about we tried to teach a morality which was not really founded in faith.

As to advising my children with regard to their children, I would say to them that with each succeeding generation which tries to teach it in this fashion to its children, morality becomes further and further removed from what I believe is the only ultimate source of morality. I feel sure that morality itself begins to dissipate and disintegrate and loses its content, and I would say to them that for the sake of their children I feel they should give them what I would call a more dogmatic education and a more dogmatic upbringing than I myself gave them.

It seems to me that that is one of the questions of the seminar. We talk about Christian education. I think it was raised, probably in a very acute form, by Professor Harbison in his paper, when he gave his opinion that a Christian education could never quite be a liberal education, that liberal education could never quite be a Christian education. It seems to me that it left out of account one very great question. The great question was, what must we do in the state, the condition, of man as we find it now, the condition of ourselves?

I feel that our education would have to be much more specifically Christian than it is. That is really the point I was going to make. Or I would almost feel that my own children in regard to their children would have to make up their minds whether they were to be Christian or not Christian, and that a kind of halfway position, surely, we have seen is untenable.

VOICE: But even in the home I myself would hesitate with my own children to demand a commitment one way or another at a given stage of their development. I would do with my children as I would do in the school, and say, "Here is what I believe, here is what the school stands for," arguing it out, and let them make up their minds.

I gathered from what you said—and perhaps I misunderstood you—that you would, to use the word that has been bandied about, dogmatize to the extent of saying, "Well, you make up your minds one way or another."

MR. PATON: Our professor of education used to say that he felt it was his duty to give to his child the bare outlines of religion. Then as for those who might wish to discard it, that would be their concern. I would state very strongly that view because I have a great revulsion against an attempt to make children be something. I don't think I meant that. But I would tell them specifically where I stood and what I believe. I would say that I felt these things were the rocks upon which my life was founded.

VOICE: One point I think Mr. Paton was making in his way, and which was made by Professor Shepherd in his way, is that actually you have got to be in a community to learn anything, to be truly educated. You have got to be a member of the community. That is the way a child starts, that is the way a child learns. If we can agree to that, we have at least got some kind of start, haven't we?

VOICE: May I ask the gentleman who said he would not require his children to accept and believe in Christianity per se, if he would not expect them to know what Christianity is?

VOICE: Certainly.

VOICE: That is quite a different thing.

VOICE: Wouldn't the community situation, as Mr. Paton has described it, pretty well eliminate the business of just cracking the whip and saying, "Damn it, you have got to do this"? Isn't that the whole point of the community situation, that you don't do that? It is authority under the aegis of love, manifested under the control of law.

MR. PATON: In some communions the child is almost immediately introduced into the life of the church and in other denominations that isn't done, it is done in some other way. But in the church to which I belong, for example, the child is baptized, and at the confirmation he confirms the vows that were made for him at the time of baptism when he really knew nothing of what was happening.

VOICE: I would agree with you that you would say, "Here is the reading, the knowledge that you ought to have, and read the opposite viewpoint by all means. The decision is yours; that is all."

MR. PATON: I would agree with that too. But looking back again to my own experience, I don't think that we made it clear to our children that there would have to be some kind of commitment. That is what I think. I think that is where we failed. I think it was more or less because of the state of faithlessness in which we were that we couldn't throw away the outward appearance of being Christians. On the other hand, we discarded much of what was inward. I think, therefore, that we were afraid to say to the children, "You ought to make up your minds, not just that you should know about it but that you have to make up your minds about it, you have to commit yourselves to it in some way."

VOICE: Whether it is now or ten years from now.

MR. PATON: Yes, it wouldn't make any difference. I think that is where we failed. When we returned to a committed position again ourselves and then tried to restore the things that we had omitted, we couldn't help wondering whether it was possible—and I remember they say that it is in the first seven years that the child is made.

To return to the question of schools, I think you know that in Great Britain Parliament adopted quite a different attitude toward Christian education.

VOICE: Would you state that for us briefly?

MR. PATON: I will tell you where it is fully stated, in a book by Spencer Leeson.[2] As you know, in Great Britain you still have the closest association of state and Church. I

2. Spencer Leeson, *Christian Education*, London, New York, Longmans, Green, 1947.

think that the rising rate of delinquency, the rising rates of divorce and this general feeling of the fact that Britain was losing something, the fact that the influence of the Church itself was probably at its lowest, so affected Parliament— and I suppose a lot of the people in Parliament were people who were not particularly active themselves in any Christian sense—that they passed their Education Act, which gave to the schools the directive that religious education should become much more a matter of active participation than it had been, no longer a matter of the passive acceptance of information, but actual worship and living.

One must be humble here and not pretend to know what the effects of such legislation will be, but it was a fact that many of the teachers of Great Britain were disturbed, and they themselves felt that it was necessary.

VOICE: Ever since you discussed the community, I have been thinking of a book by Erich Fromm in which he points to some communities I have not heard of before, over in Europe—I can't identify them now, but they were small communities mostly built around some industry; communities built on a humanistic basis, that seemed to be quite successful. They seem to be rather impressive evidence of a minor sort for the success of a community based on a humanistic ethic.

MR. PATON: I think one can point to many individual communities that are successful. There is a copper belt in Northern Rhodesia where the mines are the only communities and they are very successful communities. They are only partial communities, but they are extremely successful.

I was not thinking of that so much as of the fundamental basis on which to found a community. You know, for example, that the African people had the most beautiful simple communities, and the community took responsibility for almost every important thing that ever happened in a man's life. There was nothing of the anxiety and strain that we experience in our own communities. There was an extraordinary obedience to the tribal authority, and yet at the same time when pictures were taken of these people one saw an extraordinary air of freedom.

Yet they were absolutely terror-struck, terror-ridden by witchcraft and by their belief in spirits. And as a matter of fact, even that society was almost shattered by a tyrant whose name was Chaka. It is an extraordinary picture of a society which with all this external beauty produced, perhaps not art by European standards, but many kinds of art, and everyone who came into contact with them became admirers or worshipers. This society was just destroyed by one man in the course of a few years.

VOICE: I understand your experience in South Africa in a community was in a reformatory that had mostly Negroes, native Africans. I have been thinking of what this experience must have been like in terms of what the potential was of these particular individuals. I am not sure what their education was, I am not sure of what their background was on the average; but how complete a community was this one that you dealt with? What was the capacity of these particular boys that you encountered in this situation, for achieving among themselves any meanings that might approach, say, Christian meanings?

MR. PATON: You asked in the first place about their education. Some of them had had no formal education at all. Others had had very little. For example, say that out of six hundred boys there would probably have been forty who had reached what you would call the eighth grade.

Secondly, in regard to language, they spoke six different languages, but luckily one language would be spoken by seventy per cent and another language by fifty per cent, which was a great help.

In regard to the assuming of the responsibility that was

given to them, I found them no different from any other persons, not lacking in any way whatsoever.

Christianity has made a very large number of converts among the African people of South Africa. That doesn't necessarily mean anything very important, but it does mean that there were certain Christian ideas which were readily understood. For example, even in their own societies they had had a supreme being; they believed in a supreme being, and he was remote and unapproachable. But they accepted the Christian belief that this supreme being was not remote and unapproachable, but had actually become man, part of man's history.

I should think that one of the great characteristics of their religion was the tremendous humility in worship. That strikes me as something that we have lost. It is quite an ordinary sight to see people prostrating themselves as they enter a church.

You see, we are talking about study, worship, and living. As far as study was concerned, their equipment was almost nil. But when it came to worship, they were the most humble of creatures. It has a very profound effect on society, on sophisticated people who worship with them. It is a very humbling experience to worship with such people. But there is just one thing I was thinking about while we were talking here in regard to student responsibilities. Of course their student responsibility was very different in content from the kind of student responsibility that is taken in a place like Kent. However, a very special part of our education was devoted to that, to the preparing of a boy to assume responsibility when he had the responsibility; and especially when he had authority, to teach him how to use it. It was a very important part of the education, and even some attempt was made to formalize it, and it became construction as well.

I would like to add one more comment. That is, to revert

to the question of morality and faith. It is a very interesting thing that in South Africa where the supreme moral value is racial survival, this permits us to do all the kinds of things that you think are so terrible when you read about them in the papers.

It is a very interesting reflection, as a matter of fact, that we are enabled, if we regard racial survival as our supreme value, to commit almost any other kind of immorality and feel that we are doing a good thing too.

The Liturgy and Christian Education

BY MASSEY H. SHEPHERD, JR.

THE INVITATION to participate in this symposium on "The Christian Idea of Education" imposed upon me a particular term of reference: "To show the place which the liturgy holds as the integrating, coordinating, and harmonizing factor underlying the Christian concept of education." In particular, within the context of the present program of these discussions, this address is designed to serve as an exposition of the significance of the Solemn Eucharist in which the school and conference have just engaged as a community of Christian disciples and believers. We are summoned therefore to consider Christian education from the vantage point of Christian worship, to explore the way by which the Christian liturgy embodies concretely the essential meaning of education from a Christian perspective. Such an approach makes clear at the outset of our discussion that the liturgical custom and practice of the Church are not a mere illustration or a useful resource for promoting an idea or an ideal of Christian education. On the contrary, the liturgy is the quintessence of Christian education itself, the focus of its inspiration and its fulfillment.

Schools and colleges of Christian foundation have consistently centered their corporate life about a chapel. The rhythm of daily life in the school community has been informed by the common offices of worship in this chapel. The chapel building may not always have been so large and imposing a structure as the library, the laboratory, or the athletic stadium. The faculty and students of the school may not always have found the services of the chapel the most interesting and memorable occasions of their years together. Indeed they may have found the obligation of chapel attendance in many instances irksome and dull by comparison with the book, the experiment, the game. Christian institutions do not invariably live up to their ideals. Lectures and class discussions are often more perceptively stimulating than hymns and prayers and ceremonial acts. Friendships molded in fraternity and club are often more closely felt than the bonds knit by a common religious faith and sacramental experience. We neither deny nor argue these facts. We merely affirm that in spite of them Christian educators persist in pointing to their chapels as the symbols and centers of their schools' wholeness of purpose, values, and enduring achievements. It is an intention of this discussion to suggest that in holding to this ideal, however difficult it may be in realization, Christian educators are not victimized by the self-deception of their own wishful thinking.

BY WAY OF DEFINITION

We begin by defining certain of our basic assumptions about religion in general and Christianity in particular. For it is well to bring them into the open at the outset. Systems of belief and codes of behavior are integral elements in all religion. Taken by themselves, however, they do not constitute religion in its essence. They may even exist in detachment from religious practice as mythology, theology, or philosophy. The unique and integrative factor of religion is worship, the act whereby man seeks rapport and communion with that ultimate reality which he calls God. We are not concerned here with the intriguing question of religio-historical research regarding what comes first, whether in logical or temporal priority, creed or cult. Doubtless the two are in some measure always found together. A man's creed inevitably affects the character of his cult, as in turn his cult practices give suggestion to the shape of his beliefs and ethical attitudes. But it is participation in worship, even though it be only a private exercise of prayer and meditation, that makes a man religious. One may believe in the existence of God as a philosophical or scientific truth, but this belief does not make one religious unless it issues from or in an act of reverence. One may follow an ethic of love as a pragmatic principle of behavior, but the virtue of charity is not religious unless it is motivated by obedience to an imperative accepted worshipfully as the re-vealed will of God.

There is no need to sidetrack our discussion at this point by the question whether or not religion must be theistic. There are, to be sure, atheistic religions that can be identified—classic Buddhism, certain types of humanism, and in some measure the dialectical materialism of modern Communism. But these are religions, and not merely philosophies, only to the extent that they involve for their devotees experiences that partake of the nature of cult. Our concern here, in any event, is with Christianity, a theistic religion that proclaims a supernatural revelation and a suprahistorical judgment, not as philosophical postulates but as imperatives of devout contemplation. The truths of Christianity, both theological and ethical, though they may be the subject of rational inquiry, are basically apprehended and applied to all men, irrespective of their native intelligence or formal education, in the context of adoring faith.

Now faith is a great deal more than a working hypothesis. It is a quality of personal relationships, in which the object of faith is counted worthy of trust and the subject of faith worthy of being trusted. Religious faith is closely bound up with worship. In the religious experience of Christians, the divine-human encounter occurs most intimately in a worship-ful context. It is an intercommunication of persons in unreserved fidelity and trust and in unselfish love and service. It involves the wholeness of life, coordinating strength of body, singleness of mind, and purity of heart, and thereby it in turn enhances life in its wholeness. Worship, when grounded in faith, is the response of man in total commitment to God who is ever ready to give Himself to man as the ground of his existence, the arbiter of his destiny, and the final succor of his self-fulfillment. For the Christian, such worship can be mediated only through Jesus Christ, who is in His divine-human natures and person the prototype, the judge, and the savior of his life.

When considered in this perspective, the experience of Christian worship is clearly one and the same with the goal of Christian education. It is what the Gospel calls salvation: the wholeness of the human person as he fulfills his truest self in responding to God as creature, child, and servant. For this reason, the concern of Christianity with education has primarily to do with personal character in all its responses to interpersonal relationships, both to God and to men. It cannot view education merely in terms of the acquisition of information, scientific research, or the promotion of technical competence. Christianity, of course, does not despise these lesser interests of the educational process, for it cannot be negative toward any knowledge of the natural world since it accepts the natural world as the creation of God. There have been times when Christian leaders have shown themselves hostile to or contemptuous of humane learning; but their repugnance to science has been a reaction to the claims of science to an absolute value or to the use of science for an amoral purpose. *Scientia,* in the Christian scheme of things, is worth while only as it is ordered by *sapientia,* that wisdom which is the highest gift of the Spirit of God. Wisdom is more than information and technique. It is the very image of the mind of God, in Whom knowledge is enfolded in understanding, and activity is directed by love. To have the mind of Christ, Who is the Wisdom and the Power of God, is to be able to discern the things that differ and to do the work of reconciliation.

Since man is not an autonomous, self-sufficient individual but a social animal, his religion in all its more developed forms is communally ordered. This is particularly true of Christianity, since it claims to be the community of the people of God, an *ecclesia*. All the Biblical metaphors and analogies regarding the Church make this clear, such as the figures of the vine and branches, the building with its several, knit-together stones, the bodily organism with its many members. No one can be a Christian in isolation. Communion and fellowship are part of the givenness of Christian life. Hence the worship of Christians is basically communal and corporate. Even in the innermost secret of his private devotion and prayer, a Christian is never alone. The very fact that all his worship is addressed to God through the Lord Jesus Christ is a sufficient reminder that he is a member of a body of which Christ is the Head, and that what affects one member of the body affects all the members.

From the very earliest days of its existence the unique and distinguishing characteristic of Christian discipleship was the meeting together for common acts of worship. "They continued steadfastly in the apostles' teaching and fellowship, in breaking of bread, and in prayers" (Acts 2:42). This gathering together of Christians marked them off at once from the wider community of Judaism, though the wider world community for a generation hardly distinguished them as anything more than a party or sect within the parent religious group. It is significant, too, that in later times the Roman government discerned the peculiar offense of Christians in their assemblies for worship. Roman emperors and magistrates cared little what Christians believed about Jesus of Nazareth, and they were singularly loath to make any investigation regarding the moral and social behavior of their Christian subjects. Their unfailing identification of true adherents of Christianity was participation in the Christian cult. For this reason they were generous to apostates simply because they knew that apostasy forever excluded a baptized Christian from any further communication in the Church's public worship.

We use the word liturgy in this discussion to describe this public, corporate, and, in a broad sense, official worship of the Church, in which Christians are bound by the very nature of their religious profession and adherence to participate. In particular we employ the word liturgy to denote those sacramental acts given to Christian disciples, according to the Gospel tradition, by Jesus Christ Himself. In this case the exception only proves the rule. For despite the opinions of various individuals and groups in the course of Church history regarding the value or dispensability of the Gospel sacraments, the fact remains that the vast majority of Christians today of all ecclesiastical persuasions still consider that participation in these sacraments is a *sine qua non* of visible membership in the Church of Jesus Christ. They are accounted as generally necessary to salvation, and the peculiar witnesses of an open adherence to corporate Christian life. In order to understand clearly the implications of Christian liturgy for any idea of Christian education, it will be necessary to consider first something of the original, and therefore fundamental, nature of Christian worship, and secondly the significance of actual participation in it. We may then draw certain conclusions as to the ends or goals which the Christian liturgy is designed to fulfill.

BY WAY OF ORIGINS

The Christian liturgy did not come into being suddenly without seed or root. It developed out of patterns and perspectives already long established in ancient Judaism. We are not concerned here to trace the organic evolution of liturgical forms or the successive enrichments of interpretation brought to Christian worship in later ages. There is, however, one formal characteristic of both Jewish and Christian worship that is shared in common and that sets this tradition of liturgical practice apart from other types of religious cult. We refer to the large place given to instruction within the context of corporate worship. Jewish and Christian worship are in large measure a communication of the Word of God through the reading of the Scriptures and the prophetic proclamation of preaching. It is true that the primary purpose of such proclamation is to set forth the glory of God by the recital of His mighty acts among men and for their salvation. At the same time, the reading and interpretation of the Word of God have fulfilled a catechetical function, and the materials have been of both a theological and an ethical content. In both Judaism and Christianity the cultic act has always been intimately associated with the sacred Word.

Even in the ancient cultus of the Jewish Temple, the varied types of sacrificial acts were accompanied by the Psalms, which interpreted the significance of the action to the offerer. The same was true of the annual round of festivals. For example, the Passover meal was not eaten in silence. The father of the family or friendly group recited the story of deliverance and covenant-making not only to the praise of God but also for the instruction of the younger members of the circle. The service of the synagogue was actually described by eminent Jewish teachers, such as Philo of Alexandria, as a school. Many students of synagogue origins consider that the institution was at first intended to serve for instruction in the Law of God, and only later enshrined its teaching sessions in a setting of praise and prayer.

Christian liturgies exhibit the same characteristics. The sacramental actions are always prefaced or accompanied by Scriptural words. Prophesying and teaching have always been an integral element in the public worship of the Church. The forepart of the Eucharistic liturgy, the Mass or Holy Communion (whatever term one wishes to call it), has since the earliest days been particularly designed for catechumens, by its ordered course of reading and preaching from the Scriptures. The daily offices of Christian congregations and monastic communities are nothing less than an ordered course of reading in the Bible set within a framework of praise. The "lesson" is a fundamental element in all Christian liturgies, whether Orthodox, Catholic, or Protestant. There is no corporate act of Christian worship but what one of its purposes, even though secondary, is to inform, to instruct, and to edify.

This pedagogical element, if we may call it such, in both Jewish and Christian liturgy arises from a fundamental principle that they have in common; namely, they are religions based upon a covenant. A covenant, in the Biblical sense of the term, is a meeting of persons who engage to give themselves one to the other in mutual communion, and who by binding words and ceremonial actions pledge to one another full fidelity and devotion. Though the two parties to the covenant are free, and hence responsible, agents, they are by no means equal. Not only does God take the initiative, in His self-disclosure and promise, but He also sets the conditions by His demands. But insofar as man is capable of apprehending Him, God in His revelation and grace gives Himself utterly and unreservedly. Man on his part responds to the initiative of God by his own free pledge of fidelity, his ready acceptance of God's demands, and the giving of himself through representative offerings. Man's response is also entire and all-inclusive. The Word of God given to man in the covenant is not merely relevant to the actual occasion of the covenant-making and meeting, but embraces the whole of man's life. Similarly, man's response cannot be fulfilled only in the cultic act of pledge and offering, but must include all his thoughts, words, and deeds.

To the Jew, the record of God's convenanting with His people was inscribed in the Old Testament, and in particular in the Torah or five books of Moses, wherein were contained both the narrative of God's actions in history that brought into being the covenanted people, and the law that detailed God's Word and demands. The prophetical and other writings spell out the story of man's breaking of the covenant, his punishment, his renewal, and his hope of its ultimate fulfillment. It is important to note that in the Torah, as throughout the Old Testament, the historical and prophetical elements, the liturgical and ethical injunctions are woven together. There is no separation of them into distinct levels of value or significance. The ceremonial and moral laws were of a piece, being derived from the one God who gave them. Thus the Scriptures provided at one and the same time a world view, a philosophy of history, a code of behavior, and a form of worship. Worship and life were always for the Jew in a dynamic relationship. Every cultic act, whether it be sacrifice in the Temple or meditation in the synagogue, was a renewal of the covenant once made, and this renewal was both judgment and healing to the whole of life.

The covenant so made between God and His people was binding for all time, anchored as it was in the unchangeable faithfulness of God.

> He hath been alway mindful of his covenant and promise, that he made to a thousand generations.   (Ps. 105:8)

> The merciful goodness of the Lord endureth for ever and ever upon them that fear him; and his righteousness upon children's children; Even upon such as keep his covenant, and think upon his commandments to do them.
> (Ps. 103:17–18)

Man in his sinful self-centeredness was continually breaking his agreement, was continually being renewed and forgiven in his penitence and offering. But the covenant could never be annulled. It could only be fulfilled. It is in this hope that Israel abides unto the present day.

It is the faith of Christianity, in distinction from Judaism, that the old covenant was fulfilled and thereby superseded by a new covenant—again through the divine initiative, in the God-man Jesus Christ, in Whom alone perfect love is met by the perfect obedience of man. We are not concerned here to expound or to argue the Christology of the New Testament, but only to note the translation of the covenant theme in the context of Christian worship and life. It is impossible, however, to understand any aspect of Christianity unless one bears in mind always that the Christian community, the new Israel of the new covenant, comprehends its own existence in the twofold perspective of being in the world but not of the world. For the Christian sees in the incarnation, death, and resurrection of Jesus, the Son of God, not only the critical turning point of history but the end of history; not only the fulfillment of an age but the inauguration of the age to come. And furthermore, not only is the resurrection of Christ decisive for the historical process, it is even cosmic in its scope, being nothing less than the first fruits of a new creation.

The whole theology of the New Testament is permeated by this twofold dimension. The New Testament proclamation (the *kerygma*) of the Gospel is a recital of the mighty acts of God "in the last times," when the prophecy and hope of the old covenant have been fulfilled in the coming of Jesus Christ, Who at the same time stands ready to come in glory to judge the world. Indeed, in the Johannine writings the judgment of Christ is viewed as having taken place already in the saving events of His passion and resurrection. But whether the New Testament writers present the end as impending or as accomplished, they are at one in viewing the act of God in Christ as the overthrow of sin, evil, and death, and the opening of the Kingdom of Heaven to all believers.

The ethic of the New Testament stems directly from this theological proclamation. The commandment of love is both a law for this life and an inner principle exhibiting the character of life in the Spirit which is the mark of the new age to come. It fulfills the law of the old covenant at the same time that it breaks through every legalistic moral system. It is both absolute and relative: absolute as the norm by which all living is judged, relative in its varied applications to every concrete situation of personal relationships. New Testament savants sometimes break their heads together in argument over whether the ethical teaching of Jesus is an ideal of a future age, a guide for the interim between the two comings of Christ, or a code for the historic Christian community. The fact is that it is none of these things by itself, and all of them together. It is the ethic which produces from St. Paul the apparently paradoxical responses: "Wretched man that I am! Who will deliver me from this body of death?" (Rom. 7:24) and "I can do all things through Christ who strengtheneth me" (Phil. 4:13).

The Christian liturgy, replacing the rites of the old covenant, is the focal point in which God and His people meet together to ratify, to renew, and to celebrate the new covenant established in the death and resurrection of Christ. The essential forms and actions of this liturgy were given to His disciples by Christ Himself. Without any explicit repudiation of the old order of rites and ceremonies, certain familiar patterns of Jewish cult were selected by Christ to bear the full significance of His new covenant: the bath of baptism and the intimate fellowship of the Supper. It would take us too far afield to speculate upon the peculiar appropriateness of these symbolic cult actions, free as they are from the particularities, not to say the grossness, of the bloody ceremonials of the old law, and so easily comprehensible and applicable to all mankind. What is germane to our purpose is to note that in both cases, of baptism and Eucharist, the significance given them by Christ is a participation in, a sharing in His death and resurrection. They are therefore more than outward and visible signs of an historical, religious community. They are also instruments by which this community experiences in the here and now the suprahistorical, supernatural realities of eternal life in the age to come. By them the Christian is not only made a member of the Church, he is also given citizenship in the Kingdom of Heaven. He is reborn into "newness of life," and tastes "the powers of the world to come."

At a very early time the Church ordered this liturgy in a pattern of time that pointed to its eternal significance. Each year at the Paschal anniversary of the mighty acts of God in Christ, the full sacramental liturgy was celebrated in renewal of the death-resurrection experience. New converts, thoroughly catechized in the Christian gospel, were baptized and sealed into the covenant, and joined with the whole Christian community in the Eucharistic feast. The baptism was a once-for-all, never-to-be-repeated experience. It marked the change from an old, corrupt order of life into a newness of life in deathless relationships. It admitted the initiate into the full privileges of the covenant community, and it made him an heir of an eternal inheritance. It thus had a significance not only for all time but for all eternity.

But the second part of this Easter mystery, the Eucharistic feast, was renewed again and again throughout his life, in the meeting of the community on the first day of each week. Thus the original covenant bond was continually confirmed and strengthened, not only as an individual experience but also as a corporate participation. The fact that this renewal of the covenant bond took place on Sunday and not on the Jewish Sabbath was itself highly significant. The observance of the Sabbath had been one of the distinguishing characteristics of the old covenant of Israel. The Sabbath was God's gift of respite from the toil of time-existence, a symbol of the rest of God Himself at the conclusion of His toil of creation. It was also the promise of the coming bliss when time should be no more, and toil and labor should cease. The Christian Sunday, on the other hand, recalls the Easter event. Its note is not so much rest from toil as it is joy in reconciled fellowship. It marks not the end of the old creation so much as the beginning of the new creation of which Christ is the first fruits of many brethren. Sunday, too, like the Jewish Sabbath, looks forward to the coming end of the world—not as an unfulfilled hope but as a foretaste in the here and now. The Sunday Eucharist of the Church in the time-dimension of this world thus transcends the bonds of time. It recalls the past event of Christ's death and resurrection into the present, and at the same time realizes in the present the future consummation. The presence of the living Christ in the midst of His own assures the Church that it not only communes together on the level of a this-world existence but is also seated with Him in the heavenly places whence it judges the world. "Ye are they," said Jesus to His disciples at the Last Supper, "who have continued with me in my trials; and I appoint unto you a kingdom, as my Father hath appointed unto me: that ye may eat and drink at my table in my kingdom, and sit on thrones judging the twelve tribes of Israel" (Luke 22:28–30).

BY WAY OF PARTICIPATION

We do not maintain for a moment that the Eucharistic assembly of the Church is the only time and place in which God communes with His people in the new-covenant relationship. The meeting takes place wherever two or three are gathered together in the name of Christ, to pray, to seek for truth, to witness for the truth, to give in charity out of a pure heart. We do maintain, however, that the Eucharist is a peculiar meeting place of God with His people, and distinctive of Christian religious practice. This is true not only because of its institution by Christ and the historic use of the Church from generation to generation. An analysis of the structure and the implications of participation in the Eucharist reveals it to be an inclusive epitome of Christianity itself. Not least among its

manifold meanings and ends is the education of those who
share in it with open minds and hearts, until they come "to the
measure of the stature of the fullness of Christ."

The Eucharist is a personal encounter between God and His
people, as they seek reconciliation and communion one with
another. In it are revealed the grace and demand of God, and
the loving response of man in word and in deed. In the Eucharist, the Word of God, who is also Christ, is proclaimed and
offered to men in the fullness of divine grace: the forgiveness
of sin, renewal of the Spirit, and participation in eternal life.
But the Eucharist also proclaims the demand of God: the fulfillment of the law of love to God and to neighbor, and the
consecration of the whole of man's desires, talents, and possessions. Both the grace and the demand are total. Man's response, on the other hand, is also total. Through the material
elements of his own handiwork upon God's created gifts, man
offers himself entirely in penitence, faith, obedience, charity.
Though it last only for the few moments required for this sacramental act, man experiences in this meeting the selfless love
that unites him in intimate communion with God and with his
fellows. In this experience of reconciliation man comprehends
the reality of the Kingdom of God. In thus apprehending the
wholeness of his life he glimpses the infinite possibilities of his
finite existence.

The structure of the liturgy itself provides the several
stages by which the reconciliation is accomplished. In the
classic form that underlies all the historic rites of the Church,
the Eucharistic liturgy consists of two complementary parts.
In the first, the Word of God in all its fullness of recital and
demand is proclaimed: in lesson, in creed, in sermon. This part
of the liturgy, as we have already noted, is pre-eminently catechetical. It is open to all men, baptized and unbaptized alike.
It is the heralding to the Church and to the world of the Gospel, of the new covenant offered by God to men in the community of Jesus Christ. It demands a response, either of ac-

ceptance or of rejection. To be indifferent to this proclamation is only one way of rejection. Man is confronted with a choice, a decision. He either commits himself to it or passes it by. He cannot ignore it.

The second part of the liturgy provides the means of response, not alone in word but in very deed. It is an act involving an offering, a consecration, and a communion. Only those who respond to the Gospel by believing it and being joined to the covenant community can take part in this act. It is not enough to say that one accepts it. Those who accept it must here and now live it together. The Eucharist is thus more than a symbol of what Christianity is; it is an instrument for carrying it out in action. A Christian does not merely contemplate and meditate upon the Gospel in the Eucharist, think beautiful thoughts and be stirred to charitable feelings by some outward, visible, and concrete presentation or image of the Gospel. He is involved in its very life by active participation in its drama of offering, consecration, and communion. The Eucharist makes the social, communal character of the Gospel actual and real, an historical fact.

It is important also to bear in mind that in the Eucharistic action the Church does not act for itself alone. As the saving act of Christ is all-embracing, so too is the Eucharist. The Church acts in this sacrament, albeit proleptically, as the representative of all mankind, indeed of all nature. It realizes the end of the redemptive process as well as the beginning. It experiences both the all-inclusive mercy and the sovereign judgment of God in Christ not only upon itself but upon the cosmos.

The initial stage in the Eucharistic drama is the offertory. The Church takes the substance of creation, initially given by God, and with the imprint of its members' lifework upon it presents it to God in the form of bread and wine, food and drink, sustenance and nourishment in the basic need of physical existence and survival. This offering is made by each individual as God's steward and his brother's helper. But the offering is also corporate, for each one gives of his own life to the common life. In the offertory the Christian acknowledges God's claim upon His own creation, upon man's work upon His creation, upon man's whole life itself. At the same time man acknowledges the interdependence of his work with that of others, for the enhancement and enrichment of his own life as of the life of all society. The material elements are symbols and instruments both of his personal fulfillment and of his social obligations. Thereby he lifts the inert and inanimate objects of nature to a new level of personal and social significance. No matter how large or small the individual's field may be, no matter how great his vocation and place in the social and economic order, his offering is necessary and hence important and significant in the larger wholeness. At the risk of using a much overworked word, one may say that the offertory of the Eucharist exhibits the true and actual democracy of the people of God.

The second stage in the Eucharistic action is what is commonly called the consecration. The community of disciples now hands over to God itself and its offerings as one body. It places itself, in and through its gifts, in God's hand that it may be made holy and thereby become the instrument of God's purpose. It is taken up, so to speak, into the entire and selfless offering of Christ to be the instrument of a higher reconciliation: that of man with God. All this is done in the context of a solemn thanksgiving. For by thanking God for the gifts both of nature and of grace, the Church publicly acknowledges that they belong to God; and if they belong to God, they are sacred and holy. The thanksgiving is also made as a memorial: not only a memorial of the saving act once for all done but a calling to remembrance of the hope that is yet to be revealed in glory.

At this point it is only honest to remind ourselves, by way of parenthesis, that Christians are not of one mind regarding the precise definition of what happens in the consecration. And it is certainly not the province of this discussion to enter into the delicate theological issues involved. Nor can we claim that any exposition of what is effected at this stage of the Eucharistic liturgy will be entirely satisfying or acceptable to all and sundry Christian believers. We are entering the realm of unseen and mysterious realities where adoring faith must of necessity take hold of what is evident to sense and to reason. If, as we suggested, the offertory action brought together the natural world into the wider and fuller context of personal and social meaning and significance, we may press on to say that the consecratory action lifts this level once more into the larger realm of supernatural grace and divine-human relationships. That this is effected not by the power and competence of men but by the Word and Spirit of the living God is a postulate of Christian faith, grounded in the promise of Christ. We shall not argue the point. We shall simply leave it at this assertion, as part and parcel of the Christian testimony and experience.

The third and final stage of the Eucharistic drama is communion. Communion is the realization of reconciliation and wholeness. In the act of communion every level of existence is brought into harmonious order and union and peace. For once the will of God is done on earth as it is in heaven. The Kingdom of God is manifest. Nature is the instrument of grace, and selfless charity binds man to man and man to God. Again we would emphasize that communion is not a mere feeling or thought, or even a word, but a deed. Faith and charity are one.

BY WAY OF ENDS

If we address ourselves now to the basic question of this discussion, What has the experience of Christian worship to do with the Christian idea of education? we may note at least three principles or ends of education which the liturgy of the Church provides:

1. Throughout our analysis of the corporate, sacramental

action of the Christian community, we have pointed to the *wholeness* of the worship experience in its integration of nature, man, and God. In the liturgy man finds himself in harmonious relationship with every level of his existence—material, personal, social, and supernatural. He takes hold of the natural order of material things not as an exploiter for selfish ends or even as a mere consumer of goods for his own health and happiness. He is not the be-all and end-all of creation. He is the steward of a higher Lord and the servant of a larger welfare. In the context of the liturgy, man employs the material creatures of bread and wine to enrich and to satisfy his own person only to the extent that he makes them vehicles for the enhancement of all possible personal relationships, both with God and with his fellow men. For the wholeness of a man's life is not contained in himself or in his relation to things, but to its fullest extent it comprehends all his interpersonal and social relations. Any competent writer of biography knows this. A man's life does not consist solely in how many years he lived, what he said and what he did, how much he owned and how much he spent. In involves much more—how much he owed and how much he gave to his family, his teachers, his fellow workers, his community, his race, and his cultural inheritance and environment; and we may add also, the way he prayed: whether, like the Pharisee, he prayed with himself, or, like the publican, he prayed, "God, be merciful to me a sinner."

Let us look for a moment at bread and wine by themselves, viewing them as representative symbols pointing to several possible ends. If these fruits of man's labor upon nature are taken to be the summation of man's values, man makes himself thereby an idolator. But material idols are useless and wasteful, being subject to corruption in time, and, far worse, being destructive of society itself, by making people of less worth than things. If, on the other hand, the fruits of man's labor upon nature are recognized as means, but as means only to human or social ends, man merely sets up another kind of idol in himself or in a utopia of his own imagination. He is incapable of exorcizing the demon of selfishness, and ends by making himself, or his party, a very strife unto his neighbors. The world we live in today is a terrifying illustration of humanistic idolatry, teetering on the edge of destruction by bowing down before man-centered, society-centered, race-centered gods.

The Christian liturgy offers us the true vision of wholeness from the perspective of the Kingdom of God, where means and ends are properly identified and related. But it is not only vision that it offers, an ideal inspiring, stimulating, but nonetheless unattainable. The liturgy offers also the realization of the ideal in the action of life: in a representative act, to be sure, but an act all the more real and concrete by reason of its representative character. In the representative act the Christian does more than contemplate the vision of peace. He makes peace, by the help and grace of God.

2. The Christian liturgy provides a framework and laboratory for *creative activity*. It gives man a share in the creative work of God, in bringing cosmos out of chaos. There is no insight of knowledge, no novel opportunity of charity that cannot be incorporated into the Eucharistic action of offering, consecration, and communion. The liturgy is not a celebration of a closed system, either of natural or of moral philosophy. In its reverence for material things as the cooperative handiwork of God and men, the liturgy offers the widest scope to science. In its enhancement of personal and social well-being, the liturgy affords perspective and judgment upon every scheme for the better ordering of political, economic, and cultural pursuits. Upon the Church itself, the liturgy brings God's judgment for every obstacle it has blindly put in the way of the advancement of knowledge and the broadening of social justice.

Nothing has been more destructive in modern civilization than what has been called "the warfare of science and theology." It has contributed to the unnatural separation of much of our educational endeavor from religious practice. It has produced sterile researchers who accumulate knowledge without understanding. It has debased our language to serve for manipulating propaganda rather than for communicating truth. It has emptied much religious piety of any real contact with everyday life. It has encouraged many men of good will to believe that ethical standards can remain stable apart from faith in God. It has even built such a barrier between the classroom and the sanctuary that many Christian teachers have become afraid to speak out, for conscience' sake, what they believe to be true and right.

No creative solution to the world's life can come out of such a situation. Mankind will dream loftier dreams of a better standard of living, only to have them shattered by the nightmares of poverty and involuntary unemployment. Man will be more and more astonished at the technical achievements of science, only to haunt himself with the dread of destruction of his art and industry. To this dilemma the Christian sacramental liturgy, when properly understood, offers a simple but profound answer. It is to take all the creative work of man's head and hand, and in faith and charity give it over into the re-creative hand of God, by whose Word and Spirit alone can it fulfill its proper ends.

> For as the heavens are higher than the earth, so are my ways higher than your ways, and my thoughts than your thoughts.
>
> For as the rain cometh down, and the snow from heaven, and returneth not thither, but watereth the earth, and maketh it bring forth and bud, that it may give seed to the sower, and bread to the eater:
>
> So shall my word be that goeth forth out of my mouth: it shall not return to me empty, but it shall accomplish that which I please, and it shall prosper in the thing whereto I sent it.   (Is. 55:9–11)

3. Finally, the liturgy provides room for endless *growth*, to single and to on-going generations. For every individual participant it is a lifelong discipline, searching to know the mind of God, stretching out to meet the charity of God. The liturgy offers no graduation diploma either in knowledge or in character. Yet it is a perpetual commencement. For each Eucharistic act, fulfilled in itself, opens new vistas of possibility and so becomes a preparation for another. This is the true meaning of abundant life, that it is ever a wellspring of fresh adventure.

To the sensitive offerer and partaker in the Eucharistic action, an imaginative consideration of how his life, bound up in the gifts of bread and wine, is related in manifold ways opens almost limitless horizons. He contemplates an ever-widening circle of communal bonds, his membership in a family circle, the employer-employee relationships of his daily job, his significance as a voter in his local community, state, and nation, his international obligation as a churchman. In addition to these basic communities, he is more likely than not a working member of many, more voluntary, associations: an athletic and social club, a literary or cultural society, a professional organization or trade union; not to speak of the part-time engagements in neighborhood and civic leagues, political action groups, and institutional boards.

If the worshiper is a particularly sensitive one, he will not see all these activities and organizations that fill his waking hours as so many impersonal forces, pressures, and strains but will translate them into the concrete images of living persons like himself, seen and unseen, near and far. All of them, like himself, are making bread and wine out of the resources and with the talents at their disposal, to feed themselves and their loved ones, to make friends and enjoy companionship, and to provide basic securities that free them from want and fear. To visualize all these people concretely as individuals known and loved by God, and to see the manifold ways by which all natural and humane sciences can be brought to the service of their well-being, is a never-ending prospect for the growth of a man's mind and heart. One can sustain the vision and act decisively to realize it only as the charity of man is undergirded and strengthened and increased by the boundless charity of God.

The goals of Christian education are not essentially different from the disciplines of Christian worship. Both of them aim to set us in the direction that leads to the fullest participation, according to each individual's capacity, in the creative purpose of God as it unfolds in a world that has been happily called God's "workshop." This is to see the relatedness to the whole of all the bits of knowledge, and to sense the worth of every contribution, however small and ordinary, of each fellow worker in the venture. It is, above all other things, to make the great discovery that fills life with a radiant wonder, of finding God Himself as the Teacher and Companion, the Lover and the Judge, in every true and good and beautiful experience of nature or of history, of science or of art, of word or deed of men who are made in His image and called to share the likeness of His Only-begotten Son.

DR. MASSEY H. SHEPHERD, JR., DISCUSSES THE
QUESTION OF CHAPEL ATTENDANCE IN
SCHOOLS AND COLLEGES.

DR. SHEPHERD: The matter of chapel in schools or colleges has been referred to once or twice. I have always abhorred the idea of any compulsion in religious worship. I suppose the trend in modern education is to get away from it. Yet I have this curious quirk in my mind: If compulsion is to be applied to chapel worship in connection with the school community, it should not be applied to students but to the faculty. It seems to me that there is nothing worse than to have students required to go to chapel when the faculty are merely asked, at their leisure, to take turns.

I talked to a friend of mine who for many years had been a chaplain at a private school, not a denominational one. I seriously suggested to him when he was discussing problems of this nature that it might be a good idea if their chapel were planted right in the middle of their campus and every morning the faculty were seen attending chapel, and if then it were left up to the students to do as they pleased.

Again I say that I am certainly against compulsion. There is no reason to force a man to participate in an act of that sort against his conscience. I'm curious to know what would be your general reaction to my thought.

VOICE: Shouldn't there be a clear difference or a clear distinction made between the levels you happen to be dealing with? The lower secular schools may be acting *in loco parentis.* There would be a different problem with the other schools or universities.

DR. SHEPHERD: I include the matter of the parent, too, in this consideration. There is the question of whether you will force your child to go to services, a question which sometimes

147

irks both parents and children. Certainly I could never bring myself to have the child go if the parents didn't go too.

VOICE: That isn't exactly what I mean. I mean at the secondary level the school takes responsibilities which a university may hesitate to take.

DR. SHEPHERD: I'm sure that there is a different problem at different age levels, but I think there must be a basic principle somewhere.

VOICE: I think it again depends upon the context. We have the secular school and we have the multi-faith schools, and I think the problems can be considerably different. In most cases, you would expect your faculty in a church school or college to go to chapel with more regularity than you would in a nonchurch school or college. The atmosphere in a school that was statedly Christian would be quite different.

DR. SHEPHERD: Let us take, for example, theoretically, to satisfy my own curiosity, a school like M.I.T., which is not in the category of religious schools but which furnishes religion in the sense of providing a chapel. A certain proportion of its faculty are Christians. To what extent is it feasible or advisable for those of the faculty who are Christians to discipline themselves voluntarily to regular worship in the context of the school community?

VOICE: On a voluntary basis it would be most desirable. I wouldn't think it would be a good thing to pursue on an administrative basis.

DR. SHEPHERD: I don't think it would be good to require it but I think it could be kindly suggested. The chapel is always referred to as the center of the boys' lives. I think as active Christians in the community, people on the faculty should also make the chapel a center of their lives in terms of Christian action. I think the situation is somewhat different when you are treading on what people might call academic or religious freedom in a school which is not statedly Christian. If it were a voluntary thing, I would say that it probably would work, but otherwise I would be against it.

VOICE: I once heard this same subject debated at a Friends' institution, and there were strong comments against compulsion. Nevertheless they wanted a real and active community worship and wanted to say to outsiders, "If you want to come to chapel, register as a student. If you for any reason don't want to, and if we tell you please don't register, understand that is no rejection of you, but we all do go to chapel and therefore if you come, you will too."

DR. SHEPHERD: I once had an interesting experience in writing to a school. It is true that it was a church school. I wanted to live there for a while and do some special study. The dean wrote back and said that he would be very glad to have me but said that there was one rule: all visitors had to participate in chapel. He stated as a reason that that was his way of incorporating them into the community of the school. He said, "You don't have to eat any meals with us. You don't have to come home at night with us, but one thing the visitor has to do is to attend chapel."

I think we have lost something in this modern age through freedom of religion. That practice, it seems to me, has affected many Christian scholars or teachers as well as other Christians in a very adverse sense. We have no feeling, it seems to me, in most of our schools and even in some specifically Christian schools, of the representative nature of corporate worship. I'm thinking, for example, of a very moving paragraph in Gregory Dix's book, *The Shape of the Liturgy.* He deals with medieval religion and he points out all of its many bad features, but he also points to the fact that day after day in cathedrals and the larger churches there were groups of persons who considered it their primary obligation, morning and evening, to come together to perform an act of praise and worship to God as the Redeemer, as the representatives of all mankind and all creation.

I don't think that many people, even Christians, look at it that way today: that there is a Christian obligation on Christians to live together in any kind of corporate community, in school or otherwise, even though they may be few in number, and day by day, as part of the Christian community, to worship in this representative capacity.

I have a feeling that if that idea ever were developed once more in Christendom it would be of far greater value than all kinds of school rules of compulsion and so forth. It might remain a small group, but it becomes a group that stands for something which cannot be ignored.

VOICE: It seems to me that if you establish first of all the need or the right for such a daily worship service there would be no feeling of compulsion. With that as a basis for your faculty and your students, as a body, attending such a service, you would have the Christian community you want.

DR. SHEPHERD: I think undoubtedly a large number of people go to church as a matter of need. The point of motivation is where you have to begin. I do feel in the case of, let us say, the faculty, who have a greater responsibility, that if they are convinced Christians, apart from how they may particularly feel about it, there is a point at which one can begin with a sense of duty and discipline as Christians and an obligation as Christians, one to another. And I would say that, even though they may be a school group, insofar as they live in community life together, that community life necessarily involves the obligation of worshiping together, and then the need is seen.

VOICE: I was thinking of those people on the borderline who are not actually committed Christians.

DR. SHEPHERD: In some cases the thing is carried on partly because it is a principle of the school and somebody is there to see that it is kept going somehow. I know of one school in which daily chapel is not largely attended, but they have a paid person who is responsible for seeing that the services go on. He may ask people to assist him. Most of the people who assist him are members of the faculty—that is, those who are willing. However, the thing that horrified me in this situation was that the members of the faculty expect to receive a fee.

This is an extra. It is not what they were hired to do by the university. They are asked to do it. And it is a policy in this institution that any member of the faculty or any Christian minister in the community—anybody who is asked to take the service—receives a fee, which seems to me to destroy the whole thing.

VOICE: You say it is the policy of the university?

DR. SHEPHERD: Yes, it had been a policy of the university. This is stated, you see, in a letter which goes out to faculty members asking them if they would take such-and-such a date and that the honorarium would be so-and-so.

VOICE: It seems to me, Dr. Shepherd, that your idea about the representative aspect of worship is an excellent one. The parallel of intercessory prayer as contrasted, let's say, to sheer egocentric petitionary prayer comes to my mind.

The Christian Idea of Education

JOHN COURTNEY MURRAY, S.J.

IT IS SOMETIMES instructive to examine the dynamism of an idea in its first origins. I propose therefore to look at the Christian idea of education in its first institutionalized form, as it took shape in the Christian School of Alexandria in the early decades of the third century.

The forehistory of the school includes the name of Clement of Alexandria (who would himself deserve a special study) and also the more shadowy name of Pantaenus. Both of them conducted what we would today call "private schools." But the proper history of the School of Alexandria, as the first officially "church-related" school, begins with Origen, the gigantic intellect who towers over the third century and indeed over the whole of Christian antiquity.

His story starts, modestly enough, in A.D. 203, when Demetrius, Bishop of Alexandria, put him in charge of the diocesan catechesis, at the age of eighteen. Doubtless the bishop had no intention of starting an intellectual revolution; that is not the sort of thing that bishops ordinarily do. But Origen happened to be a genius. And a particular moment in history had arrived. The time was at hand when the Church, still preaching the Word of God in all the simplicity of its divine wisdom, had to move onward and outward into the complex world of human intelligence where many words, pretending to be wise, were being spoken. Origen was the man who spectacularly made this crucial move.

His initial task was spiritually thrilling but not intellectually ambitious. He taught the elements of Christian doctrine to catechumens preparing for baptism in the shadow of the edict of Septimius Severus which threatened death to Christian converts. In time, however, a problem arose that was also intellectually exciting. "When I devoted myself to the Word," Origen later wrote, "and the fame of my proficiency went abroad, there came to me adherents of the various schools of thought, and men conversant with Greek learning, particularly with philosophy. It seemed therefore necessary that I should examine the doctrines of the schools and see what the philosophers had said concerning the truth." In this simple, almost casual way Origen describes the beginning of the full-scale historic encounter between Christianity and the ancient world of intellect. Out of this encounter the first Christian school was born.

We can, without excessive fancy, construct Origen's problem. The men who came to him, wanting to be Christians, were living in the seething heterogeneity of contentious cultures, philosophies, and pieties that was third-century Alexandria. They had frequented the famous Museum and its fabulous library—the twin institutions that together had made Alexandria the capital of "the creative half of the Empire." These cultivated men—Egyptians, Jews, Greeks, Romans, Orientals —were troubled and confused as they heard Origen discourse on the Christian creed and on the history behind it.

Their philosophy raised questions about God and immortality, the finite and the infinite, the nature of morality, and the content of the good life. Their nascent discipline of philology created difficulties about the text of Scripture and its sense. The science of the Ionian epoch had known a revival in Alexandria, and consequently these men had questions about the Christian view of the material universe. They knew history and had theories about its meaning; they would therefore want to inquire into the Christian sense of history. They were skilled in politics and law and therefore were desirous to know the situation of the Church, visible as an institution with its own

structure of government, in the face of the empire. The great
desire for redemption from evil that had become central in all
the religions of the time had touched them, and they had questions about the Christian interpretation of evil and the Christian meaning of redemption. Their Roman masters had fixed
their minds on an ideal of citizenship; but was there a relation
between the service of an earthly city and a citizenship in the
Kingdom of God? And did the ascetic otherworldliness of the
Christian life leave a place for the art and music and literature
that they had learned to love? They were men to whom Hellenism had taught the primacy of the life of reason; how then
was their love of intelligence to be reconciled with the obedience of Christian faith and the acceptance of great mysteries?

In short, these men were asking one searching question.
What was the relation between the Museum of Alexandria
and the Church of Christ, between the human wisdom that lay
accumulated in the scrolls of the library and the divine wisdom
of which the books of the Bible were the repository? It was a
most valid question that demanded an answer. A journey
to Rome about A.D. 212 further convinced Origen that Christianity was challenging the best intelligence of the time and
was in turn being challenged by it, either with hope or with
hostility. Therefore on his return to Alexandria he reorganized
his catechesis into a *didaskaleion,* a proper school, and em-
barked upon a new course.

Eusebius tells us that there were two levels in the new program. Origen put his average students through the general
education of the freeborn Greek youth—in grammar, rhetoric
and logic, in arithmetic, geometry (which included geography
and some rudimentary biological science), astronomy (including what was known of physics), and music. These were
the "Hellenic disciplines" (Eusebius), ἡ ἐγκύκλιος παιδεία, the
"circle learning" of Francis Bacon, the arts and sciences that
made the free man and the citizen, equipped with the intellectual tools on which civilization depends, possessed of the hu-

manist heritage that man had so far accumulated. However, Origen struck a new note when he told his students, as Eusebius reports, "that this general education would be of no small help to them in the study and understanding of the divine Scriptures."

Origen broke the old "circle"; or, if you will, he included it in a circle of a wider sweep. He affirmed the old humanism to be valid still, but he denied its adequacy. The traditional *paideia* was to be retained; it was a true culture that enriched the mind. But it left the soul still in poverty, for now the materials for a higher culture were available in the doctrine of Christ. Therefore Origen's school had for its ulterior purpose the transmission of the Christian heritage of faith whose depository was the Church. And his general education stood in relation to this higher purpose; it would be "no small help" in the assimilation of Christian truth. The statement is laconic; and it raises many problems, with which Christian educators have struggled ever since.

It was, of course, no such simple matter as that of teaching people to read in order that they might read the Scriptures (itself an admirable idea). Nor was it the equally simple combination of two unrelated jobs that was recommended by the sturdy colonial American Calvinist when he said: "The Bible and figures—that's all I want my boy to know" (a better idea, at that, than just "figures"). Origen's purpose was the civilization of intelligence in order that it might be able to receive a fuller understanding of the doctrines that simple catechetical instruction by the Church had already made known to it.

Christian faith can of course be received into an intelligence altogether rude; on the other hand, it does not necessarily spring up in a cultivated intelligence. It is a gift of God. But what is given is truth, and the gift is made to a human intelligence. Therefore it makes on intelligence the demand that the truth, thus given, should be understood, insofar as intelligence can encompass its understanding. In this process of understanding a civilized intelligence is "of no small help." The civilization of intelligence is a humanistic and scientific process; the understanding of Christian faith is a religious and supernatural one. The processes are distinct, but they ought to be related; for they go on within the same one mind and soul. It was therefore the essential function of Origen's school to relate them, under the primacy of the process in which faith, a higher gift than intelligence, involves the Christian. Origen wanted his students to grow into an intelligent Christianity; but to this end it was necessary that intelligence itself should grow in them. And there could be no other means of growth than the acquisition of the intellectual skills, the assimilation of the body of knowledge, and the initiation into the traditions of civility, that made the society around them civilized.

There was a further cognate task, reserved for those who were up to it. "When he perceived that any persons had superior intelligence," Eusebius writes, "he instructed them also in philosophic disciplines." Here Origen really came to grips with the problem of the day. Christianity, he knew, was not the Grecian art of being human, or a sentimental touch of universal brotherhood added to a Roman ideal of citizenship; still less was it an ineffable, incommunicable, self-authenticating, individual inner experience of "salvation," that stood in no intelligible relation to what the Alexandrian Museum was thinking and saying. Christianity was fundamentally a Word, a doctrine, a gnosis (so Origen called it), something that one knows, and knows to be the law of life, normative in all the problems of human thought and purpose. Christianity of its essence presumed to occupy intellectual ground; and in third-century Alexandria it found the ground to no small extent already occupied.

There was the ancient lore of Egypt and the East; there was the revealed wisdom and sacred law of the Jew; above all, there was Greek reason and "all that the philosophers had said concerning truth." The problem was not some rude dispossession of these tenants of intellectual territory. The Library of Alexandria was not to be burnt, as Justinian later thought, in a stupidity of zeal rather Vandal or Mohammedan than Christian. The question, as Clement of Alexandria had already put it, was whether there is "one river of Truth"; whether the two Testaments are finally One; whether the Logos, the Word, Who had come as Christ to be the Light of the world, was not somehow also the light that had beckoned to the soul of Egypt, burst upon the prophets, and illumined the intelligence of Greece. The question was whether Christianity, like Christ, was the Truth in which all truths are ultimately One.

This was the ultimate question with which Origen's best students were put to wrestle, and he with them as their guide. He was, as Eusebius notes, "celebrated as a great philosopher even among the Greeks themselves." And his first step with his students is described by one of them, Gregory of Neocaesarea, a lawyer and later a bishop, in the famous *Panegyric of Origen* that was his valedictory to his alma mater and its master: "He introduced us to all schools of thought and was determined that we should be ignorant of no type of Greek doctrine," Stoic, Pythagorean, Platonist—all except the Epicureans, who, as atheists, had no answers to the questions a Christian might ask and asked no questions a Christian had not already answered. "Nothing," Gregory writes, "was forbidden us, nothing hidden from us, nothing inaccessible to us. We were to learn all manner of doctrine—barbarian or Greek, mystical or political, divine or human. We went into and examined with entire freedom all sorts of ideas, in order to satisfy ourselves and enjoy to the full these goods of the mind. When an ancient thought was true, it belonged to us and was at our disposition with all its marvelous possibilities of delightful contemplation." This was the first task—the acquisition of an all-inclusive knowledge. But with it went a more stringent task. Origen himself, Gregory says, "went on with us, . . . directing us, pointing out to us all that was true and useful, putting aside all that was false." This was the work of discernment and order that is proper to the Christian intelligence. It is the task of making an inclusive knowledge also universal in the true sense —that is, *"uni-versum,"* turned into one, fashioned into a unity.

Gregory's account catches something of the spirit of the five years he spent with Origen. One feels the pulsation of that active energy upon whose release and discipline the success of the educational process depends. One recognizes the excitement inherent in the free search of the mind for truth, wherever it is to be found. But one recognizes too the greater excitement inherent in the mind's search for intellectual order, for the hierarchy in the order of truth, for the inner hidden unity that must somehow join in a many-splendored, differentiated pattern all the fragments of truth, human and divine, that the intelligence of man can encompass.

This was the highest responsibility accepted by the School of Alexandria—a responsibility for establishing intellectual order, for constituting the unity of truth, for communicating the Clementine vision that "there is one river of truth, but many streams fall into it on this side and on that." This is the Christian "view," in Newman's later sense of the word. What the human spirit endowed with Christian faith permanently needs is to view all its knowledges, acquired within the Church and within the Museum, as ultimately ordered into one. For to the Christian the word "truth," like the word "God," is a word that in the final analysis has no plural, despite all the distinctnesses that exist, unconfused, within the compass of its unconfined infinitude.

The tools for the achievement of this work of order and unity were philosophical, as the word itself was a work of intelligence. Nevertheless, this intellectual work was profoundly religious. Its ultimate dynamism was what Gregory calls "piety," a piety of intellect as well as a piety of will—a love of the truths that may be found amid all the chaos of philosophical opinion, and a will to subsume all these truths under "the Holy Word, the loveliest thing there is" (in Gregory's exquisite phrase). This love of the ordered wisdom of the Gospel, guiding intelligence—itself greatly loved—in all its free ranging, was for Gregory the glowing heart of his school experience. It remains forever the heart of the school experience, ✓ when the school is Christian.

This brief sketch of the Christian School of Alexandria reveals, I think, the two related ideals that have traditionally been the inspiration of Christian education. There is, first, the⌐ ideal of the civilized intelligence, a certain ideal of rationality that embraces (a) a perfecting of the powers of man—his reason, imagination, and taste; and (b) a vision of things as they are, a view of reality that reaches to fundamental certainties. Second, there is the ideal of the unity of truth, a vision of the realm of truth as an order, a universe, all-embracing in⌐ its scope, unified in its character.

The first ideal was the basic inspiration of the Church's century-long efforts at popular education. These efforts began in the sixth century after the wreck of the imperial school system; they were renewed at the Carolingian renaissance, and again renewed as the Iron Age ran out under the impulse of the Cluniac reform. The efforts were slack enough at times, and always enormously hampered, not least by the stubborn other half of Aristotle's famous half-truth that "all men naturally desire to know." The Church which could not compel men to believe could hardly compel them to know. It could not even compel its priests to obedience to the canon law, whose origins were in A.D. 529, that they should establish schools in their parishes. Nevertheless, that the success was considerable is known to all except those to whom myths are important. In his classic three volumes on the medieval universities Rashdall has made it clear that the lofty apex of medieval education which was the university—populous, widespread, and, for all its limitations, vigorously alive—rested on a broad base. In the later Middle Ages, he says, even the small-town boy "would never have to go very far from home to find a regular grammar school." In fact, Leach has estimated that there were relatively four times as many schools in pre-Reformation England as there were in 1864. One of today's accrediting associations would doubtless look down its nose at them; but its nose has a twentieth-century length. They remain an impressive embodiment of the perennially vital idea first launched in Alexandria —the relation between Christian faith and the civilized mind and manner.

The second aspect of Origen's idea is even more important. The first church-related school came into being in answer to an inner need of the human spirit as it was caught in the clashing encounter between Christianity and all the knowledge symbolized by the Alexandrian Museum. This encounter is permanently joined, for "the Museum" is a permanent institution and so too is the Church. They continue to present mankind with two forms of knowledge, each of which is autochthonous, subject in its growth to its own laws and to its own dynamism. One knowledge issues from reason and the experience of the senses; the other from divine revelation and the experience of faith. And what the human spirit endowed with Christian faith permanently needs is that these two knowledges should somehow be related in a universe of intellectual order. Out of this permanent inner need there springs the permanency of the dyad, Church and school. Actually, what Origen's school sought to provide was, in modern terminology, a unity of educational experience, issuing in that unity of intellectual and spiritual life which is by definition freedom and is likewise, when shared by a people, culture. The principle of unity was the primacy of "the Holy Word, the loveliest thing there is," and the sternest too. For this Word, the whole developed wisdom of the Church, requires to be made somehow relevant to every problem of intellectual discernment and moral decision that a school exists in order to raise.

This need of inner spiritual intellectual unity is doubtless felt most sharply on what we call the higher levels of education, when the full exigencies of "the liberal life" seek harmony with the full exigencies of the Christian life in terms of that most precarious of all syntheses, a Christian humanism. Nevertheless, the inner need is always there, inescapably to be met. What makes the difference is simply the principle (stated by Whitehead, agreed to by all sensible men) that no one is to be taught more than he can think about at the time. Your Christian, be he first-grader or graduate student, has always to enter more intelligently into the Church's life of faith and into the life of thought proper to the Museum. Between the two lives there is no automatic harmony. Indeed there seems to be a certain tension (which was deeply experienced, for instance, by John Henry Newman, who was continually caught between the visions of loveliness opened by human learning and the vision of the Word, the loveliest thing there is). Possibilities of seeming conflict are forever being disclosed, which center around changing foci. In these conflicts the growing mind is inevitably caught, and it is troubled and confused, as Origen's students were. Crises of growth are recurrent. The Christian school therefore undertakes to provide an area of experience in which the Church may meet the Museum in deliberate encounter.

The school is not the Church nor is it the home. It is a sort of city—an area both of protection and of prudent exposure. Within it all youth's confusions and crises may be consciously created, not simply allowed to happen, and then faced and solved under the guidance that only piety, in Gregory's sense, can give. It is a city of freedom in which intelligence may be released freely to grow. And it is a city of order in which the growing intelligence freely gives itself to the guidance of what is lovelier than itself to be led to the higher freedom with which the Word of God makes men free.

In his Bampton Lectures, *The Christian Platonists of Alex-*

andria, Charles Bigg says of the school there: "It may be doubted whether any nobler scheme of Christian education has ever been projected." It still is the essential Christian scheme, presenting the essential Christian school-ideal—a universal knowledge, founded on a broad basis of fact, integrated by a philosophic view, this view itself being then vitally related to the organic body of Christian truth. When it comes to the realization of the ideal, the most stubborn enemy has always been the sheer nobility of the ideal itself, which—even apart from hindering circumstances—tends to defeat performance. The failures of Christian education are normally multitudinous, sometimes scandalous, and occasionally spectacular. Even at its best a school is only a school, one milieu of influence among others, able to do only what a school can do. What matters in every age is the idea that inspires its efforts, and the integrity of these efforts.

Bibliography

I. SPECIAL

H. E. F. Guerike, *De schola quae Alexandriae floruit catechetica,* 2 vols. Halle, 1824–25.

W. Bousset, *Jüdisch-christlicher Schulbetrieb in Alexandria und Rom,* Göttingen, 1915.

C. Bigg, *The Christian Platonists of Alexandria,* Oxford, Clarendon Press, 1886.

W. J. Gauche, *Didymus the Blind. An Educator of the Fourth Century,* Washington, Catholic University, 1934.

J. Salaverri, "La filosofía en la Escuela Alejandrina," *Gregorianum, 15* (1934), 485–99.

P. Leturia, "El primo esbozo de una universidad católica o la escula catequética de Alejandria," *Razón y fe, 106* (1934), 297.

G. Bardy, "Pour l'histoire de l'Ecole d'Alexandrie," *Vivre et penser, 2* (1942), 80–109.

G. Bardy, "L'Eglise et l'enseignement pendant les trois premiers siècles," *Revue des sciences religieuses, 12* (1932), 1–28.

L. Allevi, "Il *Didaskaleion* di Alessandria. La piú antica università cattolica," *La scuola cattolica* (1924), pp. 309–28.

P. Camelot, "Les idées de Clément d'Alexandrie sur l'utilisation des sciences et de la littérature profane," *Recherches de science religieuse, 21* (1931), 38–66.

G. Bardy, "Aux origines de l'Ecole d'Alexandrie," *Recherches de science religieuse, 27* (1937), 65–90.

II. GENERAL

Hastings Rashdall, *The Universities of Europe in the Middle Ages,* ed. Powicke and Emden, 3 vols. Clarendon Press, 1936.

A. Dwight Culler, *The Imperial Intellect. A Study of Cardinal Newman's Educational Ideal,* New Haven, Yale University Press, 1955.

William F. Cunningham, C.S.C., *The Pivotal Problems of Education,* New York, Macmillan, 1940.

Jacques Maritain, *Education at the Crossroads,* New Haven, Yale University Press, 1943.

Leo R. Ward, *Blueprint for a Catholic University,* St. Louis, B. Herder Book Co., 1949.

John J. Ryan, *The Idea of a Catholic College,* New York, Sheed and Ward, 1945.

Commission on American Citizenship, *Better Men for Better Times,* Washington, Catholic University, 1943.

THE REVEREND GEORGES FLOROVSKY DISCUSSES
ASPECTS OF THE PAPER OF THE REVEREND
JOHN COURTNEY MURRAY, S.J.

VOICE: This is the question I would pose to Father Florovsky: Can we hope in the future for some synthesis? What is
our hope for a Christian philosophy, a Christian center for
knowledge?

FATHER FLOROVSKY: I think I may start with some remarks on Father Murray's presentation. My general impression was that he was unduly optimistic. He emphasized the
contribution of Origen as a pioneer, but he did not say enough
about the contradictions in which Origen was involved, and
neither did he mention that we can trace in what you call the
history of Christian thought a tendency to challenge Origen's
endeavor in principle.

At a certain period the whole problem of Hellenism in
Christianity was very sharply put, and the feeling was expressed that probably the results of the Hellenic or Graeco-
Roman liberal education were looted or contaminated by
Christianity. There was a basic tension between the two men-
talities, between these two approaches, and a premature, precip-
itate synthesis even at the time of Origen. Afterward, those
who were not converted to Christianity resented very much the
Christian handling of Greek philosophy. They felt that it was
perfidious, and educators felt strongly that Christians were
ruining the Greek philosophy by using it for purposes for which
it was not intended.

On the other hand, the remaining Christians felt it was a
bad thing to mix things that were incompatible—and so it
continues through the ages, and now in our days the question
is again discussed with great vigor and probably with one-
sidedness.

In a number of books published in our lifetime, we find
164

theologians opposing and contrasting two incompatible words, "spirituality" and "intellect." The former is Biblical-Christian, Judaeo-Christian, and the latter is Hellenic, and if you were to ask whether a synthesis is possible, many would say no, it is utterly undesirable, dangerous, and disruptive, because you cannot bring two mutually exclusive principles together.

It is the tension between these two words, and between these two roots of our civilization, about which Dr. Pollard was speaking. Historically, there are these two roots, but the question is raised whether it was a good thing or bad that there are. I think I can say without offense and exaggeration that one may almost identify the Catholic with the synthesis of these two trends and the Protestant with their careful separation.

If you put together Christian Platonism, is it an ugly monster or a successful synthesis? Or Christian aestheticism, taking into consideration Aristotle's conviction that the world was eternal and not created; is it an ugly monster, a hybrid, or is it a successful synthesis? Or Christian Stoicism, taking into consideration that Stoicism bred indifference to suffering? Nobody would deny that these things existed and that they do exist now; that there are Christian Platonists, Christian Aristotelians, and Christian Stoics, and I don't know what else; but is it a good thing, is it a right way, or is it an impasse, a misleading way, which cannot lead anywhere except into error?

Father Murray simply did not mention it, but this is a problem which has troubled people since Origen's time. Thomas Aquinas was about to be condemned in his own time for heretical convictions. He was almost condemned in France, but he was upheld in Rome.

VOICE: How do you feel yourself? Do you feel that Christian Platonism is possible?

FATHER FLOROVSKY: I am afraid I don't believe it is possible. I don't believe that one can simply put Platonism or Aristotelianism into one form and Christian theology in the other form and say we have achieved a synthesis. A sharp student can immediately discern that they are two different things under one cover. I was a bit astonished that Father Murray did not bring in the name of Augustine at all. I would not say that Augustine was absolutely successful; probably he was not, but he was a bit more successful than Origen and a bit more successful than Thomas—for a very simple reason: because he did not attempt synthesis. What he attempted was a conversion of the Greek mind, and I think this is the key word.

The point is not that we should synthesize, which I think is impossible. It does not appeal to me at all. Greek mentality or Greek intellect, as it was inherited by us, is a sum of knowledge with a certain disposition of mind and certain attitudes. Consider the concept of time in Greek philosophy and the concept of time in Christian philosophy. What is the measure of time, circular or linear?

You look at your watch and you have the symbol of Hellenic circular time which always returns, morning and evening, morning and evening. You have it in the stars, in everything, a rotation of spheres. We haven't gotten very far away from the ancient astronomy. As a matter of fact, in our immediate observation nature rotates. There are springs and summers and winters and again springs and summers, so we build up our concept of time on the immediate observation of nature. We come to the conclusion that the course of time is a rotation.

When we open the Bible and read it, we find that in the beginning was the Creation and everything else, culminating in the Gospels. Out of nothing there was something, and it ends, and there will be no more time. It is a moment from beginning to end, and the symbol of this is an arrow which moves from a beginning. It was started. It did not start itself in eternity. It was started and it aims at a goal.

But now a completely different conception arises. We may find that the human mind continues with the concept of rotation, and there is always a temptation to believe in the recur-

rent cycles and so on, but nevertheless we cannot get rid of this
Biblical concept of a moving arrow.

But here we have the question: Can you synthesize the two
things? What is involved in this cyclic conception? If you view
history as a cyclic pattern it has no purpose and no goal and
never moves anywhere. It returns upon itself and then everything will come again.

In the Biblical concept, history moves and something is
achieved. Here we have a different idea. Our minds have been
converted from one conception to another. Augustine was quite
emphatic on this point. He exclaimed, "Well, but all these
things, these cycles, are exploded," and we turn our minds
from this dream.

So here is an example. Augustine, who was quite great, sufficiently Hellenic, and sufficiently Platonic, did not avoid the
point at which there was a definite conviction that you must
impose conversion upon the Greek mind without denying the
use of intellect. He would not look for a compromise at this
point, he would simply demand conversion.

VOICE: But Thomas did compromise.

FATHER FLOROVSKY: Thomas did compromise.

*The Discussion Shifts to the Relevance of the Theme of Eternal
Life in Christian Education.*

FATHER FLOROVSKY: Every Christian believes that history has a content, and that man has a historical destiny in
one way or another. All Christians believe that there is another
life. What is the relation between this life and the other life,
between this one and the one to come? It is not enough simply
to struggle with the physical question, because it immediately
influences our interpretation of history from a very practical
point of view. We have three possible solutions.

First, that this life and the other life have no relation whatever because a future life is a life of grace and depends upon the sole will of God and upon the terms of election which was done without provision, without taking into account the actual life here. Then you have an absolute divorce, and therefore nothing in history has any eternal relevance, but eternity absolutely is disconnected from this life.

Secondly, that what is happening in history, although history is meaningless and does not lead to anything, is a very good training school. You train an abstract virtue and describe it in an abstract way. So it is not important what is done in history. The content of history is absolutely irrelevant, but it results in the formation of human character. It is therefore man's training for eternity, a training of virtues and punishment of vices and nothing else. So also the contents of a civilization are absolutely irrelevant. That solution, in the strictest sense, I could never accept.

The third concept is that history is not only the training ground of our character and our testing in the virtues but also, in some sense which we probably cannot fully apprehend, an accumulation of the content of human activity. In eternity it will be present in some changed form, but in any case the age to come will be a consummation of the present age in a certain sense. I would add that this is through personalities and not through objective structures.

Now the concept of Christian education will be different in these three different cases, because in the first case, you see, there is no chart for Christian education except the preaching of penitence and divine right. There is nothing else you can do.

In the second case, you would emphasize the educational aspect as distinguished from instruction, because everything you teach belongs to this world and will pass away with this world. Its aim will be just to make good people.

In the third case, you can really press for a synthesis because you are at the middle, at least in principle. You admit the presence of certain genuine values in what is going on in the cultural process. It doesn't mean everything, and discriminations should be made, but you admit certain values in principle.

Niebuhr definitely inclines to the solution that what is important is whether a man was penitent in this life or not because, from the Lutheran point of view, everything man is doing is bad, since it is God who must be the only actor and man simply appears in the scene. Therefore what is important is training in certain virtues, especially in the virtue of repentance. Repent, and know that you are dust and ashes, and this is the only thing to expect to achieve. You must keep people in an ecstasy of repentance. That is all.

The other concept, which is in a sense Augustinian, and which appeals to me most of all, is that there is a meaning, not only in our attitude to things but in things themselves. I think it is much more compatible with the belief that the world was created by God and intended for some purpose. Even if God's wishes are mutilated, still it remains God's world and belongs to God. It is at this point, of course, that Augustine was not so strong.

If you start with the idea of man as a miserable sinner in the hands of God, if this is your pattern of history, I don't see very much chance for religion in education. You cannot just repeat every day to the children in the class, "You are miserable nothings and God is angry with you," and nothing else. New England preachers in the seventeenth century used to do that every Sunday.

VOICE: As I understand it, the first point of view is that there is nothing in common between the next life and this life. You go by grace from one to the other.

The second position is that this life is regarded simply as a training ground for the next, a moral training ground, let us say.

The third position is one in which the actual history we

live in this life has eternal value, is important to the next life.
Would that be a fair summary?

FATHER FLOROVSKY: I would put it this way: In both
my second and my third cases, history is relevant to the life
to come, but relevant in different senses.

VOICE: May I say something on this? I think I am the
horrible example in this group, because I feel that I am at
the foot of the ladder somehow. This kind of discussion is so
far over my head and so far removed from my own experience
that I find it exceedingly difficult to follow.

So many of you men have had courses in theology and
courses in philosophy, and you have dwelt in this refined
atmosphere so long that a very humble person like myself
who is running a school and dealing with the everyday problems of boys finds it very difficult to follow you.

I have no hesitancy in speaking out because you are very
kind to me, but my feeling is that, frankly, I am not very
much concerned about the future life; that in my school I
am very much more concerned about what goes on now, and
I have a feeling that our task is somehow to grow in spirit
through unselfishness and through a life devoted to the people
with whom we are associated.

VOICE: Here is a real question: Is it a part of education
to talk about the next life and make it the center, or isn't it?

FATHER FLOROVSKY: We are supposed to discuss the
concept of Christian education. There may be another education respectable in many senses. There may be very respectable Stoic education, and the Stoics were good educators.

However, the concept of eternal life belongs to the essence
of Christian education, and I think it belongs simply because
it belongs to the essence of historical Christianity. It belongs
to the essence of Biblical Christianity. It belongs to the Gospel.

Whether other things are respectable and good from other
points of view is not the question. Sacrifice is possible without

belief in God, and sacrifice seems to be a good thing, but don't call it Christian virtue because this it is not.

VOICE: Father, what was the position of Calvin in this matter? Wasn't it the difficulty of even discussing these things that made him take his drastic view?

FATHER FLOROVSKY: You see, the point of Calvin is that the human attitude is irrelevant unless it is relevant to God's attitude. What is relevant to God's attitude—that alone is relevant. Man's attitude to himself is absolutely irrelevant. Man's attitude to God is relevant in some sense, but in a limited sense. The attitude of a non-elect of God is irrelevant because it cannot change God's election, but the attitude of the elect does not add very much to God's election.

VOICE: Then there is a contradiction in the history of the disciples, because they insisted very much on education. They were very good educators, and if education can do nothing—

FATHER FLOROVSKY: Well, obviously, you see, there is sometimes a lack of consistency in conceptions, but Calvinist education, like Lutheran education, is education in virtue.

VOICE: Where then is the fountainhead of the strong doctrine of vocation that you get in Calvinism?

FATHER FLOROVSKY: Yes, and you find the same in Lutheranism, but here vocation again is from the same abstract educational point of view, you see. We may distinguish education and instruction. Education by obedience—you must follow your vocation, but this vocation may be ultimately meaningless, you see, except as an occasion for exhibiting certain virtues of obedience and so on.

VOICE: Isn't my vocation, at least in the Calvinistic view, an occasion for glorification of God, whether I dig ditches or preach the Gospel?

FATHER FLOROVSKY: Yes. You see, whatever you do, the content is comparatively irrelevant because everything passes away, but the fact that you are obeying God is relevant, and so to say, enhances the glory of God.

Of course, here is a contradiction, because the glory of God is absolutely supreme. No human glorification can be of any real significance, and here is an inherent contradiction, because Calvin's contention was that there should be and there is but one real actor in reality—God. Everything else really is impotent. It cannot do anything. This is the Calvinist conception, a combination of the first two of the three attitudes I described toward this life in relation to eternal life, and a view which, as I said before, I could never accept.

On Some Typical Aspects of Christian Education

JACQUES MARITAIN

I

IF WE WISH TO PERCEIVE what a Christian philosophy of education consists of, it is clear that the first thing to do is to try to bring out what the Christian idea of man is.

The Christian idea of man has many connotations and implications. Let us point out some of them.

For Christianity there is no transmigration; the immortality of the soul means that after the death of its body the human soul lives forever, keeping its own individuality. It is not enough, moreover, to say that the human soul is immortal; faith holds also that the body will rise up and be united with the soul again; and Thomas Aquinas goes so far as to insist that in the state of separation from its body the soul is no doubt a substance, but one in which human nature does not come to completion; therefore the separate soul does not constitute a person. All this means that soul and body compose one single substantial unit; as against Hinduism and Platonism, Christianity forcefully emphasizes the unity of the human being, and any recurrence of Platonism—for instance the way in which Descartes ("I or my mind") separated the soul (that is, according to him, the Thought or the Mind) from the body (that is, according to him, geometrical Extension) and lodged the mind in the pineal gland, like a waterworks

engineer in the midst of his machines—is but a distortion of
the Christian idea of man.

Similarly any education of the Cartesian or angelistic type,
any education dealing with the child as with a pure mind
or a disembodied intellect, despising or ignoring sense and
sensation, punishing imagination as a mere power of deception,
and disregarding both the unconscious of the instinct and the
unconscious of the spirit, is a distortion of the Christian idea
of education. Christian education does not worship the human
body, as the ancient Greeks did, but it is fully aware of the
importance of physical training as aiming at a sound balance
of the whole human being; Christian education is intent on
making sense-perception, which is the very basis of man's
intellectual life, more and more alert, accurate, and integrated; it appeals confidently to the deep, living power of
imagination and feeling as well as to the spiritual power of
reason; it realizes that in the development of the child hand
and mind must be at work together; it stresses the properly
human dignity of manual activity.

At this point I am not thinking only of the educational
value that the various sorts of crafts taught on the campus
have even for future doctors, lawyers, or businessmen. What
I mean to say is that, in a more fundamental way, Christian
education knows that despite the basic unity of the educational
process the task of the school in preparing the young person
for adult life is twofold. On the one hand it must provide
the equipment in knowledge required by that kind of work
—both of the hand and the mind—which the ancients called
servile because it is more obviously manual, and which in
reality is not servile at all but rather the common human
work, the kind of work most natural to man. On the other
hand the school must provide the equipment in knowledge
required by that kind of activity—both of the hand and the
mind—which the ancients called liberal because it is more
obviously mental, and which should rather be characterized

as *more exacting human work.* I shall come back to this question at the end of my lecture, my point being that in our age genuine liberal education should cover both of the two fields I mentioned.

Thus does Christianity lay stress on the fact that man is flesh as well as spirit. But the Christian idea of man has further, and deeper, connotations. Christian faith knows that human nature is good in itself but that it has been put out of order by original sin; hence it is that Christian education will recognize the necessity of a stern discipline, and even of a certain fear, on the condition that this discipline, instead of being merely external—and futile—should appeal to the understanding and the will of the child and become self-discipline, and that this fear should be respect and reverence, not blind animal dread. And Christian faith knows that supernatural grace matters more than original sin and the weakness of human nature, for grace heals and superelevates nature and makes man participate in divine life itself; hence it is that Christian education will never lose sight of the grace-given equipment of virtues and gifts through which eternal life begins here below. Aware as it is of the fact that in the educational process the vital principle which exists in the student is the "principal agent," while the causality exercised by the teacher is, like medicine, only cooperating and assisting activity, Christian education does not only lay stress on the natural spirituality of which man is capable, it does not only found its entire work on the inner vitality of human nature; it makes its entire work rest also on the vital energies of grace and on the three theological virtues, Faith, Hope, and Charity; and if it is true to its highest aim, it turns man toward grace-given spirituality, toward a participation in the freedom, wisdom, and love of the saints.

A Christian philosophy of man does not see man as a merely natural being; it sees man as a natural *and* a supernatural being, bearing in itself the pitiful wounds of Adam and the sacred wounds of the Redeemer. There is no natural perfection for man. His perfection is supernatural, the very perfection of that love which is a diffusion of God's love in us, and the example of which Christ gave us in dying for those he loved. The task of the Christian is to enter Christ's work: that is to say, in some way to redeem his fellow men, spiritually and temporally; and redemption is achieved by the Cross.

Accordingly, Christian education does not tend to make a man naturally perfect, an athletic, self-sufficient hero with all the energies and beauty of nature, impeccable and unbeatable in tennis and football as well as in moral and intellectual competitions. It tries to develop as far as possible natural energies and virtues, both intellectual and moral, as tied up with, and quickened by, infused virtues, but it counts more on grace than on nature; it sees man as tending toward the perfection of love despite any possible mistakes and missteps and through the very frailty of nature, praying not to be put to trial and sensing himself a failure, but being at the same time more and more deeply and totally in love with his God and united with Him.

Christian education does not separate divine love from fraternal love, nor does it separate the effort toward self-perfection and personal salvation of others. And Christian education understands that at every level of human life, from the moral situation of the monk to that of the poet or the political leader, the Christian must take risks more or less great, and is never sheltered, and at the same time must be prepared to fight to the finish for his soul and life in God, using the weapons of the Cross every day. For it is up to us to make any suffering imposed by nature or by men into a merciful cross, if only we freely and obediently accept it in love. And furthermore the cross is there, at each and every moment in our life when we have to undergo that rending and agony in which, even with respect to small things, the choice between good and evil consists.

All this does not concern adult life only or adult education only; it begins in a more or less dim way very early for man. That is why the integral idea of Christian education, the idea of Christian education in its wholeness and as a lifelong process, already applies to the child in a way adapted to his condition, and must guide school education as to the general orientation of the educational process and the first beginnings which the child is capable of.

II

I should like to distinguish in Christian education two categories of requirements. In the first place Christian education involves all those requirements which characterize in general any genuine education truly aiming at helping a child or man attain his full formation or his completeness as a man. I have discussed these general points on other occasions and do not intend to do so today. In the second place Christian education, insofar as it is precisely Christian, has a number of specific requirements, dependent on the fact that the young person with whom it is concerned is a Christian and must be prepared to lead his adult life as a Christian. It is with respect to this second category of requirements that I shall now submit some observations. The first point will have to do with the curriculum in general; the second, with the development of Christian intelligence; the third, with the ways in which religious knowledge and spiritual life are to be fostered.

The first point has to do with the problem of Christian culture recently raised by Mr. Christopher Dawson in several interesting and challenging articles.[1] Is a curriculum in the humanities fitted to the education of a Christian if it is only or mainly occupied with the Graeco-Roman tradition and pagan or merely secular authors?

Before tackling the question I cannot help remembering

1. Cf. Christopher Dawson, "Education and Christian Culture," *The Commonweal* (Dec. 4, 1953); "Problems of Christian Culture," *The Commonweal* (April 15, 1955)

that the teacher in philosophy of the Angelic Doctor was the pagan Aristotle. In a more general way, and in relation to deeper considerations, I should like to observe that in general one of the aspects of the universality proper to Christianity is the fact that Christianity encompasses the whole of human life in all its states and conditions; Christianity is not a sect, not even in the sense of a sect dedicated to the purest perfection. Let us think for instance of those Essenes who a few centuries before Christ lived up to high moral standards and about whom we have learned many interesting details from recent archaeological discoveries. The Essenes were a closed group, a sect. Christians are not a sect, and this is the very paradox of Christianity; Christianity says, Be perfect as your heavenly Father is perfect, and Christianity gives this precept not to a closed group but to all men, whatever their state of life may be, even to those among us who are most deeply engaged in the affairs and seductions of this world. That is why, required as they are to tend to the perfection of love, Christians, as I observed a moment ago, have to confront the world and to take risks at every stage or degree of human existence and human culture. They are not of the world but they are in the world, as really and profoundly *in* as any man can be. They must be secluded from nothing, save from evil. All the riches of Egypt are theirs. Everything valuable for man and for the human mind belongs to them, who belong to Christ.

Coming now to education and our problem of Christian culture in the curriculum, I would say that in my opinion what is demanded is to get rid of those absurd prejudices which can be traced back to the Renaissance and which banish from the blessed land of educational curricula a number of authors and matters under the pretext that they are specifically religious, and therefore not "classical," though they matter essentially to the common treasure of culture. The writings of the Fathers of the Church are an integral part of the humanities as well as, or more than, those of the Elizabethan dramatists; St. Augustine and Pascal matter to us no less than Lucretius or Marcus Aurelius. It is important for young people to know the history of astronomy or the history of Greek and Latin literature, but it is at least as important for them to know the history of the great theological controversies and the history of those works about spiritual life and mystical experience which have been for centuries jewels of Christian literature.

Yet, it is my conviction as well as Christopher Dawson's that, once this point has been clearly established, the curriculum in the humanities of a Christian college must deal still more than that of a secular college with the whole of human culture. The significant thing, and what causes our approach to be Christian, is the perspective and inspiration, the *light* in which all this is viewed.[2] To know the great works produced by the human mind in any spiritual climate—and not only as a matter of information but in order to understand their significance and to *situate* them in the great starry universe of the intellect—is a requirement of that very universality of Christianity which I just spoke of. To tell the truth, that with which the traditional, classical Graeco-Roman humanities are to be reproached is mainly their narrowness and *provincialism*. In our age the humanities do not only extend beyond literature; they extend beyond the Western world and Western culture, they must be concerned with the achievements of the human mind in every great area of civilization; nay, more, with the prime and basic human apperceptions and discoveries which are obscurely contained in the myths and symbolic imagination of primitive men. Our watchword should be

2. ". . . the sociological problem of a Christian culture is also the psychological problem of integration and spiritual health. I am convinced that this is the key issue. Personally I would prefer a Ghetto culture to no religious culture at all, but under modern conditions the Ghetto solution is no longer really practicable. We must make an effort to achieve an open Catholic culture which is sufficiently conscious of the value of its own tradition to be able to meet secularist culture on an equal footing." Dawson, "Problems of Christian Culture," p. 36.

enlargement, Christian-inspired enlargement, not narrowing, even Christian-centered narrowing, of the humanities. The history of civilizations, and anthropology, may play in this connection—here again I am in agreement with Christopher Dawson—a basic introductory part, if they are viewed and understood in an authentic philosophical and theological light.

Incidentally, I should like to touch upon another question, which does not have to do with the humanities but rather with that notion of Christian inspiration and Christian light which I just alluded to. It is obvious that any matter dealing with the meaning of existence or the destiny of man can be illumined by Christian inspiration. But what about all these matters in which no metaphysical or moral value is involved? Has the notion of Christian inspiration or the idea of Christian education the slightest significance when it comes to the teaching of mathematics, astronomy, or engineering? The answer, I think, is that there are of course no Christian mathematics or Christian astronomy or engineering; but if the teacher has Christian wisdom, and if his teaching overflows from a soul dedicated to contemplation, the *mode* or manner in which his teaching is given—in other words, the mode or manner in which his own soul and mind perform a living and illuminating action on the soul and mind of another human being—will convey to the student and awaken in him something *beyond* mathematics, astronomy, or engineering: first, a sense of the proper place of these disciplines in the universe of knowledge and human thought; second, an unspoken intimation of the immortal value of truth, and of those rational laws and harmony which are at play in things and whose primary roots are in the divine Intellect.

The second point relating to the requirements of Christian education as such is concerned with the development of Christian intelligence. May I recall a saying of a great Dominican friar, Father Clerissac, who was my first guide and to whom I shall always feel indebted? "La vie chrétienne est à base d'intelligence," he said. "Intelligence is the very basis of Christian life." If it is true that school training has primarily to do with the intellect and the equipment of intelligence, this saying of Father Clerissac is for Christian educators a clear warning of the particular importance of school training, assuming that school training does not prove false to its ideal essence.

In this connection, what is true of education in general is especially true of Christian education. It is a sacred obligation for a Christian school or college to keep alive the sense of truth in the student; to respect his intellectual and spiritual aspirations and every beginning in him of creative activity and personal grasping of reality; never, as St. Thomas puts it, to dig a pit before him without filling it up; to appeal to the intuitive power of his mind, and to offer to him a unified and integrated universe of knowledge.

It is not irrelevant to expose at this point an illusion which seems to me to be particularly insidious. Just as it is often believed that in society no human person, no man invested with public office and charged with applying the law, but only the law itself, that abstract entity which is the law, has to be obeyed and to exert authority, so it is often believed that in the school no human person, no man invested with teaching authority and charged with conveying science, but only science or scholarship itself, that abstract entity which is science or scholarship, has to be listened to and to exercise the task of instructing minds. As a result, many teachers hold that it is their duty to dissemble and put aside as far as possible, or even to atrophy, their own convictions, which are the convictions of a given man, not the pronouncements of abstract science or scholarship. And since these so-called pronouncements exist only in the books written by the various scholars, and in the form (as a rule, and especially when it comes to the humanities and philosophy) of conflicting statements, the task of the teacher, modestly throwing himself into the shade, boils down to presenting to the student a carefully and objectively prepared picture of incompatible opinions, between which only subjective taste or feeling appears apt to choose. What is the effect of such teaching? To blunt or kill all that I have just described as requiring a sacred attention from the teacher, and to make the student grope from pit to pit. The first duty of a teacher is to develop within himself, for the sake of truth, deep-rooted convictions, and frankly to manifest them, while taking pleasure, of course, in having the student develop, possibly against them, his own personal convictions.

Let me now turn our attention toward a distinction which has, to my mind, crucial practical importance; namely, the distinction which I have emphasized elsewhere between natural intelligence, or intelligence with its native power only, and intelligence perfected by intellectual virtues, that is by those acquired qualities or energies which are peculiar to the scientist, the artist, the philosopher, etc. My contention is that intellectual virtues and skills, which are terribly exacting and require therefore an absorbing special training, are to be acquired during the period of graduate or advanced study, whereas school and college education is the proper domain of natural intelligence, which thirsts for universal knowledge and progresses more spontaneously than technically or scientifically, in vital unity with imagination and poetic sensibility. Hence the notion of *basic liberal education,* which is concerned with *universal knowledge* because it has essentially to do with *natural intelligence,* and which does not try to make the child into a scholar, a physicist, a composer, etc., albeit in a diminutive way, but endeavors only to make him understand the *meaning* and grasp the basic truth of the various disciplines in which universal knowledge is interested. As a result, the scope of the liberal arts and the humanities would be greatly enlarged, so as to comprise, according to the requirements of modern intelligence, physics and the natural sciences, the history of sciences, anthropology and the other human sciences, with the history of cultures and civilizations, even technology (insofar as the activity of the spirit is involved) and the history of manual work and the arts, both mechanical and fine arts. But on the other hand, and to compensate for this enlargement, the manner of teaching and the quantitative, material weight of the curriculum, as regards each of the disciplines in question, would be made less heavy: for any effort to cram the mind of the student with facts and figures, and with the so-called integrity of the subject matter, by dint of useless memorization or shallow and piecemeal information, would be definitely given up; and the great thing would be to develop in the young person genuine understanding of, and active participation in, the truth of the matter, and those primordial intuitions through which what is essentially illuminating as to the basic verities of each discipline learned is definitely and unshakably possessed.

As applied to Christian education, the aforementioned remarks have, it seems to me, a special bearing on the teaching of philosophy and theology, both of which should be the keystone of the edifice of learning in a Christian college, dedicated as it is, by definition, to wisdom. Common sense and natural intelligence, sharpened by the infused virtue of faith, are enough—not to be a philosopher and a theologian, to be sure—but to understand philosophy and theology, intelligently taught. Philosophical training, as I see it, might be composed of two main courses, supporting one another: on the one hand, a course in the relatively few basic philosophical problems, as viewed and illumined in the perspective of Christian philosophy and as related to the most pressing questions with which the age is concerned; on the other hand, a course in the history of philosophy, intent on bringing out the central intuition in which every great system originates and the more often than not wrong conceptualization which makes these systems irreducibly antagonistic.

As to theology, it is not to form a future priest or minister

that it has to be taught in a Christian college, it is to equip
laymen's reason in such a way that they will grasp the content
of their own faith in a deeper and more articulate manner, and
use the light and wisdom of a supremely unified discipline
to solve the problems with which a Christian is confronted in
the accomplishment of his mission in temporal society. This
theological training, as I see it, should be especially connected
with the problems raised by contemporary science, by the
great social movements and conflicts of our age, and by
anthropology, comparative religion, and the philosophy of
culture. I should like to have special seminars in which students in philosophy and theology would meet representatives
of the most various schools of thought: scientists, artists,
missionaries, labor leaders, managers, etc. For it is not with
books, it is with men that students must be made able to
discuss and take their own stand. An inviolable rule would
be that, after such meetings, the discussion should continue
in further seminars between the students and the teachers of
the college, until they have completely mastered the problem
and brought out the truth of the matter.

I should like to make a final remark in relation to our present question, namely, the question of the development of
Christian intelligence. This remark deals with the Holy
Scripture, especially the Old Testament, and modern exegesis.
During college years Christian youth should be given serious
knowledge of the meaning of exegesis, and of the distinction
to be made between what is valid result and discovery and
what is arbitrary construction in the exegetical comments of
our contemporary scholars. They should be shown how the
main problems of exegesis can be solved in the light of a
sound theory of divine inspiration, and how our approach
to the Biblical text is thus made at the same time more realistic
and purer. The question here is not to cultivate vain learning
but to go in—with greater awareness of all that is human in
the human instrument and greater faith in the divine truth

taught by the principal author—for that assiduous reading of the Scriptures which has been a sacred custom in Protestant countries and is now being practiced more and more among Catholics, and which is an invaluable asset of Christian life.

I believe, moreover, that the contact with the Holy Scripture must be at the same time so full of reverence and so deeply personal that it is not advisable to make the teaching of which I am speaking part of the compulsory matters of the curriculum. It would be much better to have this teaching given, as an elective matter, to students really eager to get it, who would constitute for this purpose one of those self-organized groups whose importance I shall stress in a few moments.

There is a third and final point to be made in the second part of this lecture: it has to do with the ways in which religious knowledge and spiritual life are to be fostered in a Christian school or college.

It has often been remarked that, in eighteenth- and nineteenth-century France, for instance, a number of the most violent adversaries of religion had been in their youth either seminarians or pupils of great Jesuit colleges. This is no serious argument against the methods of the seminaries and of the Jesuit Fathers, for, as an old saying puts it, *quid quid recipitur, ad modum recipientis recipitur,* anything that is received is received according to the mood and capacity of the receiver. Yet a more general and surprising fact remains, namely the fact of the religious ignorance in our contemporary world of a great number, I would say of a majority of people educated in religious schools and denominational colleges. Why is this so? Because, in my opinion, religious teaching, however carefully given, remains too much of a separate, isolated compartment, and is sufficiently integrated neither with the intellectual interests nor with the personal life of the students. As a result, it is received by many in the most superficial stratum of the soul

and forgotten almost as soon as it has been shallowly memo-
rized.

It is through its vital connections with philosophy and theology that religious training can be really integrated with the
general mental activity and the intellectual interests of the
student. Though a Christian college in which the cosmos of
knowledge is not crowned by theology may have the best
courses in religion, the religious teaching it metes out is but a
leaf which goes with the wind. But it is especially about the
integration of religious training in the personal life of the students that I should like to say a few words now.

My contention is that the proper way in which such an integration may be achieved is the development of liturgical life
on the campus and the participation of the student population
in the liturgy of the Church.[3] The succession of feasts which
celebrate divine mysteries and the events of our redemption, or
commemorate the days on which the saints have been born to
eternity, the prayers, the songs, the sacred rites of liturgy, compose a kind of immense and uninterrupted sign through which
the heaven of religious truths symbolically penetrates our daily
life. Breathing in this kind of heaven provides the student with
the oxygen he needs to have the religious teaching given in
the classroom integrated with the depths of his own personal
life.

I do not wish to see all the students of a Christian college,
dressed like monks, officiating in the chapel. Nor do I wish to
hear all of them, on Sundays, collectively answer the priest at
Mass—I am afraid the automatic display of the vociferations
of boys or the cooing of girls is more liable to disturb than to
quicken adoration and thanksgiving. What I wish is to have
liturgical study groups freely organized on the campus, and to

3. Cf. *ibid.*, p. 35: ". . . it seems to be clear that the key of the problem
is to be found not in philosophy but in *worship*. . . . In that case the fundamental 'classics' are not St. Thomas and St. Augustine, but the Bible, the
Missal, the Breviary and the Acta Sanctorum." Let us replace "not, but" by
"not only, but also," and all this is true.

have a certain number of the members of these groups, inspired by the example of the Benedictine monks, form sorts of brotherhoods and choirs in order actively to participate in liturgical ceremonies, especially in the celebration of High Mass. Thus, I assume, a sufficient emulation or stimulation regarding liturgical life would take place in the whole student population.

The best things must develop on a free basis. It is so with liturgical life, it is so with daily attendance at Mass and the reception of Holy Communion. (I note in passing the striking improvement which it has been possible to observe in the student population of Notre Dame, after it was decided to give the Eucharist in all the chapels of the campus and at any time in the morning to any student desiring to receive it.) In the groups of which I am now speaking, whose aim would be the knowledge and practice of liturgy, a brief seminar would be held every day on the lives of the saints mentioned in the Breviary.

Next to these liturgical groups there would be other groups, probably fewer in number but exercising a more important action as a hidden ferment, which would be dedicated to studying the doctrine of theologians and great spiritual writers on mental prayer and mystical experience, and learning the rudiments of contemplative wisdom. I think that the most useful task of such groups would be to foster among their members that daily reading of the Gospel which is the normal way toward wordless prayer and the very nourishment of spiritual life.

III

In the third and last part of my lecture, I should like to discuss two issues: first, concerning the moral formation of the youth; secondly, concerning liberal education for all.

With respect to the first issue, it is to be noticed that school or college education is only a part and a beginning of man's education, especially because it is more concerned with intelligence and knowledge than with the will and moral virtues, or with telling young people how to think than with telling them how to live. According to the nature of things, moral education is more the task of the family, assisted by the religious community to which it belongs, than the task of the school.

Now what is normal in itself is not always what occurs most often in fact. As a matter of fact, it is too easy to observe today that, especially in the social and moral conditions created by our industrial civilization, the family group happens frequently to fail in its moral duty toward children, and appears more liable either to wound them or at least to forsake them in their moral life than to educate them in this domain. Thus the school has, in some imperfect and partial way, to try to make up for the lacks of the family group in the moral formation of youth. But what can be the power and efficacy of teaching and classrooms in such matters?

It is at this point that we may realize the crucial importance of the grouping of students in self-organized teams. In an essay written for the *Yearbook* of the National Society for the Study of Education I have already insisted on the part to be played by these teams in the life of that kind of republic which the school or the college is. The teams in question are different in purpose and in structure from the study groups whose role is also essential in academic life and some examples of which we have just considered. These self-organized teams, of which I am now speaking, are responsible for the discipline of their members and their progress in work. They are

> formed by the students themselves, without any interference from school authorities; they elect their own captains; they have regular meetings—which no teacher attends—in which they examine and discuss how the group behaves and the questions with which it is con-

fronted. Their captains, on the other hand, as representatives of each team, have regular contacts with the school authorities, to whom they convey the suggestions, experiences, and problems of the group. So the students are actually interested in the organization of studies, the general discipline, the "political life" of the school or the college, and they can play a sort of consultative part in the activity of the educational republic.[4]

But in a Christian college—and this is my point—the self-organized teams which I have just described would also have another and more essential function. They would have to enforce and carry into being, in all occasions and incidents of daily existence, the requirements of Christian charity. It is on the exercise of mutual charity that the attention of everyone in them would be focused. And so these teams would make up in some way for what might be lacking in the moral education provided by the family—and they would be, so to speak, workshops in the evangelical rules of mutual love.

To make things more precise, let me point out a custom which the teams in question might find the greatest advantage in borrowing from the daily life of religious orders. The custom I have in mind is that of the *chapter* in which all the members of a religious community gather together for the purpose of a common self-examination. Each one must make known the faults—not, of course, the faults depending on the *forum internum,* the inner tribunal of conscience, but those depending on the *forum externum*—that he has committed during the day; and each one has similarly to make known the same kind of external, visible faults or mistakes he has observed in others. There is thus a sort of general wash, presided over by the abbot or prior, who metes out the soap of suitable exhortation: thereafter everyone goes back smart and lively into his own cell.

4. From my essay "Thomist Views on Education," *Modern Philosophies and Education,* National Society for the Study of Education, Yearbook 54 Pt. I (University of Chicago Press, 1955), p. 77.

Well, our self-organized teams, as I see them, would imitate this wise custom, fittingly adopted or modified, and hold chapters of their own—I know of Christian families which did so for many years, and with considerable moral profit—laying stress especially on all that concerns the requirements of mutual respect and love in the matters of conscience, be they serious or minor, of which the group is made aware. And the captain of the team would play the part of the prior in giving the moral direction and explanations he deems necessary. The benefit of the custom is twofold: I mean to say, on the one hand the development of the sense of responsibility and moral awareness, and the progress in Christian charity; and on the other hand the psychological relief caused by the fact of giving expression to that perception and experience of the lacks of others which, if it had to remain repressed, might, slight as the matter may be, embitter one's soul.

All this talk about self-organized teams is not simply theoretical. I have personally known a place in which the experiment was made, and with full success.

I have emphasized the importance of two different kinds of self-organized groups: the self-organized teams of students of which I just spoke, concerned with the moral and political life of the educational republic, and operating independently from teachers; and the self-organized study groups, which could and should develop in connection with a large variety of matters, and in which the teachers play a necessary part, but more as counselors and guides than as professors and lecturers. When I think of the necessity of these diverse self-organized groups and of the way in which they are likely to grow in actual fact, in proportion as their significance is recognized, I come to the idea that the educational structure of future schools and colleges will be different from the present one: instead of one single system, there would be two coordinated systems of forces or formative energy—two nervous systems, so to speak, confronting and complementing one another; the first system being composed of those various centers, starting from above, of teaching authority which are the faculties, departments, schools or institutes; the second being composed of those various centers, starting from below, of autonomous study and self-discipline which are our freely self-organized groups or teams of students. The unity which schools and universities are looking for [5] is not a unity of mechanical centralization; it is a spontaneous, star-studded unity of harmony in diversity.

To conclude my lecture I have still a few remarks to submit about the other issue that I have mentioned, namely the question of liberal education for all.

The notion of liberal education for all is, in my opinion, one of those concepts which are in themselves close to the requirements of natural law, and appear obviously valid once we think them over, but which were long repressed, so to speak, or prevented from being uttered in consciousness, because social conditions and social prejudice, condemning the greater number of men to a kind of enslaved life, made such concepts impracticable, which is as much as to say unthinkable. This concept of liberal education for all is a late fructification of a Christian principle, it is intimately related to the Christian idea of the spiritual dignity of man and the basic equality of all men before God. "Education directed toward wisdom, centered on the humanities, aiming to develop in people the capacity to think correctly and to enjoy truth and beauty, is education for freedom, or liberal education. Whatever his particular vocation may be, and whatever special training his vocation may require, every human being is entitled to receive such a properly human and humanistic education." [6] No educational philosophy should be more dedicated to the ideal of liberal education for all than the Christian philosophy of education.

Coming now to practical application, I must first of all make clear that, in saying "liberal education for all," it is of *basic*

5. Cf. John U. Nef, *The Universities Look for Unity,* New York, 1943.
6. "Thomist Views on Education," *Modern Philosophies,* p. 77.

liberal education—basic liberal education for all—that I am thinking. This concept of basic liberal education has already been stressed in a preceding part of my lecture. It gives practical value and feasibility to the concept of liberal education for all. For on the one hand basic liberal education, covering as it does the field of the achievements of the human mind in science as well as in literature and art, has nothing to do with the old notion of liberal education as an almost exclusively literary education. On the other hand the resulting broadening of the matters of the curriculum is compensated for by a considerable alleviation in the very approach to these matters, which is henceforth adjusted to the needs and capacity of natural intelligence—more intuitive, therefore, and freed from any burden of pseudo science. Furthermore, if it is a question of college years, it appears that the college has to insure both basic liberal education in its final stages and the development of a particular state of capacity: so it would be normal to have the college

> divided into a number of fields of concentration or fields of primary interest, each one represented by a given school (or *"institut,"* in the French sense of this word). In effect, this would be to have the college divided into a number of *schools of oriented humanities* all of which would be dedicated to basic liberal education, but each of which would be concerned with preparatory study in a particular field of activity, thus dealing with the beginnings and first development of a given intellectual virtue or a given intellectual skill. And basic liberal education rather than this preparatory study would be the primary aim. But precisely in order to make basic liberal education fully efficacious, the manner in which it would be given, and the teaching organized, would take into consideration the particular intellectual virtue, or the particular intellectual skill, to be developed in the future scien-

tist or businessman, artist, doctor, newspaperman,
teacher, lawyer, or specialist in government.[7]

But what about the main difficulty, namely the fact that for
many boys and girls intellectual life, liberal arts, and the humanities are only a bore, and that as a result liberal education,
in proportion as it is extended to a greater and greater number
of young people, seems condemned to degenerate and fall to
lower and lower levels? I am far from believing that all the
boys and girls in question should be rated as duller students.
In any case it may be answered that good educational methods
are intended to stimulate the natural interests and intelligence
of normal students, not to make the dull ones meet the standards. The clear maxim in these matters is, as Mortimer Adler
put it in his seminars on education, "The best education for
the most gifted person in the community is, in its equivalent
form, the best education for all." As a rule, to ask men to
maintain themselves at a level of real humanity is to ask a
little too much of them, a little more than they are capable of.
That is why what have been called heterogeneous schools or
classes (segregating the brighter and the duller) must be considered a bad solution in every respect. Better to have homo-
geneous courses—I mean adapted, according to the principle
I just mentioned, to the highest possible level with respect to
the capacity, not of the duller, but of the good average student;
and to assist in a special way the brighter students by allowing
them freely to group together in extracurricular units—study
clubs or academies—under some tutorial guidance.

All that is true, but it is insufficient and does not reach the
root of the matter. It is necessary to go further. As long as the
problem is posed in classical education's usual terms, I mean
in terms of the student's greater or lesser capacity to enjoy the
pure activities of the intellect and progress in them—in other
words, as long as pure intellectual activity is considered the

7. *Ibid.,* p. 81.

only activity worthy of man, and those who do not enjoy it are considered to be necessarily duller—no really satisfactory answer can be given. A deeper and more general principle must be brought to the fore. What principle? The Christian principle of the dignity of manual activity. This principle, which the monks of former times perfectly understood, was long disregarded by reason of social structure and ideological prejudice, both of which kept more or less the imprint of the times when manual labor was the job of slaves (as is still manifest in the expression "servile work"). As against such prejudice, let us not forget that St. Paul made a living as a tent-maker— not to speak of Jesus Himself, Who was a carpenter. The principle of the dignity and human value of manual work is now in the process or being at last realized by common consciousness. We have to understand that genuine manual work is neither the work of a beast of burden nor that of a robot, but human work in which both body and mind are at play— as they are also in the intellectual work of a writer, a lawyer, a teacher, a doctor, etc., who cannot perform his own task without a certain dose of bodily exertion. The difference is that in one case (manual work) bodily activity plays the part of a (secondary) "principle agent" activated by the mind, and in the other case (intellectual work) the part of a merely "instrumental agent" moved by the mind. So both are, like man, made of flesh and spirit; manual work and intellectual work are equally human in the truest sense and directed toward helping man to achieve freedom. We have good reasons to believe that a general rehabilitation of manual work will characterize the next period of our industrial civilization.

If we take all these things into consideration, we shall see that such a crucial change in perspective, which is Christian in itself and in its first origin, will inevitably reverberate in education, and must be of special interest for the Christian philosophy of education; and we shall realize better the bearing of the remarks that I submitted at the beginning of this lecture, when I observed that the task of the school in preparing the young person for adult life must involve a twofold function: on the one hand it must provide the equipment in knowledge required by the vocations and activities which consist mainly of manual work; on the other hand it must provide the equipment in knowledge required by those vocations and activities which consist mainly of intellectual work.

These things have been recognized for centuries, but in creating an invidious opposition between a so-called *popular* education, preparing for manual vocations, and *liberal* education. My point is that in a somewhat distant future *liberal* education, on the contrary, will permeate the whole of education, whether young people are prepared for manual or for intellectual vocations. In other words popular education must become liberal, and liberal education must become popular. Is it not clear that "liberal education for all" means liberal education for prospective manual workers as well as for prospective intellectual workers? The very possibility of this supposes considerable changes in our social and educational structures, a result of which would be to make some more democratic, probably gratis equivalent of our present colleges available to all.

The *unipolar* conception of liberal education would then be replaced by a *bipolar* conception; and here we have the answer to our problem. We would no longer have to choose between either obliging students unconcerned with disinterested knowledge to trudge along in the rear of classes which are a bore to them or diverting them toward other and supposedly inferior studies by reason of a lack, or a lesser capacity. We would have these students enter into a different but equally esteemed and appreciated system of study, and steer spontaneously, by reason of a positive preference, enjoyment, and capacity, for a type of liberal education which, while remaining essentially concerned with humanities, prepares them for some vocation pertaining to manual work—not, of course, by making them apprentices in any of the innumerable manual vocations but rather by teaching them, theoretically and practically, matters concerning the general categories into which manual service can be divided, such as farming, mining, craftsmanship, the various types of modern industrial labor, etc.

Thus education, especially college education, would be organized around two opposite centers, a center of manual service training, and a center of intellectual service training, each one with its own various institutes or schools of oriented humanities. And though intellectual service is in itself or in its nature more spiritual and therefore of greater worth than manual service, the fact remains that with respect to man and therefore to the humanities the one and the other are equally worthy of our esteem and devotion and equally apt to help us fulfill our destiny. They would be on a completely equal footing in the educational system.

As I see it, the choice between the two master directions I have just pointed out would take place preferably at the end of high school, possibly earlier or later. And the two centers in question could materialize either in one single, sufficiently large institution or in a variety of different colleges, vocational institutes, or advanced schools specializing in one matter or another. The important thing, moreover, is that in any case manual service training as well as intellectual service training should be permeated with liberal arts and the humanities, though in a different way.

Of course some dull or lazy or psychologically inept people would always be found in one place as well as in the other. But I am convinced that interest, intellectual curiosity, and understanding with respect to the whole field of the humanities and liberal arts would exist as a rule in the students of the manual service training as well as in those of the other center, on the condition that the mode or way of approach be fittingly adapted. For if to most of these students matters pertaining to disinterested knowledge, the liberal arts, and humanities are liable to appear a bore, it is only insofar as they are matters of *formal teaching.* If the approach becomes informal and unsystematic, everything changes for them.

In my book *Education at the Crossroads* I laid stress on the division between the *activities of learning* and the *activities of play* in the school, and on the essential part which play has in school life.[8] For play possesses a value and worth of its own, being activity of free expansion and a gleam of poetry in the very field of those energies which tend by nature toward utility.

Now I would like to go much farther than I did in that book, and, while broadening considerably the notion of the activity of play so as to comprise in it the notion of *informal* and *unsystematic* learning, I would submit that, on the one hand, training in matters which are of most worth and have primacy in importance may take place through the instrumentality of the activities of play as well as of the activities of learning; and, on the other hand, the relationship between activities of learning and activities of play would be reversed or opposite in the schools of the intellectual service training center and in those of the manual service training center. In the first case the humanities, liberal arts, and philosophy are matters of formal learning; and craftsmanship, for instance, and any kind of manual work, including painting and sculpture, are matters of informal learning or play. In the second case it is the manifold field of manual service training which would be a matter of formal and systematic learning, whereas the humanities, liberal arts, and philosophy would be matters of informal learning or play: a situation which would in no way mean any diminution in intrinsic importance but which would quicken and set free the intellectual interest and understanding of the category of students in question with respect to these things.

My working hypothesis, then, is that in the schools of the manual service training center education in all matters pertaining to the humanities and liberal arts would be surprisingly

8. Cf. *Education at the Crossroads* (New Haven, Yale University Press, 1943), p. 55.

successful if it were given not by way of formal teaching but by way of play and informal learning. With respect to informal learning, I would say that the teaching (formal teaching) of gardening, for instance, offers every opportunity to give students, by way of digressions or comments, a most fruitful informal and unsystematic teaching in botany and biology, not to speak of economics, the history of architecture, the history of civilization, etc. It is the same with the teaching (formal teaching) of the various skills and kinds of knowledge required from labor by modern industry and the informal and unsystematic teaching of physics and chemistry, nuclear physics, engineering, mathematics.

With respect to play, I would say that facilities given to students to read great books of their own choice and for their own pleasure, then seminars in these readings, in literature, in philosophy, then concerts and theatrical performances with appropriate comments, all these things conceived of and managed as a preparation for having the adult worker make profitable use of his leisure time constitute a genuine education in the humanities and intellectual life in the form of that activity of free expansion which characterizes play.

You will, I hope, excuse me for having indulged in dreams of my own regarding the future of our school system. As to myself, I am grateful to you for hearing on the subject of education a man who feels more and more, in growing old, that he is unable to educate anybody, but badly needs to be educated himself.

THE REVEREND JOHN COURTNEY MURRAY, S.J.,
DISCUSSES FURTHER ASPECTS OF HIS OWN
PAPER, AND TOUCHES UPON THAT OF
PROFESSOR MARITAIN

VOICE: Would you be good enough to restate the thesis of your paper, Father Murray?

FATHER MURRAY: I think Mr. Maritain expressed it himself this morning: the fact that intelligence lies at the root of Christianity. Definitely that would lead to some explanation and doubtless it would be open to challenges that you would want to offer, but that was really the thesis I was pursuing. This notion of Christianity, of what comes to us through Christianity, the Christian revelation, is a knowledge and a wisdom, too. Indeed, it is more than that, but it is that which takes root in human intelligence and therefore since the seat of faith is intelligence, at least in part, it is also in the will. Therefore, human intelligence necessarily has to cultivate itself as an instrument for the understanding of the gift that God has made to it. That point is what I call the civilization of intelligence itself as a Christian task imposed by faith itself.

My second proposition, I think, was the ideal of the unity of truth as the lodestar of the Christian educator and the Christian scholar, too; at least to make an honest attempt to integrate the whole of human knowledge under the primacy of the word of God, making the word of God relevant to all the departments of human thinking as well as, of course, to all the departments or aspects of human action in life.

I think I concluded by saying that we are at the moment in a fairly discouraging situation by reason of the fact that our ideal of the unity of truth has, to say the least, suffered very considerably, you might say fatally, in consequence of the last four or five hundred years of intellectual history; but nonetheless the ideal, I should maintain, still remains as ideals always do. Even though the conditions for the realization of the ideal seem to be discouraging, in a sense they may not be much worse than they ever were. We sometimes tend to exaggerate the desperate situation in which we are, whereas human conditions are always fairly desperate. There are the famous words that described that in the Viennese spirit: "The situation is desperate but not serious."

I think that if you believe in God at all you believe in Him as the author of all truth. Therefore all truth, somehow, is one. I might not be able to put together the pattern of the unity but I do believe that it exists. In fact, I myself would maintain that the pattern of the unity cannot be put together by human intelligence invested with faith and that any synthesis it may make during any given historical epoch is destined to be shattered. The unity of truth is a golden idea forever receding from our grasp, but the validity is established.

I think I made the suggestion that nothing can be done with any perfection in this regard; that Christian education is always a limping, defective, faulty, very fluid kind of thing. What one does is what one can, and it seems to me at the moment that the best one can hope for in the intellectual line, which is the line of the school, is what I call piecework: an effort to relate truths of Christianity to various disciplines ranging from art down to psychiatry, if you will. Whether psychiatry should be at the bottom or at the top, I don't know, but there should be a constant effort on the part of the educator to ensure that his students, as they absorb all the knowledge that the school puts at their disposal, or the college, or the university, should somehow be integrated into the Christian view. I think I used the word "view" several times because I rather like it. It is Newman's word, and the general idea, as you know, is that you have a view when you have established your intuitions in the natural order or your faith in the supernatural order on an intellectual basis, so that this organized, articulated body of thought that you hold can not only be presented but also defended and explained, because it has roots in reality. Newman makes the distinction, as you know, between having views and being simply "viewy." I think that "viewyness" is a very common phenomenon today. We have all kinds of opinions about everything. We are always compelled to have them and ofttimes our opinions are not really solidly rooted in fact or in faith, as the case may be; whereas a view has made contact with reality and has become part of one's total intellectual apparatus, part of one's very soul, so that it is a solid kind of thing.

It is this effort to construct the Christian view, to integrate everything in a Christian view, that would seem to me to be the cardinal ideal of Christian education.

You have to make a distinction between a school that explicitly professes itself to be Christian, a school which really lives up to the designation, and other schools which by no means make such a profession but nevertheless have on their faculties Christian men and women engaged in the work of education. This point has come up in the discussions which I attended previously. There are represented in this seminar all different types of schools ranging from the Roman Catholic school, which is definitely committed to the whole Catholic view, off in every direction you want to move on the spectrum to, let's say, the American public school.

Therefore you have several tasks to define. You could define the task of the Christian educator, the Christian man or woman teaching in the public school system or in some manner of nondenominational or interdenominational schools, and what it would be for him as a Christian within the educational milieu in which his work is cast. He has the Christian vocation no matter where he is. But then you have the other thing, in a place like Kent, which is definitely a church-affiliated school and therefore is committed to the tradition of the Church.

What are the school's ideals and the teacher's ideals within this latter educational milieu that would vary from the ideals possible within some less well-defined type of educational institution? It has been a constant problem, I guess, all through this seminar, that there are so many different kinds of schools represented, and the same description would apply to all of them with varying degrees of exactitude, even as far as the professed aims of the schools go.

You might have a group of Christian men and women in, let's say, a Midwestern public school, who would be doing a better job of religious education than you might find in a church school. It is possible.

MR. COLE: [1] That is one of the things that has puzzled me: What was in the minds of the planners in setting up these groups? The fact that we were not broken down into those of us who are in church schools on the secondary level and college level and those who are in the so-called secular institutions has made me assume that they are looking for some kind of a broad statement. I think that this is one of the things from which our difficulty stems. I think it is extremely difficult to try to formulate a statement which is going to be applicable in any kind of situation one finds himself in.

FATHER MURRAY: I would doubt if you could draw up any manner of definition of a Christian school or Christian education that would be applicable to the whole range of schools represented in this seminar. I myself, of course, have maintained that you don't really have a Christian school in the proper sense of the word unless that school is explicitly pledged to the transmission of the Christian religion and the intellectual heritage of Christianity in an organized, integrated form.

MR. COLE: That touches on the second question that we have been sort of kicking around the table. I mean, is the integration of the content of Christian tradition and the teaching thereof the whole task of education? What is the relationship of the kind of Christian values that we have been talking about in terms of respect for personality and all the rest of it to the task of education, and to what extent, even in the Christian

1. William Graham Cole, Chaplain, Williams College.

school where what you are doing is transmitting a certain body of tradition—to what extent are you working for commitment to that tradition? That is obviously the problem in any school where you can't very well mark students on the basis of their acceptance of the dogma. You can't do that, can you? You can't give the student who accepts the dogma an A and the one who questions it an F. I know it is more complex than that.

FATHER MURRAY: Did you get into the question of content? That was one trouble, one problem that the other groups seemed to be stumbling over. In this pluralistic society, in the pluralism of schools represented here, there seemed to be the disposition to throw the burden of Christianity, of Christian education, on the teacher and to equate the Christianity of a school simply with the radiance of the teacher's own faith. Of course no one will deny the validity and value of such a manner of personal influence. It is when we come to the actual content that trouble starts. Is Christianity taught in a given school, at least in one or another of its existent versions or traditions?

We have in our schools formal courses, four-year-long high school and four-year-long college courses, organized courses in Catholic doctrine, Scripture history, medieval history, documents of the Church and so on. The whole thing is an organized course. In four years you would have presented to you the totality of Catholic belief and practice, liturgy, theology, and all the rest of it. The unfortunate thing is that most of the time it is taught badly. We make it the worst taught subject in the whole curriculum.

FATHER MARTIN: [2] How far can these Christian ideas be carried in a given school which is not Christian, within the terms of our definition?

FATHER MURRAY: Of course, from the point of view of my own faith a Christian school is quite flatly and frankly an instrument of the Church and it participates, to some extent at

2. Charles Martin, St. Alban's School, Washington, D.C.

any rate, in the mission of the Church, both as a prophetic mission and also as a pastoral mission. The Church has a prophetic mission. It preaches simply the Word of God looking to the salvation of the soul, and its pastoral ministry consists in the guidance of the soul toward its eternal destiny.

Now this prophetic mission of the Church addresses itself to intelligence, at least in part. The message of the Church is answered by understanding on the part of the people to whom it is addressed. The school does the same work but from a different angle. It does give its students some pastoral care—guidance, if you will. They bring their personal problems and they are assisted in their solutions and they raise practical difficulties about the conduct of life and they are instructed out of the Christian tradition as to how to handle them. That is what you might call the counseling part of the school's work—the pastoral part.

But then the school undertakes to impart to the Catholic faith its proper intellectual dimensions and this is a department of understanding that cannot be achieved except in a school. It cannot be achieved in a church where you have the priest preaching from the pulpit, because all that happens is that people sit and listen, if indeed they do listen. Moreover, although the Catholic dioceses have organized programs of instruction that run through the whole year, the prophetic mission of the Church is not necessarily an organized course of study. The effect is not directly to organize and integrate the whole body of Christian doctrine. One Sunday one point will be made clear and the next Sunday something else will be clarified. There is a certain amount of doctrine and a certain amount of moral instruction together with a certain amount of liturgical instruction, whatever it may be.

The school tries to organize the whole thing in a pattern, all the truths of Christian faith; and it undertakes also to establish them as truths by referring them to their sources in the Revelations, and to introduce the student on different levels to the great Christian thinkers who have elaborated on the treasures and truths of faith in some intellectual fashion. The great doctrines of the Church are brought in in accordance with the age level and the maturity of the students with whom you are dealing. Therefore, as I say, the essential fact from the Catholic point of view is that your school is a kind of scholastic instrument of the Church. I should think that the same situation would prevail in any other frankly church-affiliated school. It would commit itself to the organization of the faith of the church to which it was affiliated and would stand in pretty much the same relation to the pulpit of that church as the Catholic schools stand in relation to the pulpit of the Catholic Church.

When you use the word "Christian" in its full and integral sense then, of course, you run into the problem of the schools that have no such affiliation and are not thus committed to be the aid or the instrument in the mission of the Church, but are either multidenominational or nondenominational or, as is the case of the public schools, just secular.

VOICE: Are we defining the term "Christian" as institutional Christianity?

FATHER MURRAY: I am; yes.

MR. COLE: I think that we who are Christians are sometimes inclined to neglect one doctrine of Christianity: that is, that God is at work even outside the bounds of that which we label Christian education, regardless of where it is taking place. I think the problem here is that the relationship between the transmission of Christianity as a faith must be considered together with the transmission of Christianity as an attitude toward persons, as an interpersonal relationship. I think that is where the basic problem lies.

FATHER MURRAY: In other words, your idea of a Christian school would vary according to your idea of Christianity?

MR. COLE: That is right.

FATHER MURRAY: Then it would be as simple as that.

For instance, if you take the religious views of a man like Schleiermacher, I'm sure that his idea of a Christian school would be quite different from mine.

I would certainly agree that even in the most secularized institutions you could have many Christian acts performed and many Christian attitudes revealed, but we couldn't redesignate Public School 88 as a Christian school. It just isn't, to my way of thinking. Or else perhaps the whole title of this seminar should be changed and we should be discussing the Christian idea of an educator. Then you could perhaps talk meaningfully about the manner in which a Christian man or woman would endeavor to transmit his Christianity. However, if we keep the title "The Christian Idea of Education," then I think we are committed to defining the thing at its maximum and must simply admit that you can find fragments of this idea elsewhere. Newman's definition of the word "idea" is "the inner form, the life principle which gives substance and form and dynamicism to a total enterprise." I don't think you find that in Public School 88.

VOICE: With regard to the subject matter taught in a literature course that examines various writers whose ideas are to a greater or lesser extent hostile to institutionalized Christianity, if not Christianity as a whole, how should a Christian teacher attack that?

For instance, how should a Christian teacher approach Sartre? Should he perpetually try to hold up an author to a standard of Christian ideas of philosophy, compare his ideas piece by piece with Christian philosophy, or should he in the case of Sartre discuss him and then at the end point out the divergence in thought?

FATHER MURRAY: I think he would owe something to his own integrity and also to the integrity of scholarship. Two things are involved: his own Christian integrity and his own discipline. His teaching has to be critical, and he himself as a Christian has definite standards of criticism. Therefore, to take your example, he would have to teach Sartre somehow, one way or another. Don't touch him unless you are really going to convey to the class what this man has to say. However, somewhere along the line, at the end or anywhere, you have to bring out that Sartre's existential concept, the philosophy that you see in his works, is not the Christian idea of man. How long you prolong it into a philosophic debate will depend upon what kind of an audience you have. In your secondary school you might not want to prolong it too far. Would there be any dissent from that point?

Obviously there is no Christian science, as such. There is science. Science, however, has a Christian premise and has Christian values. There are certain destructive and unchristian aspects of science as pursued by scientists. Your scientists or your technologists are frankly out to assert human mastery over nature. That is the aim of science, to harness and control the forces of nature and put them at the disposal of man. The scientist can do this on the premise of Prometheus or he can do this on the premise of Christ and Christianity.

VOICE: Is there any reason why this can't be done in P. S. 88?

FATHER MURRAY: It certainly could be done by the individual teacher. There is no question about that. A man teaching social science or any of the branches of theology, who is convinced of the Christian premise, a convinced Christian, would be teaching this premise over the years and it could not fail to be apparent to his class if he did not fall into the trap that Professor Maritain pointed out where you hold back and reveal nothing, which is a common thing in the academic world. I have run into that very often.

I recall a conversation I had with a man who said he thought that the different systems of philosophy should be taught by a man who is sympathetic to them but doesn't avow them, is not committed to them. There is also the theory that the Catholic should explain what the Protestant believes and the Protestant should explain what the Catholic believes. For God's sake, why don't we let each man speak for himself and reveal that he is committed to something? The widespread attitude is that we should not have any commitment to anything. If a teacher is committed right down the line, his commitment cannot fail to show itself in his teaching.

FATHER MARTIN: Speaking from the Quaker view of religion, speaking from the nonliturgical view, what can be and should be transmitted?

FATHER MURRAY: The Quaker has a clearly defined concept of education. I remember that a friend of mine who is a Friend gave me a most interesting booklet many years ago. I don't recall what it was now, but I remember being impressed at the time that this was a very carefully worked-out concept and that they knew pretty well what they were trying to do. It was impressive.

Dr. Shepherd brought up an interesting point yesterday morning when he said that in order to profit by the experience of living you have got to have an awful lot of formal education. He spun out beautifully the educational value of the liturgy. A Roman Catholic could listen to a pontifical High Mass and the things said either would leave him completely blank or might have any number of emotional or intellectual effects on him if he understood how this all happened and what is the meaning of the thing which has to be articulated in doctrinal terms. I think the same point was made apropos of the Quaker time of silence. The Quaker time of silence requires instruction; it doesn't explain itself.

MR. COLE: It seems to me that one of the virtues of the Catholic position is the recognition of the importance of a man's loyalty to the truth as he sees it. Doesn't the Christian idea of education have to include a profound respect for the search for truth, the honest and earnest search for truth in the whole educational enterprise, however wrong we may think it is from the Christian point of view? We have to affirm the validity of the whole enterprise of the secular mind as it seeks for the truth, even though it doesn't acknowledge it as God.

FATHER MURRAY: I think that is valid. I am thinking of what Newman said: that a university is no good to the Church unless it is a good university and its goodness as a university is established in autonomous terms of scholarship; and, similarly, the search for truth is a Christian value, there is no doubt, requiring affirmation. Your ability as a Christian, according to your station and opportunities and without making too much of a nuisance of yourself, is to point out where you think some particular search for truth has gone awry. There is an old saying that goes something like this. "Let the professor point out the ways in which the men of his own time are seeking the truth and why they wander from the truth." That is a difficult thing to do. It is much easier simply to refute what you think is erroneous than to try to understand that this came from a search for truth which was honest and sincere but somehow went wrong, and that it is up to you to show why it went wrong. That takes a considerable amount of doing individually. That is the Christian mold of education.

When my students are old enough they have to understand, let's say, the whole history of heresy and how and why it all happened, not only in terms of theology, because frequently, as we know, the basis of heretical deviation is sociological. You have to explain why all this happened.

FATHER MARTIN: What needs to be transmitted in the way of Christian tradition and Christian truth at the university or college level? There seems to be an agreement that there is a body of truth to transmit according to our understanding of that truth.

FATHER MURRAY: You are always transmitting the same body of truth but you do it with varying degrees of what today is called sophistication according to the level of intellectual maturity at which your students have arrived.

For instance, in the last two years of your Catholic college

—there has been some prior instruction in philosophy—there is made a conscious attempt to convey a philosophical intelligence of the faith which you couldn't attempt to do in grammar school or schools on a secondary level or even with freshmen. At that point we start instruction in the dogma of the Trinity in terms of metaphysical concepts of relation. It is a beautiful piece of intellectual construction.

VOICE: Is there any intellectual spot where the defense of the Trinity ends and you can't go any farther?

FATHER MURRAY: It ends with the creedal formula; that is, the formulated faith, the dogma as such.

VOICE: Can you throughout Christian doctrine find other truths that end at a particular spot where no research will take you any further? Suppose you give only partial substance to second-formers on some doctrinal point and say, "This is it, and you'll find out more later on." Do you eventually find out everything about it so that therefore it becomes the truth?

FATHER MURRAY: Take the idea of the sacrifice of the Mass. The little child is taught that the Mass is a sacrifice. What does it grasp when it reads that? The teacher asks the pupils to repeat after him. Then, to skip all the intervening scales, you get up to the top level of properly developed theological instruction where you analyze the concept of sacrifice and where you identify the reason why the Mass is properly called the sacrifice and what are the premises and what are the facts and what manner of participation it calls for. You are filling out the dimensions of the idea that had been present only in some germinal fashion in the youthful mind, and yet, to be truthful, I must say that the child believes as much as I believe. He can't explain it, but he believes all that I believe.

I would like to put forth this idea: Suppose we did draw up a syllabus. Would that help us in our task which is to define the Christian idea of education? Would you want to say that education is Christian if and only if it transmits at least this much of the Christian body of truth?

FATHER MARTIN: I don't think we can come to a resolution like that here. What I wanted to get here was an aspect of the idea of Christian education. Namely, that the font of certain fundamental truths is the basis for the Christian idea of education.

FATHER MURRAY: It seems that it would not be impossible to draw up some fairly general statements on the Christian idea of education in a frankly church-affiliated school, whatever the church may be with which it is affiliated. That is by no means impossible. The school would put down in this syllabus, "This is a Christian school," and then it would justify its ideas in terms of the rest of the syllabus. Such a form or such a syllabus could be drawn up in a generalized enough way to cover all manner of church-affiliated schools—Roman Catholic, Presbyterian, and so on.

It seems to me that much material has come across this table today that would go toward defining what a Christian man is, and what should be done in his teaching function, no matter where he is—in a public school, a nondenominational school, or whatever you have.

MR. COLE: I think it is perfectly possible to develop such a bipolar idea. You will never get anywhere unless you develop some such dichotomy. In fact, it would be multipolar, if you want to pursue it further, but bipolar would do. The divisions would be broad and general.

Your second idea wouldn't be too difficult to put across. That is, that a Christian ought to bring into his teaching in any field and in any school at least the Christian concept of man, the idea that Maritain mentioned this morning. He may not be able to bring in the Trinity or the full doctrine of the Redemption, but he can bring in, and must bring in, in fact, his concept of man in his teaching.

FATHER MURRAY: I think I would have to start with the idea of the school as the instrumentality of the Church for the transmission of this religious and intellectual heritage in a manner that cannot be accomplished either within the family or within the Church proper.

FATHER MARTIN: That is one pole.

FATHER MURRAY: It is much more than that.

FATHER MARTIN: That is the catechism.

FATHER MURRAY: There is the liturgical aspect of it as understood in various analogous fashions, according to your understanding of the Sacrament. In other words, your Christian school ought to have an atmosphere of prayer and worship that is somehow tangible and made tangible in terms of certain stated exercises which would vary according to the particular church. In other words, worship is not by any means alien to the idea of the Christian school. On the contrary, we are also schooled in worship within the school.

Then there would be the element of moral guidance by mature men and women of your own commitment and out of the depths of your own tradition, into whose moral aspects you are thus initiated fully as the problems of adolescence and youth press upon you.

Those are the several avenues of generalities that I dare say may well be acceptable to any manner of church-affiliated schools. They don't touch upon any particular sectarian thing and they allow for sufficient breadth of specific understanding by each.

Another thing I would say is that Christian schools should have a devotion to honesty and integrity of scholarship. The first thing a Christian school should consider is being as good a school as possible, which means a high level of intellectual excellence on the part of both master and student.

With regard to the Christian educator, man or woman, not within the special church-school environment, I would say that the transmittal of the Christian concept of man is extremely important, and if both his scholarship and his personal dealings with his students and fellow faculty members are on a high level then he is fulfilling his duty as a Christian educator.

Faith and Culture

GEORGES FLOROVSKY

I

WE ARE LIVING in a changed and changing world. This
cannot be denied even by those in our midst who may be un-
willing or unprepared to change themselves, who want to
linger in the age that is rapidly passing away. But nobody can
evade the discomfort of belonging to a world in transition. If
we accept the traditional classification of historical epochs into
"organic" and "critical," there is no doubt that our present age
is a critical age, an age of crisis, an age of unresolved tensions.
One hears so often in our days about the "end of our time,"
about the "decline of the West," about "civilization on trial,"
and the like. It is even suggested sometimes that probably we
are passing now through the "great divide," through the greatest change in the history of our civilization, which is much
greater and more radical than the change from antiquity to the
Middle Ages, or from the Middle Ages to modern times.

If it is true at all, as was contended by Hegel, that "history
is judgment" (*Die Weltgeschichte ist Weltgericht*) there are
some fateful epochs when history not only judges but, as it
were, sentences itself to doom. We are persistently reminded
by experts and prophets that civilizations rise and decay, and
there is no special reason to expect that our own civilization
should escape this common fate. If there is any historical future
at all, it may well happen that this future is reserved for another civilization, and probably for one which will be quite
different from ours.

It is quite usual in our days, indeed quite fashionable, to say that we are already dwelling in a "post-Christian world," whatever the exact meaning of this pretentious phrase may actually be—in a world which, subconsciously or deliberately, "retreated" or seceded from Christianity. "We live in the ruins of civilizations, hopes, systems, and souls." [1] Not only do we find ourselves at the crossroads, at which the right way seems to be uncertain, but many of us would also question whether there is any safe road at all and any prospect of getting on. Does not indeed our civilization find itself in an impasse out of which there is no exit except at the cost of explosion?

Now what is the root of the trouble? What is the primary or ultimate cause of this imminent and appalling collapse? Is it just "the failure of nerve," as is sometimes suggested, or rather a "sickness unto death," a disease of the spirit, the loss of faith? There is no common agreement on this point. Yet there seems to be a considerable agreement that our cultural world has been somehow disoriented and decentralized, spiritually and intellectually disoriented and disorganized, so that no over-arching principle has been left which could keep the shifting elements together.

As Christians, we can be more emphatic and precise. We would contend that it was precisely the modern "retreat from Christianity," at whatever exact historical date we may discern its starting point, that lies at the bottom of our present crisis. Our age is, first of all, an age of unbelief, and for that reason an age of uncertainty, confusion, and despair. There are so many in our time who have no hope precisely because they have lost all faith. We should not make such statements too easily, however, and have to caution ourselves at least at two points.

First, the causes and motives of this obvious "retreat" were

1. Antsirintanes, *Toward a Christian Civilization.* A draft issued by the Christian Union of Professional Men of Greece (Athens, Damascus Publications, 1950), p. 19.

complex and manifold, and the guilt cannot be shifted exclusively onto those who have retreated. In Christian humility, the faithful should not exonerate themselves unconditionally, and should not dispense too summarily with the responsibility for the failures of others. If our culture, which we used, rather complacently, to regard as Christian, disintegrates and falls to pieces, it only shows that the seed of corruption was already there.

Secondly, we should not regard all beliefs as constructive by themselves, and should not welcome every faith as an antidote against doubt and disruption. It may be perfectly true, as sociologists contend, that cultures disintegrate when there is no inspiring incentive, no commanding conviction. But it is the content of faith that is decisive, at least from the Christian point of view. The major danger in our days is that there are too many conflicting beliefs. The major tension is not so much between belief and unbelief as precisely between rival beliefs. Too many "strange gospels" are preached in our days, and each of them claims total obedience and faithful submission, and even science poses sometimes as religion. It may be true that the modern crisis can be traced back to the loss of convictions. It would be disastrous, however, for people to rally around a false banner and pledge allegiance to a wrong faith. The real root of the modern tragedy is not that people lost convictions but that they deserted Christ.

Now, when we speak of a "crisis of culture," what do we actually mean? The word "culture" is used in various senses and there is no commonly accepted definition. On the one hand, "culture" is a specific attitude or orientation of individuals and of human groups, by which we distinguish the "civilized" society from the "primitive." It is at once a system of aims and concerns, and a system of habits. On the other hand, "culture" is a system of values, produced and accumulated in the creative process of history, and tending to obtain a semi-independent existence, i.e. independent of that creative

endeavor which had originated or discovered these "values."
The values are manifold and diverse, and probably they are
never fully integrated into one coherent whole: polite manners
and mores, political and social institutions, industry and sani-
tation, ethics, art and science, and so on. Thus, when we speak
of the crisis of culture, we usually imply a disintegration in one
of these two different, if related, systems, or rather in both of
them.

It may happen that some of the accepted or alleged values
are discredited and compromised, that is cease to function and
no longer appeal to men. Or, again, it happens sometimes that
"civilized men" themselves degenerate or even disappear altogether, that cultural habits become unstable and men lose
interest in or concern for them, or are simply tired of them.
Then an urge for "primitivism" may emerge, if still within
the framework of a lingering civilization.

A civilization declines when that creative impulse which
originally brought it into existence loses its power and spontaneity. Then the question arises whether "culture" is relevant
to the fulfillment of man's personality or is no more than an
external garb which may be needed on occasions but does not
belong organically to the essence of human existence. It obviously does not belong to human nature, and normally we distinguish clearly between "nature" and "culture," implying that
"culture" is man's "artificial" creation which he superimposes
upon "nature," although it seems that in fact we do not know
human nature apart from culture, from some kind of culture
at least. It may be contended that culture is not actually artificial, that it is rather an extension of human nature, by which
human nature achieves its maturity and completion, so that an
undercultural existence is in fact a subhuman mode of existence. Is it not true that a "civilized" man is more human than
a "primitive" or "natural" man? It is precisely at this point
that our major difficulty sets in.

It may be perfectly true, as I personally believe is the case, that our contemporary culture or civilization is "on trial." But should Christians, as Christians, be concerned with this cultural crisis at all? If it is true, as we have just admitted, that the collapse or decline of culture is rooted in the loss of faith, in an apostasy or retreat, should not Christians be concerned primarily if not exclusively with the reconstruction of belief or a reconversion of the world, and not with the salvaging of a sinking civilization? If we are really passing in our days through an "apocalyptic" test, should we not concentrate all our efforts on evangelism, on the proclamation of the Gospel to an oblivious generation, on the preaching of penitence and conversion?

The main question seems to be whether the crisis can be resolved if we simply oppose to an outworn and disrupted civilization a new one or whether in order to overcome the crisis we must go beyond civilization, to the very roots of human existence. Now, if we have ultimately to go beyond, would not this move make culture unnecessary and superfluous? Does one need culture, and should one be interested in it, when one encounters the Living God, Him Who alone is to be worshiped and glorified? Is not then all "civilization" ultimately but a subtle and refined sort of idolatry, a care and trouble for "many things," for too many things, while there is but one "good part," which shall never be taken away but will continue in the "beyond," unto ages of ages? Should not, in fact, those who have found the "precious perle" go straight away and sell their other goods? And would it not be precisely an unfaithfulness and disloyalty to hide and keep these other possessions? Should we not simply surrender all human values, if into the hands of God?

This questioning was for centuries the major temptation of many sincere and devout souls. All these questions are intensively asked and discussed in our days again. We say "temptation." But is it fair to use this disqualifying word? Is it not rather an inescapable postulate of that integral self-renunciation, which is the first prerequisite and foundation of Christian obedience? In fact, doubts about culture and its values arise and emerge not only in the days of historical trials and crises but also in the periods of peace and prosperity when one may find oneself in the danger of being enslaved and seduced by human achievements, by the glories and triumphs of civilization. They arise so often in the process of intimate and personal search for God.

Radical self-renunciation may lead devout people into the wilderness, into the caves of the earth and the deserts, out of the "civilized world," and culture would appear to them as vanity, and vanity of vanities, even if it is alleged that this culture had been christened, in shape if not in essence. Would it be right to arrest these devout brethren in their resolute search for perfection and to retain them in the world, to compel them to share in the building or repair of what for them is nothing else than a Tower of Babel? Are we prepared to disavow St. Anthony of Egypt or St. Francis of Assisi and to urge them to stay in the world? Is not God radically above and beyond all culture? Does culture after all possess any intrinsic value of its own? Is it—whether as service or play, obedience or distraction—vanity, luxury, and pride, ultimately a trap for souls?

It seems obvious that culture is not, and by its very nature cannot be, an ultimate end or an ultimate value, nor should it be regarded as an ultimate goal or destiny of man, or probably even as an indispensable component of true humanity. A "primitive" man can be saved no less than a "civilized" man. As St. Ambrose put it, God did not choose to save His people by clever arguments. Moreover, culture is not an unconditional good but rather a sphere of unavoidable ambiguity and involvement. It tends to degenerate into "civilization," if we may accept Oswald Spengler's distinction between these two terms, and man may be desperately enslaved in it, as modern man is supposed to be.

"Culture" is human achievement, is man's own deliberate creation, but an accomplished "civilization" is so often inimical to human creativity. Many in our days, and indeed at all times, are painfully aware of this tyranny of "cultural routine," of the bondage of civilization. It can be argued, as it often has been, that in "civilization" man is, as it were, "estranged" from himself, estranged and detached from the very roots of his existence, from his very "self," or from "nature," or from God. This "alienation" of man can be described and defined in a number of ways and manners, both in a religious and antireligious mood. But in all cases "culture" would appear not only to be in predicament but to be predicament itself.

Different answers were given to these searching questions in the course of Christian history, and the problem still remains unsolved. It has been suggested recently that the whole question about "Christ and culture" is "an enduring problem," which probably does not admit of any final decision. That is to say, different answers will appeal to different types or groups of people, believers and unbelievers, and again different answers will seem convincing at different times.

The variety of answers seems to have a double meaning. On the one hand, it points to the variety of historical and human situations, in which different solutions would naturally be imposed. Questions are differently put and assessed at the time of peace and at the time of crisis. But on the other hand, disagreement is precisely what we should expect in the divided Christendom. It would be idle to ignore the depth of this division. The meaning of the Gospel itself is discordantly assessed in various denominations. And in the debate about "Christ and culture" we encounter the same tension between the "Catholic" and the "Evangelical" trends which is at the bottom of the Christian schism at large.

If we are really and sincerely concerned with Christian unity, we should look for an ultimate solution of this basic tension. In fact, our attitude to culture is not a practical option but a *theological decision,* first of all and last of all. The recent growth of historical and cultural pessimism, of what Germans call *Kulturpessimismus* and *Geschichtspessimismus,* not only reflects the factual involvements and confusion of our epoch but also reveals a peculiar shift in theological and philosophical opinions. Doubts about culture have an obvious theological significance and spring from the very depth of man's faith. One should not dismiss any sincere challenge too easily and complacently, without sympathy and understanding. Yet, without imposing a uniform solution for which our age seems not to be ripe, one cannot avoid discarding certain suggested solutions as inadequate, as erroneous and misleading.

The modern opposition or indifference of Christians to culture takes various shapes and molds. It would be impossible to attempt now a comprehensive survey of all actual shades of opinion. We must confine ourselves to a tentative list of those which seem to be most vocal and relevant in our own situation. There is a variety of motives, and a variety of conclusions. Two special motives seem to concur in a very common contempt of the world by many Christians in all traditions. On the one hand, the world in passing, and history itself seems so insignificant "in the perspective of eternity," or when related to the ultimate destiny of man. All historical values are perishable, as they also are relative and uncertain. Culture also is perishable and of no significance in the perspective of an imminent end. On the other hand, the whole world seems to be so insignificant in comparison with the unfathomable Glory of God, as it has been revealed in the mystery of our Redemption. At certain times, and in certain historical situations, the mystery of Redemption seems to obscure the mystery of Creation, and Redemption is construed rather as a dismissal of the fallen world than as its healing and recovery.

The radical opposition between Christianity and culture, as it is presented by certain Christian thinkers, is inspired more by certain theological and philosophical presuppositions than by an actual analysis of culture itself. There is an increasing eschatological feeling in our day, at least in certain quarters. There is also an increasing devaluation of man in contemporary thought, philosophical and theological, partly in reaction to the excess of self-confidence of the previous age. There is a rediscovery of human nothingness, of the essential precariousness and insecurity of man's existence, both physical and spiritual. The world seems to be inimical and empty, and man feels himself lost in the flux of accidents and failures. If there is still any hope of "salvation," it is construed rather in the terms of "escape" and "endurance" than in those of "recovery" or "reparation." What can one hope for in history?

We can distinguish several types of this pessimistic attitude. The labels I am going to use are but tentative and provisional. First of all, we must emphasize the persistence of the "Pietist" or "Revivalist" motive in the modern devaluation of culture. Men believe that they have met their Lord and Redeemer in their personal and private experience, and that they are saved by His mercy and their own response to it by faith and obedience. Nothing else is needed therefore. The life of the world, and in the world, seems then to be but a sinful entanglement out of which men are glad, and probably proud, to have been released. The only thing they have to say about this world is to expose its vanity and perversion and to prophesy doom and condemnation, the coming wrath and judgment of God. People of this type may be of different temper, sometimes wild and aggressive, sometimes mild and sentimental. In all cases, however, they cannot see any positive meaning in the continuing process of culture, and are indifferent to all values of civilization, especially to those which cannot be vindicated from the utilitarian point of view.

People of this type would preach the virtue of simplicity in opposition to the complexity of cultural involvement. They may choose to retire into the privacy of solitary existence or of stoic indifference, or they may prefer a kind of common life in closed companies of those who have understood the futility and purposelessness of the whole historical toil and endeavor. One may describe this attitude as "sectarian," and indeed there is a deliberate attempt to evade any share in common history. But this sectarian approach can be found among the people of various cultural and religious traditions. There are many who want to "retire from the world," at least psychologically, more for security than for "the unseen warfare." There is in this attitude a paradoxical mixture of penitence and self-satisfaction, of humility and pride. There is also a deliberate disregard of, or indifference to, doctrine, and an inability to think out consistently the doctrinal implications of this "isolationist" attitude. In fact, this is a radical reduction of Christianity, at least a subjective reduction, in which it becomes no more than a private religion of individuals. The only problem with which people of this type are concerned is the problem of individual salvation.

Second, there is a "Puritan" type of opposition. There is a similar reduction of belief, usually openly admitted. In practice, it is an active type without any desire to evade history, only history is accepted rather as service and obedience than as a creative opportunity. There is the same concentration on the problem of one's salvation. The basic contention is that man, this miserable sinner, can be forgiven, if and when he accepts the forgiveness which is offered to him by Christ and in Christ, but even in this case he remains precisely what he is, a frail and unprofitable creature, and is not essentially changed or renewed. Even as a forgiven person he continues as a lost creature, and his life cannot have any constructive value. This may not lead necessarily to an actual withdrawal from culture or denial of history, but it makes of history a kind of servitude which must be carried on and endured, and should not be evaded, but submitted to rather as a training of character and testing in patience than as a realm of creativeness. Nothing is to be achieved in history, but man should use every opportunity to prove his loyalty and obedience and to strengthen his character by this service of fidelity, this "bondage in duty." There is a strong "utilitarian" emphasis in this attitude, even if it is a "transcendental utility," an utter concern with "salvation." Everything that does not serve this purpose directly should be discarded, and no room is permitted for any "disinterested creativity," for example for art or belles-lettres.

Third, there is an Existentialist type of opposition. Its basic motive is the protest against man's enslavement in civilization, which only screens from him the ultimate predicament of his existence and obscures the hopelessness of his entanglement. It would be unfair to deny the relative truth of the contemporary Existentialist movement, the truth of reaction, and probably the modern man of culture needed this sharp and pitiless warning. In all its forms, religious and nonreligious, Existentialism exposes the nothingness of man, of the real man as he is and knows himself.

For those among the Existentialists who have failed to encounter God or who indulge in the atheistic denial, this "nothingness" is just the last truth about man and his destiny. Only man should find this truth out for himself. Yet many Existentialists have found God, or, as they would put it themselves, have been found by Him, challenged by Him, in His undivided wrath and mercy. But, paradoxically enough, they would persist in believing that man is still "nothing," in spite of the redeeming love and concern of the Creator for His lost and strayed creatures. In their conception the "creatureliness" of man inextricably condemns him to be "nothing," at least in his own eyes, in spite of the mysterious fact that for God His creatures are obviously much more than "nothing" since the redeeming love of God moved Him, for the sake of men, to the tremendous sacrifice of the Cross.

Existentialism seems to be right in its criticism of human complacency, and even helpful in its unwelcome detection of man's pettiness. But it is always blind to the complexity of the divine Wisdom. An Existentialist is always a lonely and solitary being, inextricably involved and engaged in the scru-

tiny of his predicament. His terms of reference are always
the "all" of God and the "nothing" of man. And, even in the
case when his analysis begins with a concrete situation, namely
his personal one, it continues somehow *in abstracto:* in the last
resort he will not speak of a living person but rather about
man as man, for ultimately all men stand under the same
and universal detection of their ultimate irrelevance. Whatever the psychological and historical explanation of the recent
rise of Existentialism may be, on the whole it is no more than
a symptom of cultural disintegration and despair.

Finally, we should not ignore the resistance or indifference
of the "plain man." He may live rather quietly in the world
of culture, and even enjoy it, but he would wonder what
culture can add to religion except by way of decoration, or
as a tribute of reverence and gratitude, i.e. especially in the
form of art. But as a rule the plain man is cautiously suspicious
about the use of reason in matters of faith and accordingly
will dispense with the understanding of beliefs. What religious
value can there be in a disinterested study of any subject,
which has no immediate practical application and cannot be
used in the discharge of charity? The plain man will have no
doubts about the value or utility of culture in the economy of
temporal life, but he will hesitate to acknowledge its positive
relevance in the spiritual dimension, except insofar as it may
affect or exhibit the moral integrity of man. He will find no
religious justification for the human urge to know and to
create. Is not all culture ultimately but vanity, a frail and
perishable thing indeed? And is not the deepest root of human
pride and arrogance precisely in the claims and ambition of
reason? The plain man usually prefers "simplicity" in religion,
and takes no interest in what he labels as "theological speculation," including therein very often almost all doctrines and
dogmas of the Church.

What is involved in this attitude is again a one-sided (and
defective) concept of man and of the relevance of man's

actual life in history to his eternal destiny, that is to the ultimate purpose of God. There is a tendency to stress the otherworldliness of the Life Eternal to such an extent that human personality is in danger of being rent in twain. Is history in its entirety just a training ground for souls and characters, or is something more intended in God's design? Is the Last Judgment just a test in loyalty, or also a recapitulation of the Creation? It is here that we are touching upon the deepest cause of the enduring confusion in the discussion about faith and culture. The deepest theological issues are involved in this discussion, and no solution can be ever reached unless the theological character of the discussion is clearly acknowledged and understood.

We need a theology of culture, even for our "practical" decisions. No real decision can be made in the dark. The dogma of Creation, with everything that it implies, was dangerously obscured in the consciousness of modern Christians, and the concept of Providence, that is of the perennial concern of the Creator with the destiny of His Creation, was actually reduced to something utterly sentimental and subjective. Accordingly, history was persistently conceived of as just an enigmatic interim between the mighty deeds of God, for which it was difficult to assign any proper substance. This was connected again with an inadequate conception of man. The emphasis has been shifted from the fulfillment of God's design for man to the release of man out of the consequences of his "original" failure. And accordingly the whole doctrine of the Last Things has been dangerously reduced and has come to be treated in the categories of forensic justice or of sentimental love.

The modern man fails to appreciate and to assess the conviction of early Christians, derived from the Scripture, that man was created by God for a creative purpose and was to act in the world as its king, priest, and prophet. The fall or failure of man did not abolish this purpose or design, and man was redeemed in order to be reinstated in his original rank and to resume his role and function in the Creation. And only by doing so can he become what he was designed to be, not only in the sense that he should display obedience but also in order to accomplish the tasks which were appointed by God in his creative design precisely as the tasks of man. Although history is but a poor anticipation of the age to come, it is nevertheless its actual anticipation, and the cultural process in history is related to the ultimate consummation, though in a manner and in a sense which we cannot adequately decipher now. One must be careful not to exaggerate the human achievement, but one should also be careful not to minimize the creative vocation of man. The destiny of human culture is not irrelevant to the ultimate destiny of man.

All this may seem to be but a daring speculation much beyond our warrant and competence. But the fact remains: Christians as Christians were building culture for centuries, and many of them not only with the sense of vocation, and not only in duty bound, but with the firm conviction that this was the will of God. A brief retrospect of the Christian endeavor in culture may help us to see the problem in a more concrete manner, in its full complexity but also in all its inevitability. As a matter of fact, Christianity entered the world precisely at one of the most critical periods of history, at the time of a momentous crisis of culture. And the crisis was finally solved by the creation of Christian culture, unstable and ambiguous though this culture proved to be, in its turn, and in the course of its realization.

II

As a matter of fact, the question about the relationship between Christianity and culture is never discussed *in abstracto,* just in this generalized form, or in any case it should not be so discussed. The culture about which one speaks is always a particular culture. The concept of culture with which one operates is always situation-conditioned, i.e. derived from the actual experience one has in one's own particular culture, which one may cherish or abhor; or else it is an imaginary concept, another culture, an ideal about which one dreams and speculates. Even when the question is put in general terms concrete impressions or wants always can be detected. When culture is resisted or denied by Christians, it is always a definite historical formation which is taken to be representative of the idea. In our own days it would be the mechanized or "capitalistic" civilization, inwardly secularized and therefore estranged from any religion. In ancient times it was the pagan Graeco-Roman civilization.

The starting point in both cases is the immediate impression of clash and conflict, and of practical incompatibility of divergent structures, which diverge basically in spirit or inspiration. The early Christians were facing a particular civilization, that of the Roman and Hellenistic world. It was about this civilization that they spoke; it was about this concrete system of values that they were critical and uneasy. This civilization, moreover, was itself changing and unstable at that time—was, in fact, involved in a desperate struggle and crisis. The situation was complex and confused.

The modern historian cannot escape antinomy in his interpretation of this early Christian epoch, and one cannot expect more coherence in the interpretation given by the contemporaries. It is obvious that this Hellenistic civilization was in a certain sense ripe or prepared for conversion, and even can be regarded itself, again in a certain sense, as a kind of *Praeparatio Evangelica,* and the contemporaries were aware of this situation. Already St. Paul had suggested this, and the Apologists of the second century and the early Alexandrians did not hesitate to refer to Socrates and Heraclitus, and indeed to Plato, as forerunners of Christianity. On the other hand, they were aware no less than we are now of a radical tension between this culture and their message, and their opponents were conscious of this tension also.

The ancient world resisted conversion because it meant a radical change and break with its tradition in many respects. We can see now both the tension and continuity between the classical and the Christian. Contemporaries, of course, could not see it in the same perspective as we do, because they could not anticipate the future. If they were critical of culture, they meant precisely the culture of their own time, and this culture was both alien and inimical to the Gospel. What Tertullian had to say about culture should be interpreted in a concrete historical setting first of all, and not immediately construed into absolute pronouncements. Was he not right in his insistence on the radical tension and divergence between Jerusalem and Athens: *quid Athenae Hierosolymis?* "What indeed has Athens to do with Jerusalem? What concord is there between the Academy and the Church? . . . Our instruction comes from the Porch of Solomon, who had himself taught that 'the Lord should be sought in simplicity of heart'! . . . We want no curious disputation after possessing Christ Jesus, no inquisition after enjoying the Gospel. With our faith, we desire no further belief. For this is our palmary faith, that there is nothing which we ought to believe besides" (*De Praescriptione,* 7).

Yet Tertullian himself could not avoid both "inquisition" and "disputation," and did not hesitate to use the wisdom of the Greeks in the defense of the Christian faith. "What is there in common between the philosopher and the Christian, the pupil of Hellas, the pupil of Heaven, the worker for reputation and for salvation, the manufacturer of words and of deeds" (*Apologeticus,* 46). Tertullian indicts the culture of his time, and a specific philosophy of life, which in its very structure was opposed to faith. He was afraid of any easy syncretism and contamination, which was an actual threat and danger in his time, and could not anticipate that inner transformation of the Hellenic mind which was to be effected in the centuries to come, just as he could not imagine that Caesars could become Christian.

One should not forget that the attitude of Origen was actually much the same, although he is regarded as one of the "Hellenizers" of Christianity. He also was aware of the tension and was suspicious of the vain speculation, in which he took little interest, and for him the riches of the pagans were exactly "the riches of sinners" (*in Ps. 36*, III.6). St. Augustine also was of that opinion. Was not science for him just a vain curiosity which only distracts mind from its true purpose, which is not to number the stars and to seek out the hidden things of nature but to know and to love God? Again, St. Augustine was repudiating astrology, which nobody regards as science in our day, but which in his day was inseparable from true astronomy. The cautious or even negative attitude of early Christians toward philosophy, toward art (including both painting and music), and especially toward the art of rhetoric can be fully understood only in the concrete historical context. The whole structure of the existing culture was determined and permeated by a wrong and false faith.

One has to admit that certain historical forms of culture are incompatible with the Christian attitude toward life, and therefore must be rejected or avoided. But this does not yet prejudge the further question, whether a Christian culture is possible and desirable. In our own days one may, or rather should, be sharply critical of our contemporary civilization, and even be inclined to welcome its collapse, but this does not prove that civilization as such should be damned and cursed and that Christians should return to barbarism or primitivism. As a matter of fact, Christianity accepted the challenge of the Hellenistic and Roman culture, and ultimately a Christian civilization emerged.

It is true that this rise of Christian culture has been strongly censured in modern times as an "acute Hellenization" of

Christianity, in which the purity and simplicity of the Evangelical or Biblical faith is alleged to have been lost. Many nowadays are quite iconoclastic with regard to culture *en bloc,* or at least to certain fields of culture, such as philosophy equated wtih sophistics, or art repudiated as a subtle idolatry in the name of Christian faith. But on the other hand we have to face the agelong accumulation of genuine human values in the cultural process, undertaken and carried on in the spirit of Christian obedience and dedication to the truth of God. What is important in this case is that the ancient culture proved to be plastic enough to admit of an inner transfiguration. Or, in other words, Christians proved that it was possible to reorient the cultural process, without lapsing into a precultural state, to reshape the cultural fabric in a new spirit.

The same process which has been variously described as a Hellenization of Christianity can be construed rather as a Christianization of Hellenism. Hellenism was, as it were, dissected by the sword of the spirit, was polarized and divided, and a Christian Hellenism was created. Of course, Hellenism was ambiguous and, as it were, double-faced. And certain of the Hellenistic revivals in the history of European thought and life have been rather pagan revivals, calling for caution and strictures. It is enough to mention the ambiguities of the Renaissance, and in later times just Goethe or Nietzsche. But it would be unfair to ignore the existence of another Hellenism, initiated already in the age of the Fathers, both Greek and Latin, and creatively continued through the Middle Ages and modern times. What is decisive in this connection is that Hellenism has been really changed. One is too quick in discovering "Hellenic accretions" in the fabric of Christian life, and at the same time quite negligent and oblivious of the facts of this transfiguration.

One striking example may suffice for our present purpose. It has been observed recently that Christianity in fact achieved a radical change in the philosophical interpretation of time. For the ancient Greek philosophers time was just "a movable image of eternity," that is a cyclical and recurrent motion which had to return upon itself, without ever moving "forward," as no forward motion is possible on the circle. It was an astronomical time, determined by "the revolution of the celestial spheres" (let us remember the title of the famous work of Copernicus, who was still under the sway of the ancient astronomy: *De Revolutionibus Orbium Celestium*), and human history accordingly was subordinate to this basic principle of rotation and iteration. Our modern concept of linear time, with the sense of direction or vectoriality, with the possibility of progression and achievement of new things, has been derived from the Bible and from the Biblical conception of history, moving from creation to consummation in a unique, irreversible, and unrepeatable motion, guided or supervised by the constant Providence of the living God. The circular time of the Greeks has been exploded, as St. Augustine rejoicingly exclaims. History for the first time could be conceived as a meaningful and purposeful process leading to a goal, and not as a perennial rotation leading nowhere.

The very concept of progress has been elaborated by Christians. This is to say, Christianity was not passive in its intercourse with that inherited culture which it endeavored to redeem, but very active. It is not too much to say that the human mind was reborn and remade in the school of Christian faith, without any repudiation of its just claims and fashions. It is true that this process of Christianization of mind has never been completed, and inner tension continues even within the Christian "universe of discourse." No culture can ever be final and definitive. It is more than a system, it is a process; and it can be preserved and continued only by a constant spiritual effort, not just by inertia or inheritance. The true solution of the perennial problem of the relationship between Christianity and culture lies in the effort to convert the natural mind to the right faith, and not in the denial of cultural tasks. Cultural concerns are an integral part of the actual human existence and, for that reason, cannot be excluded from the Christian historical endeavor.

Christianity entered the historical scene as a society or community, as a new social order or even a new social dimension, that is as the Church. Early Christians had a strong corporate feeling. They felt themselves to be a "chosen race," a "holy nation," a "peculiar people," i.e. precisely a new society, a "new *polis*," a City of God. Now there was another City in existence, a universal and strictly totalitarian City indeed, the Roman Empire, which felt itself to be simply the Empire. It claimed to be *the City*, comprehensive and unique. It claimed the whole man for its service, just as the Church claimed the whole man for the service of God. No division of competence and authority could be admitted, since the Roman state could not admit autonomy of the religious sphere, and religious allegiance was regarded as an aspect of the political creed and an integral part of civic obedience. For that reason a conflict was unavoidable, a conflict of the two Cities.

Early Christians felt themselves to be, as it were, extraterritorial, just outside of the existing social order, simply because the Church was for them an order itself. They dwelt in their cities as sojourners or strangers, and for them "every foreign land was fatherland, and every fatherland foreign," as the author of the "Epistle to Diognetus," a remarkable document of the second century, stated it (*c.* V). On the other hand, Christians did not retire from the existing society; they could be found everywhere, as Tertullian insisted, in all walks of life, in all social groups, in all nations. But they were spiritually detached, spiritually segregated. As Origen put it, in every city Christians had "another system of allegiance" of their own, or in literal translation, "another system of fatherland" (*c. Cels.* VIII.75).

Christians did stay in the world and were prepared to perform their daily duties faithfully, but they could not pledge their full allegiance to the *polity* of this world—to the earthly City, for their citizenship was elsewhere, in heaven. Yet this detachment from the world could be but provisional, as Christianity, by its very nature, was a missionary religion and aimed at a universal conversion. The subtle distinction: *in* the world *but not of* the world, could not settle the basic problem, for the world itself had to be redeemed and could not be endured in its unreformed state.

The final problem was exactly this: Could the two "societies" coexist, and on what terms? Could Christian allegiance be somehow divided or duplicated, or a "double citizenship" be accepted as a normative principle? Various answers have been given in the course of history, and the issue is still burning and embarrassing. One may still wonder whether "spiritual segregation" is not actually the only consistent Christian answer, and any other solution inevitably an entangling compromise. The Church is here, in this world, for the world's salvation. The Church has, as it were, to exhibit in history a new pattern of existence, a new mode of life—that of the world to come. And for that reason the Church has to oppose and to renounce this world. She cannot, as it were, find a settled place for herself within the limits of this old world. She is compelled to be in this world in permanent opposition, even if she claims but a reformation or renewal of the world.

The situation in which the Church finds herself in this world is inextricably antinomical. *Either* the Church is to be constituted as an exclusive society endeavoring to satisfy all requirements of the believers, both temporal and spiritual, paying no attention to the existing order and leaving nothing to the external world: this would mean an entire separation from the world, an ultimate flight out of it, and a radical denial of any external authority. *Or* the Church can attempt an inclusive "Christianization" of the world, subduing the whole of life to Christian rule and authority, to reform and to re-organize secular life on Christian principles, to build the Christian City.

In the history of the Church we can trace both solutions: a flight into the desert and a construction of the Christian Empire. The first was practiced not only in monasticism of various trends but also in many other Christian groups or sects. The second was the main line taken by Christians, both in the West and in the East, up to the rise of militant secularism in Europe and elsewhere, and even at the present this solution has not lost its hold on many people. Historically speaking, both solutions proved to be inadequate and unsuccessful. On the other hand, one has to acknowledge the urgency of their common problem and the truth of their common purpose.

Christianity is not an individualistic religion and is not concerned solely with the salvation of individuals. Christianity is the Church, that is, a community, leading its corporate life according to its peculiar principles. Spiritual leadership of the Church can hardly be reduced to occasional guidance given to individuals or to groups living under conditions utterly uncongenial to the Church. The legitimacy of these conditions should be questioned first of all. Nor can human life be split into departments, some of which may be ruled by independent principles, i.e. independent of the Church. One cannot serve two masters, and a double allegiance is a poor solution.

The problem is no easier in a Christian society. With Constantine the empire, as it were, capitulated; Caesar himself was converted; the empire was offering now to the Church not only peace but cooperation. This could be interpreted as a victory of the Christian cause. But for many Christians at that time this new turn of affairs was an unexpected surprise and rather a blow. Many leaders of the Church were rather reluctant to accept the imperial offer, but it was difficult to decline it. The whole Church could not escape into the desert, nor could she desert the world. The new "Christian society"

science from the Greeks and our religion from the Hebrews. The Greeks combined a strong religious impulse with their metaphysical impulse. Aristotle's God was the rational structure of all existing reality.

Nor were the Greeks uninterested in the ethical problem, so that it would not be right to suggest that we have our moral heritage from the Hebrews rather than the Greeks. Our moral heritage combines Greek and Hebraic elements. Morality meant for the Greeks conformity to the pattern of existence. The political constitution of the *polis* sought to imitate the basic order of the universe. Hence Aristotle emphasized the importance of the constitution of the polis as a source of civic virtue. All natural law concepts in Western history are certainly drawn from the Greek idea of a basic structure or form of life to which human actions must conform. These structures were elaborated primarily in Aristotelian and Stoic thought. The common law tradition of England, in particular, with its sense of an historic accommodation of the vitalities and interests of a community, on the other hand, is certainly more Hebraic than Hellenic, though the Greeks had an interest in historically established norms.

It is not true therefore that we drew our religion and ethics from the Hebrews and our philosophy and science from the Greeks. It is true that every conception of meaning which depends upon structure, plan, or scheme is Greek in origin. But all dimensions of meaning which seek to incorporate the freedom of God and man, the uniqueness and wholeness of the person in body and soul, the responsibility which is derived from human freedom, the sin which is a corruption of that freedom, the historical configurations which men elaborate above the level of natural necessity, and the assurance of divine grace to the repentant sinner are derived from Hebrew sources.

Hebraic religion avails itself of poetic and historical symbols for the suggestions and revelations of ultimate meaning. These

symbols suggest both mystery and specific meaning rather
than the Greek identification of meaning with rational intelligibility. God, the God of the Bible, is the mysterious Creator
of the world. He is mysterious because creation transcends all
concepts of efficient or formal cause. Creation is beyond comprehension, a fact which Christian theology finally spells out
in its concept of *"Creatio ex nihilo."* But the God of the Bible
is the Creator of the world, only, as it were, as an afterthought
in the theory of the prophets. The creation of the world is
ascribed to Him to affirm that this God with whom Israel has
to do is the God above all gods, the supreme God, and not
an idol of a nation. God is comprehended in the first instance
as the sovereign of history, who reigns over the destiny of all
peoples but who has called Israel to a special mission among
the people. The fact that He has done this is, according to
Deuteronomy, inexplicable. God's covenant grace is in fact as
inscrutable as creation. No reason can be given for His acts.
These acts are the basis upon which we build all our structures of meaning. The God of the Bible is revealed not so
much in the permanent structures of life through which history
flows as in the "mighty acts," the particular events of history
which point beyond themselves to the ultimate ground and the
mystery and meaning which give significance to our existence.

Insofar as the Christian faith is grounded in the Bible it is
Hebraic rather than Hellenic. It is a faith in which revelation
appears in history and in which the revelation imparts specific
meaning to the mystery of the divine without annulling the
mystery. His thoughts are not our thoughts and His ways not
our ways, yet He is not complete mystery. We know of His
mercy and of His righteousness and of the paradoxical relation
between His righteousness and mercy. The Pope is right that
"spiritually we are all Semites," even though the Christian
community is founded upon a revelation that the Jews rejected
and that to the Christian represents the supreme and final
revelation in which the obscurities of all prophetic intimations

of the divine are clarified. A man appears in history who is at the same time the second Adam and the revelation of a divine mercy. The Agape incarnate in his life is the norm of human existence which is approximated but not fully realized in all human history. When it is realized in history it ends upon the Cross, a symbol of the fact that the norms of human history transcend the actual course of history. But the Christian community discerns by a miracle of grace that this death upon the Cross is not pure tragedy. It is also a revelation of the love of a suffering God Who takes the frustrations and contradictions and sins of man in history upon and unto Himself. That is the only possibility of finally overcoming the corruptions of human freedom which will express themselves in history until the end, and more particularly at the end (the anti-Christ), for human freedom over nature constantly develops and with it the possibilities of both good and evil. The Christian faith is not the guarantee that good will triumph over evil in history. It is a summons to responsible action in history based upon the assurance that evil will not finally triumph over God's designs. According to St. Paul, those who have not this key to the mystery of life and of God are tempted either to sleep or be drunken, to be either complacent or hysterical when confronted with the evils of history. But those who have the key are enabled to watch and be sober.

II

If we analyze the task of transmitting this faith, grounded in this revelation, as a source of grace amidst the confusions in our own day, we must be clear about the hazards which accompany the task both perennially and specifically in our day.

We must begin with the perennial embarrassments of this faith which Paul acknowledges so boldly. It is to the Jews a stumbling block and to the Greeks foolishness. It embodies the scandal of particularity, of *"Einmaligkeit."* It asserts that the ultimate mystery and meaning have been finally and definitively revealed in one person and in one drama of history. That is foolishness to the Greeks who are trying to discern a key to the meaning of life by penetrating through the flow of events in history to the structures which bear it. This faith, in contrast, asserts and affirms that the key is in a mysterious divine power in which creative and redemptive power are paradoxically united, and in which there is freedom to come to terms with all the exigencies of history, embodying the freedom of a curious creature who is called to be a creator even though he is a creature, and who invariably uses his freedom not only to create but to destroy. The affirmation upon which the Christian Church is founded is also "a stumbling block to the Jews" because it does not simply assert the triumph of the divine power over all evil in history. It affirms that the divine power cannot triumph without becoming involved in the evil and suffering of history. It asserts the absurdity of a "suffering God" rather than a triumphant God, of a God revealed in a man who uttered a cry of despair before his ultimate triumph, and thus gave an indication of how close meaninglessness and chaos are to the triumph of faith.

The essential message of the Bible, particularly in this final climax of revelation, triumphed over the Greek culture and embodied some of the wisdom of the Greeks in its system. It triumphed over the wisdom of the Greeks because, as St. Paul affirmed, it embodied the "foolishness of God which is wiser than men," because it gave a more ultimate and satisfying, above all a more redemptive, answer to the enigma of human existence than the wisdom of the Greeks. It did this because the wisdom of the Greeks had no place for the mystery of divine and human freedom, including the mystery of sin in human freedom and the mystery of divine grace in divine freedom.

But the triumph of Christianity over Greek culture did not obviate the necessity of coming to terms with the wisdom incorporated in that culture, beginning with the Johannine literature of the Bible and continuing through the efforts at synthesis from Augustine to Thomas Aquinas. The reason for this inevitable synthesis is simple. The world of both nature and history embodies structures, continuities, plans and forms, essences and entelechies which must be analyzed scientifically and metaphysically. The metaphysical analyses search for the rational structure of things above the level of efficient cause. Therefore a culture which emphasizes only freedom, contingency, and uniqueness as the Hebraic does cannot come to terms with the whole dimension of existence. The Christian faith is primarily Hebraic and does not simply compound Hebraic and Hellenic viewpoints. But it does embody Hellenic viewpoints beginning with the Johannine conception of Christ as the Logos Who is the pattern of creation and of love as an old law and a new law. It is an old law in the sense that it is the only possible law for man who is free to surpass himself but must find himself in going out from himself to the neighbor and to God. It is a new law, revealed by Christ in the sense that this law is historically illumined and clarified and its full import cannot be revealed in any structure of creation. For man has the freedom to surpass his created structure, being both creature and creator.

In dealing with the Christian content of our Western culture and the possibility of transmitting it in education, we must analyze why this subordinate Hellenic element achieved such undue emphasis in our own latter day, why it became rather un-Greek in its tendency toward a naturalistic metaphysic, and why just when these tendencies had reached their climax the historic situation required the full force of the wisdom and grace of the Christian Gospel and particularly that part of it which transcended the wisdom of the Greeks.

There are many reasons which we must enumerate for the

triumph of the Greek element in our culture over the Hebraic-Christian one.

Undoubtedly the most important cause of the gradual triumph of the Greek component in our culture over the Hebraic-Christian one must be sought in the interest of modern man, particularly since the seventeenth century, in the laws and causalities of nature and in the prestige of modern science's "conquest of nature." Nature is a realm of necessity, and its meanings can therefore be equated with rational intelligibility, particularly with rational, analyzable, efficient, and natural causes rather than the realm of history in which freedom and necessity are so curiously compounded. The very triumphs of modern science not only accentuated the Greek interest in structures but guided modern culture to deterministic and naturalistic versions of these structures, which are not characteristically Greek but are the natural by-product of preoccupations with efficient cause in which the irrationality of the givenness of things, the mystery of freedom and creation, is naturally obscured by the principle of science "Ex nihilo nihil sit." There are, of course, many sequences and causal coherences in human history and therefore scientific elements in historiography. But it is significant that the meaning of historical events has frequently been obscured not by the real historian but by social scientists who sought abortively to bring history into the realm of nature and thus deny the characteristically historical aspects of the human scene. In short, our culture has been intent upon equating history with nature at the precise moment when history revealed the dangerous possibilities of human freedom which were not at all like nature.

Secondly, the triumph of the Hellenic component over the Hebraic must be attributed to the inexactness of the pictorial and historical symbols of meaning in comparison with the scientific and metaphysical ones. This inexactness contains temptations toward arbitrariness and to obscurantism in culture.

The obscurantist corruptions of religion became particularly apparent in the nineteenth century when the Biblical idea of creation was used to challenge the scientific scrutiny into the chronology of the causal sequences in the time process and to set faith against the undoubted fact of natural evolution. But there were many less vivid but not less influential contests between obscurantist versions of the Christian faith and the scientific world view. The general effect of these contests was to persuade the modern generation that it was inevitable that religious people should have confused the permanent and necessary myths and symbols of religion, which indicate some transtemporal meaning or reality in the terms of the temporal, with prescientific myth which was a collection of symbols elaborated by the human imagination before modern science elaborated the picture of the world as governed by laws, sequences, and coherences.

We cannot fruitfully reverse the process of the past centuries and give a new dignity to the Hebraic-Christian component of our culture without working out to the last conclusion every problem which has been projected by the difference between religious and scientific symbols; and without admitting the obscurantist dangers in the use of the religious symbols.

Those of us engaged in education need only think of the heritage of suspicion which the age of warfare between science and religion has left as a deposit in the minds of the younger generation to be reminded that there can be no simple return to religion even in a catastrophic age without solving the problem of doing justice to the divine freedom, and without annulling the well-established fact that the universe is law-abiding and that we may even speak of "laws" in the realm of human history where freedom and necessity are so variously compounded.

The third reason for the decay of the Hebraic-Christian component in our culture is one which must be humbly acknowledged by the religiously inclined because it has to do with the religious value of ostensible irreligion. Our age is an irreligious one in the sense that preponderant opinion in our culture rejects the idea of a divine mystery and sovereignty within and beyond the observable phenomena of the world. It regards the world as self-explanatory and life as self-fulfilling. It may have various versions of its rejection of the God of the Bible, either naturalistic or idealistic. The God of the Bible is suspect not only because He is a suffering God (which was an offense to ancient Greeks) but because He is declared to be a person. (That is an offense to the modern Greeks.) The symbol of personality, however subject to distortion, is the only adequate description of the combination of freedom and structure in the divine life. This is an added case of permanent myth being involved in the prescientific myths of the divine, of the childish myths which picture God as an old man with a beard. The fact is that religion points to the ultimate ground of our existence and to the ultimate purpose of all our striving. It is therefore dangerous because every historic form of faith, including those in which idolatry has been overcome in principle, is bound to dignify some partial human value or end or center of meaning with the ultimate ground. There are, in short, idolatrous elements in all historic expressions of faith which make it impossible to identify belief in God with all virtue and agnosticism with vice. We must guard against all pretentious affirmations which equate piety with virtue if we would participate in the revival of religious faith. In the words of the great French Catholic theologian Delacroix, "There are wrong and right ways of believing in God," and much of modern atheism was in its inception a protest against corrupt forms of piety. The atheism of both the bourgeois and the Marxist movements was partly rooted in materialistic misconceptions and partly in an ethical impulse, the impulse to challenge the religious support of historic forms of injustice, the defense of particular human interest in the name of God.

We are all familiar with the intimate relation between medieval forms of the Christian faith and the feudal structure of society which was partly responsible (though only partly) for the atheism of the French Enlightenment and for the conviction of Diderot that injustice would be abolished if only "priests and their hypocritical tools" could be banished. We know of the moral scruples which prompted the atheism of the Russian nihilists, precursors of modern Communists, and know of the intimate relation between Protestant forms of piety and bourgeois forms of culture, and of the effort to support the interest of the latter by the prestige of the former.

Atheism in its more pristine forms usually contained an effort to guard disinterest against religiously sanctified interests. This did not, of course, prevent interests from availing themselves of scientific prestige for the guarding of their cherished values or prevent the worst form of theocracy from arising on the soil of atheistic Communism. The human heart, particularly the heart dominated by self-love, is full of guile; and it is able to use every instrument of religion and irreligion to sanctify its interests. The instruments most serviceable to it are those which have a contemporary prestige of disinterestedness.

The complexities of these involvements of the search for the ultimate with immediate interests must be understood if we would not fall into some naïve hope that the revival of the Christian faith will purge the world of evil.

We are living in a secularized Christian culture, and there are those who believe that all current evils are derived from secularism. They point to Communism as the final fruit of secularism, which is about as logical as to regard clerical absolutism as the logical and only fruit of Christianity. The fact is that secularism, as the natural consequence of a disavowal of the holy and an indifference toward ultimate issues and ends of life, creates its own problems, including pre-occupation with the immediate ends of life or the covert glorification of some immediate end as the ultimate end of human existence. We may regard the current preoccupation in America with technics and with the resultant productivity and wealth as an example of the first weakness. Communism, with its religious fanaticism without benefit of clergy, is an example of the second. The emergence of Communism in a secular age does prove that an explicit disavowal of the holy is no proof against the emergence of false sanctities in history.

But these weaknesses of secular cultures must not obscure the fact that explicitly religious cultures are subject to the errors of profanity or the corruption of the holy. It is interesting that "secular" and "profane" originally had almost identical connotations. Yet the different connotations which have developed in our language about these two words are instructive. The fact that there can be both corruption of the holy and indifference toward it must prevent both religious and nonreligious thinkers from drawing too simple conclusions about the virtues and vices of either religion or irreligion.

III

But despite the corruption within the religious cultures of the past, including our own, we are undoubtedly confronting the disintegration of the confident secularism of our era and a return to various forms of historic Christian and Jewish faith. The reasons for this return are many and various. The most obvious reason is the shock of the appearance of a secularized form of fanaticism and cruelty in the Communist movement. But there are more basic reasons for the disintegration of secularism. They are connected with the refutation by current history of the most cherished beliefs of a culture which ostensibly lived without beliefs, at least without beliefs having to do with the meaning of our existence. But modern culture proved that such a religious vacuum was bound to be filled. It was filled by various credos. But these different forms of secularized religion, which gave ultimate answers to the problem of human existence under the guise of giving immediate answers to immediate problems, can be reduced finally to two beliefs: to the idea of progress, which was the effective religion of the bourgeois world, and to the Marxist creed, which was the creed of the class of industrial workers. Their experience did not allow them to indulge in the simple optimism of the middle class world. An immediately pessimistic and ultimately optimistic interpretation of history, which predicted social catastrophe, and salvation emerging out of the social catastrophe, seemed more plausible to the workers or to the intellectuals, who regarded themselves as the surrogates for the workers. History has refuted both religions. That is, in a nutshell, the cause of the spiritual crisis of our age.

The idea of progress arose in the Renaissance and reached its climax in the nineteenth and early twentieth centuries. It was fed by many streams of thought, but two elaborations of the Hellenic component in our culture contributed particularly to the idea, which was after all quite un-Hellenic in its contrast to the Greek conception of a cyclical history. The one was confidence in human reason as the source of virtue, which was changed under modern impacts into confidence in man's increasing rationality or rational competence. In this sense the idea of progress resulted from the merger of the modern optimism with the Greek confidence in reason or in the identification of man's reason with his highest self.

The other root of the idea of progress was the modern conquest of nature based upon the Hellenic idea of an inherent rationality of nature, which made it subject to rational inquiry according to its rational coherences, and upon the Biblical idea of the incomprehensible givenness of things in creation, without which modern empiricism, inductive rather than deductive analysis could not have arisen. We are all familiar with the story of modern science's "conquest" of nature which has so altered the whole human situation that it seemed for a time as if it had altered it even more radically than it had and as if it had made man the master not only of nature but of his own destiny. The vision of human reason's elimination of ancient stupidities and superstitions and the hope of the conquest of nature to the point where human weakness would be completely overcome, these two hopes lie at the foundation of the modern idea of progress which became the effective religion of modern man, imparting meaning to this existence and promising him redemption from every evil.

The idea of progress has been refuted by the tragic events of current history. We have global wars instead of the parliament of mankind and the federation of the world. Cruel tyrannies have emerged in an era in which democracy and liberty were expected to be triumphant. And the world's enmities became the more tragic since science had given the weapons of warfare a new destructiveness through the discoveries of nuclear physics. History refuted the hopes of the past centuries because they were founded upon two erroneous beliefs. The one was that reason could be the master of interest and passion and therefore the instrument of increasingly universal interests. This was an error since reason is always intimately related to the self and is more easily the servant than the master of the self.

The other error was derived from the first. It was the mistaken belief that every triumph over nature and every consequent enhancement of human freedom would redound to the benefit of man. The error lay in regarding man's freedom over nature as unambiguously good. Yet all human freedom contains the possibilities of both creativity and destructiveness. Human history is therefore bound to develop in both dimensions to its end. Our generation has had tragic and vivid displays of this truth in the good and evil, in the increasing community, and in the increasingly lethal warfare in our experience. Thus contemporary history has refuted the too simple interpretations which have been given to both life and history by modern secularized religions. It is rather ironic that the Marxist alternative to the liberal idea of progress was closer to the Biblical apocalyptic views than were the progressive notions. It had a conception of judgment and redemption which embodied some of the paradoxes of Biblical faith. But it was even more grievously mistaken in its utopian visions than the liberal alternative, for it generated hell on earth through its dreams of heaven on earth.

It is the refutation of the "wisdom of the world" in contemporary experience and the proof that these simple explanations of the meaning of our existence are really "foolishness" which give the Christian faith new relevance in our day. The foolishness of redemption through the suffering God, the absurdity of the affirmation that we must die to self if we would truly live, the scandal of the claim that the mystery of the divine has been revealed in an historical drama and that this drama gives us the key to the ultimate mysteries, all these claims were so easily dismissed by previous generations and yet seem so much more plausible to this generation.

IV

Before engaging in the task of examining the relevance of the Christian faith in a day which has witnessed the refutation of alternative wisdoms, it will be necessary to clarify one point of apparent obscurity. It would seem as if we had identified what is known as modern secularism with the Greek component of our culture, and the religious impulse toward ultimate ends and answers to the riddle of existence with the Hebraic component. Put thus baldly, the correlation would be erroneous. Hellenism was certainly not defective in its sense of the ultimate, at least not in the thought of Plato, Aristotle, and the Stoics. Furthermore the two dominant tendencies in the credo of modern secularism, namely a naturalistic metaphysics and a progressive interpretation of the drama of history, were both in conflict with classical Hellenism. A naturalistic ontology was vanquished in the classical culture, and the idea of progress was a secularized version of the Biblical idea of a dynamic history rather than a fruit of Greek philosophy of history which was consistently cyclical in its interpretation.

Yet there is some justice in this correlation between secularism and the Greek component if it is recognized that both credos of modern culture grew up on the ground of a thoroughly Greek understanding of the rationality of the world, and both sought to reduce the meaning of life to the dimension of rational intelligibility, banishing mystery from the realm of meaning. Nature is reduced to intelligibility by explaining its events in terms merely of natural or efficient cause. And history is made simply intelligible if it is regarded as a projection of nature and if its events are seen as determined by some rational principle of movement toward a goal. In either case the mystery of freedom, particularly the freedom of man in history, is obscured. If this freedom is granted, the realm of history is immediately filled with realities which are not easily correlated in a rational scheme. Among these are particularly the incomprehensible individual and the seemingly capricious historical configuration in which human freedom and natural necessity are variously compounded.

The modern man is as defective as the classical Greek in both his comprehension of the mysteries of selfhood and the mysteries and meanings of the endless and baffling configurations of the dramas of human history. These meanings can be apprehended only by taking the responsible freedom of man seriously, even though that freedom is always partially conditioned and obscured by the various determinisms of nature and of history in which man as a creature is involved. The freedom of man also introduces another factor into the realm of meaning which cannot be easily digested in a rational system, namely his sin and guilt. There is no balm for this sin in any purely rational system but only in the assurance that there is an ultimate divine freedom of grace rising above the intelligible structures of the cosmos. Furthermore, the freedom of man—his capacity to rise above the temporal flux in which he is so obviously involved—faces him with the problem of his death and the possibility of any abidingness of his own life in the flux of time and decay. The various configurations of the historical drama can be rationally correlated on various levels, and we can speak of the rise and decline of this or that civilization of a bourgeois culture and a feudal structure.

If we look at the total human drama, we can find no conclusion within it but only the perplexing development of both good and evil possibilities. History most surely points beyond itself for the completion of its meanings and these completions can only be apprehended by faith rather than by reason. This is why the Biblical-Hebraic faith must remain the bearer of the religious content of our culture. The faith of the Bible seeks to penetrate the mysteries and meanings of life above and beyond the rational intelligibilities. It is not for this reason "otherworldly." Rather it has a firm grasp upon the meanings of life in history and does not reduce them to meaninglessness by seeking to comprehend them too simply into some realm of rationality. "Deeper than life the plan of life doth lie."

A too simple insistence on rational intelligibility on the other hand is always in danger of reducing life to a dimension in which the very realities which give life meaning, freedom and responsibility, self-transcendence and the love of the neighbor, the grace which empowers the self to love and overcomes its sin, all these realities or dimensions of reality are denied.

But we cannot conclude a consideration of the revival of

the Christian faith without considering the task which our generation, like all Christian generations, must confront anew. That is the task of relating freedom to the structures and essences of life and of correlating faith to reason. Without this task religious faith degenerates into obscurantism, and the Christian faith remains separated from modern culture and is available only to those who are too ignorant to know of the problem of the relation of God's and man's freedom to the various structures and cohesions and coherences of the cosmos. This is a formidable task in the pursuit of which we must undoubtedly avail ourselves of the help of modern process philosophies in place of the synthesis between the Christian faith and Aristotelian philosophy which was effected in the Middle Ages.

The task can be accomplished only if Christians have on the one hand a sure grasp of the wisdom of God which is contained in the foolishness of the Gospel, and on the other a humble recognition of the validity of the wisdoms of the world on their own level—namely, when they are charting and analyzing any coherence or structure of nature or of history in which rational analysis is a guide to the truth about life.

God Is the Teacher

STEPHEN F. BAYNE, JR.

THE FUNDAMENTAL THOUGHT underlying nearly everything that we would want to say about the Christian idea of education is that God is the teacher. It is He who establishes all truth; it is He who wills that men shall know the truth; He gives us curious and reflective minds to seek that truth and grasp it and use it; He even gives us the supreme privilege of helping Him in partnership both to teach and to learn. But the initiative is His, just as the truth is His; and all teachers, headmasters, trustees, students, preachers, bishops, and all the rest of the catalog do what they do because God, first of all, does what He does.

A skeptical teacher might cock an eyebrow at this idea of partnership with God, and remember that rhapsodic lady who exclaimed to the New England farmer, "How wonderful it must be to be in partnership with God in clearing the ground and growing crops on your farm!" To which the farmer is said to have answered a little sourly, "Yes, but you should have seen this farm when God had it alone." Teachers might be tempted to say something like that when they think of the long hours and the arduous work of teaching. But actually, teachers come to know very clearly what it means to say that God is the teacher, for they puzzle over the daily miracle of the discovery of truth and wonder how it is that when they clear away the underbrush, so to speak, and open the way, the mind of the student seems suddenly to be flooded with light, far more than the human teachers could ever have given him. Truth seems to speak for itself when the way is clear and the ground prepared; truth takes over; truth seizes and holds the mind; truth possesses us, accuses us sometimes, directs us, precisely as if a person were hiding in the truth (as indeed He is).

God is the teacher. He does very well by Himself when He has to. The questions He asked Job are still quite valid questions:

> Canst thou bind the sweet influences of Pleiades, or loose the bands of Orion? Canst thou bring forth Mazzaroth in his season? Or canst thou guide Arcturus with his sons? . . .
>
> Who hath put wisdom in the inward parts? . . .
>
> Wilt thou hunt the prey for the lion? Or fill the appetite of the young lions, when they couch in their dens . . . ?

This is God teaching in nature, the dumb obedient nature of stars and lions, where God necessarily has all the work to do.

But what of the free and responsive nature of man? What of the prophets and the poets? The question might well be asked as to who taught Isaiah or who put the words in Shakespeare's mind? And doubtless the answer would necessarily still be that God did it. But we would not be altogether satisfied with that, for we would know that there were many who had a share in teaching Isaiah or Shakespeare—parents, teachers, friends, books, the Church, the city. Yet their part was really still within the teaching of God; they were privileged to share this task, because God does not mean to do all this alone forever. He means to admit us into partnership with Him and to entrust us with as much as we can bear of the central task of the universe, the learning of the truth.

God is the teacher. Therefore when we look at our earthly partnership with Him, we see certain qualities that we must have, if our teaching is to be true partnership with Him.

The first test of teaching is that it tell the truth. Sometimes, when we are thinking about Christian schools or Christian teaching, we talk as if there were some special reserved area known as "Christian truth" which is to be added to the regular kind of truth, as if everybody needed to know algebra but only some people needed to know the "Our Father," or as if physics belonged to the area of general truth, and then God taught a kind of optional extra for some people, about the duty of brotherhood.

The first thing that a Christian would want to say is that all truth is one. There is only one kind of truth because there is only one God; and you don't have one test for certain aspects of truth and a wholly different one for other aspects. The history the Creed talks about is part and parcel of exactly the same history that Winston Churchill writes about; it is subject to the same tests; it requires the same understanding.

Brotherhood and the table of atomic weights and the Lord's Prayer and the history of the Hittites and the discovery of gunpowder and the Creed and the multiplication table and Heisenberg's principle of uncertainty and the Agnus Dei—all of this and all truth comes to us in one magnificent, tumbling hodgepodge, because it is all God's, and God is one.

The virtue of the Christian teacher is exactly the same as that of any teacher. It is to tell the truth, and to lead students to understand it and to learn how to master it for themselves. It is good if teachers are Christian, because it is good for all men to be Christians; but if the teacher is to teach at all, the test of his skill and his dedication, Christian or not, is the same. He is a minister of God Who is the teacher; and his primary duty is not to protect God or to add God to the curriculum but to be a good and honest teacher, which is his ministry.

The second test of teaching as the Christian looks at it is the test of wholeness. Truth is one, and man is one; no teaching is right which does not teach the whole truth to the whole man.

It is so easy to forget that man is whole and single. He has many desires, and they are conflicting desires, often; we are tempted to take them one by one and try to answer each one separately. He wants a useful job?—very well, we will help him find one. He wants a certain standard of living? we will try to give him the assurance of that, too, but he may have to change his job to get the kind of living he wants. He wants a home and children?—yet he wants also a certain dash and glamour in his life. He wants peace in the world, yet he wants also national self-sufficiency and prosperity. He wants a simplicity of life which he remembers from old times, yet he wants also the complex variety and ease of this present time.

He is a bundle of desires—he is a whole collection of people, really. But he can't be all of them, or have all the things he wants. He must choose which person he will be and what desires are the commanding ones; and this is part of what God means to teach him.

Think back over what school means to every one of us. We remember what we were like when we came; we remember how many times while we were at school our horizon lifted, and we saw more and understood more and were less satisfied with what we knew and less complacent about what we thought; we remember how we discovered new pleasures and new and unsuspected pain; we remember when we first felt ourselves to be truly in love; we remember when we discovered poetry; we remember the satisfaction of a successful experiment; we remember the successive discoveries of the power of language and its difficulties; we remember the sudden, vast light we gained from reading history; we remember the tentative exploration of new friendship and friendship at a new level; we remember great stories and plays; we remember old prayers rediscovered with new meaning; we remember awakened curiosity about life and its purposes; we remember testing our own thoughts and hopes against the experience of others— and, all this while, we were being led into the community of man, and led to see ourselves as we really are.

This is the sense of reading old books and rethinking old

thoughts, of the study of history and literature and all the rest of it—it is that we may see man as he is, single and whole, reasoning and choosing and believing, half of this world and half of some other, the only animal who must decide what kind of animal he will be, the only beast it is shameful to call a beast, whose soul, as Boethius said, "albeit in a cloudy memory, yet seeks back his own good, but like a drunken man knows not the way home." God is the teacher; and part of His purpose is that we shall learn that manhood has got to be chosen, that it is not simply the sum of the things that happen to us or the things we buy but it is a story which we write by our own choice.

The test of wholeness is the test of how well we teach and learn that all the separate needs and desires of man must come finally under the obedience of his supreme desire, for he is not many separate persons or parts of persons, but one. And the counterpart of this is that there is a like wholeness and singleness in the universe. There are so many ways to describe the universe. The physicist has a way, the psychologist has a language of his own, the poet puts his words to it, the preacher has still another description—it is not easy to remember that all of these are talking about the same thing; and it is no wonder that we are so often bewildered and perplexed, as if there were really many truths to choose from, and many different universes. But God has been teaching us from the beginning that there really is only one universe and one reality. Sometimes He teaches us by war and oppression, that there is a law and a judgment under which all human relationships must come. More often He teaches us by the dreams and hopes of men who are not afraid to imagine better things and to commit themselves to their dreams. Always He has been reminding us that there is a whole and single reality which binds all our scattered affairs into one common framework of truth and justice. And the school or the teacher who means to do God's work must, at all costs, remember that unity.

This is no academic truth. Kent School has been privileged, this past year, to have in its family two of the most courageous Christian witnesses our world knows—Father Trevor Huddleston and Alan Paton. We rightly admire and cherish their audacity and their invincible bravery. But it would be a mistake, and they would be the first to say so, to attribute their social witness merely to an unusual idealism or a particularly pure and austere character. Look to their education. They are bold witnesses not because they are simply good men. They are what they are because they see life whole and man whole; there are no separate compartments of truth to them, for all truth is one and you cannot segregate man the worker, or man the citizen, or man the Negro into one compartment and man the child of God into a wholly different compartment. There is one truth, and these men are the servants of one truth; and therefore compassion and courage are born in the singleness of their hearts.

The third test goes by the name of "excellence." Plato, that invaluable companion of all Commencement speakers, once defined education as "that training in excellence from youth upwards which makes a man passionately desire to be a perfect citizen and teaches him how to rule and to obey with justice." Plato would be a little scornful of some of what we now do in the name of education. He says "the other sort of training, which aims at the acquisition of wealth or bodily strength, is not worthy to be called education at all."

But the positive side of his definition would speak at once to all of us. We live in a time when excellence, in many things at least, is at a discount. Excellence is expensive; and our whole national economy is built upon another principle, of mass production and a wide and responsive market, which has little room for the rare and expensive. I do not say this harshly; I say it simply as a matter of fact, which has brought great blessing to masses of people. For example, I know that, if I had the money, I could have designed and made for me an automobile which would be everything a car should be. I know I cannot afford to buy such a car; I know that, despite the glittering advertisements, the only car I can afford to buy is a mediocre and poorly designed thing which will soon be outmoded, and which is designed not to meet the best standards we know but to sell in the largest quantities. Bear with me if I seem to criticize a sacred cow. Rather the contrary; I am content to buy a cheap and mediocre car because the bargain is so fantastically worth while; for a few dollars, thanks to mass production and the wide market of mediocrity, I can buy transportation and pleasure beyond the wildest dreams of the men of fifty years ago, or of the majority of people in the world even today.

But the price we pay for such a bargain should not be forgotten; it is the price of excellence. A mass market does not tolerate excellence; it seeks rather the swift nourishment of obsolescence and of the average and the mediocre. In its way, nobody wants to quarrel with this; it has been a good bargain, in automobiles and dishwashers and air conditioners and typewriters and television programs and the publishing of books and in all the myriad other things we buy and sell.

But it is a ruinous bargain in manhood. A church which adopted such a compromise with mediocrity would be the devil's own church. We know that when we seek guidance in our moral standards we need to know not what the average man thinks or wants but what is right. Two or three years ago a popular anthropologist examined the sex habits of a cross section of the American people. This is a curious pursuit for a grown man, we think, but there is no law against it. Such a study, however, is no help in facing our own decisions in our sexual life. We do not need to know what the average person does or is alleged to do; we need to know what we ought to do —and thus we are brought face to face with the excellent. Excellence is the only thing that can help us; mediocrity is our problem and our burden; if we are to be set free, we need to know what is right.

A school which adopted the philosophy of the mass market would fail of its purpose in exactly the same way. The absolute standards of truth which make science possible permit no compromise whatsoever. The multiplication table is not the decision of a majority vote. The history of mankind is not a chronicle of compromises with mediocrity; it is the story of great decisions faced and made by men who put average standards behind them, who choose the absolutes, the excellences of freedom and love and justice, and are content to abide by those excellent things to the end.

Uncompromising men who have no patience or use for the safe and the mediocre—history is the record of the impact those men made with their choices.

Supremely in the heart and the imagination of every member of Kent there must remain the image of that most excellent Person whose royal, bleeding Figure hangs over the altar in the Chapel. There He is at the center of this school—the Excellent One. His example and teaching invigorate and sustain every heart. In Him there was no average truth or middle-of-the-road virtue; He knew and served the absolutes and He taught them, and in that teaching alone is our salvation. How wonderfully He has gripped and held the hearts of men for twenty centuries, simply because He made no compromises with what was right and true and good. He is manhood, fulfilled and crowned. Let Him then be the chief Master of every school.

Let me add two more tests of Christian teaching, and then I am done. *One is that of discrimination;* of being able to tell the difference between the important and the unimportant things in life, true and false.

Sometimes I think this is a peculiarly twentieth-century task. We have made a fine art of propaganda in our time, with all of us at the mercy of the new media of communication. We read and hear and see in such prodigious quantity, and have so little time or training to help us make our own independent judgments, that it is no wonder that cynicism is so attractive an escape from responsibility for us.

"Don't believe anything you hear—it is all propaganda"— some such easy skepticism is the refuge of legions of people. My own eight-year-old stormed away from the television set the other day, muttering, "Brag, brag, brag—that's all they do is brag." This is somewhat acute social criticism for an eight-year-old. After all, the commercials are written for him and his compatriots, and the least he could do would be to express some appreciation of the distinguished efforts which are devoted to selling him depilatories and deodorants. Alas, like many another American, his first impulse is to take refuge in cynicism.

But this is an impossibly false refuge. For there is some truth behind the flood of claims and invitations, even of "commercials"; and man must of necessity make his choice on the basis of what truth he can find, whether he is buying washing machines or peaceful co-existence with another nation. He cannot be free from the choice; he therefore requires most urgently the age-old training in judgment.

For this is really not a twentieth-century task particularly. As long as there have been men and needs in the world we have had to learn in every generation what we really want, and what is true, and how to tell the true and the important from the trivial and the deceitful. If I may quote again from the Commencement speaker's great and generous friend, Plato once said, "Something there is which every soul seeketh, and for the sake of this doeth all her actions, having an inkling that it is, but what it is she cannot sufficiently discern, and she knoweth not her way, and concerning this she hath no constant assurance as she hath of other things." This endless responsibility to weigh and sift and test, to discriminate between desires and to make judgments about differences—this is a universal task of the school and the teacher.

God is the teacher, and means to lead us in self-discovery,

and in the reserved and austere use of standards of judgment, so that we may little by little grow in wisdom and in freedom "to distinguish things that differ," in the words of an old Scottish prayer. And once again, I think we test our schools by that standard. How well did we learn what our important desires were? How well did we learn the way by which we tell the good and the true, the authentic, from the cheap and superficial? All our reading of the classics, all our study of history, all our practice in words and in the other arts, all our exacting, pure experiments in science, all this is not an end in itself but a way of leading us to see ourselves and our real desires and necessities. I grant that when we learn about manhood from a great novel or a great philosopher or in the climactic pages of history, we see manhood in far greater stature than we are likely to see ourselves. That is why books are written, I suppose, so that man may be "writ large" in the sky, and we see ourselves clearly and sharply. Alfred Whitehead once said that "moral education is impossible without the habitual vision of greatness." This is true of all education; God means, by His teaching, to set us free by helping us to learn the standards of right judgment which alone make right choice possible.

Last of all, I take it that all true teaching aims to teach mankind how to take sides. This is a delicate and difficult thing to say, for we rightly prize our freedoms and our objectivity. The student in the laboratory or the writer at his desk must, for his own soul's sake, be unencumbered by petty loyalties which distract and divide. The truth must speak for itself, and we must serve the truth with purity and singleness of purpose.

But the end of truth is not neutrality; there is no neutrality in truth, really. The end of learning is that we may discover, in freedom and humanity, and with mature discrimination, how to take sides. A school is not neutral; a school is part and parcel of its community; and the community has every right to expect that the school shall teach a new generation how the humane and intelligent man takes sides for humanity against everything that would belittle and degrade him.

For the history of humanity has been a history of a fierce and devoted unneutrality. Every good gift which has come to humanity has come from free people who refused to sit back and play the spectator's part but who eagerly and courageously took sides for man against every evil and wrong and untruth. Truth is not neutral; truth breeds the boldest and bravest of all spirits. And the school or teacher who pretends to an insulated neutrality, who tries to stand inviolate and unperturbed while the current of life flows all around him, is a fool if not a knave.

Remember once again that God is the teacher. When God, in the supreme moment of teaching came into this world in Jesus of Nazareth, he came with no neutrality. In Christ, God took sides, once and for all, in the final and ultimate terms— He took sides for man in man's endless fight against heartlessness and ignorance and blindness and cruelty. Therefore the Christian teacher, trying to follow humbly and sincerely in the steps of the great Teacher, learns himself the necessity for decision and action. Our loyalties need to be great ones, not petty ones. To this end, teaching ought to be restrained and thoughtful and filled with respect for the freedom and judgment of others. But the goal before teaching is not a heartless neutrality; the goal is to teach men how to make up their minds and choose their sides and build their lives, and if need be give their lives, for the unneutral truth.

I have said that God is the teacher, and that, because this is so all teaching must then reflect the character of God. Teaching must be true and it must be whole. Teaching must lead us to the excellent, and teach us right judgment and discrimination. Most of all, true teaching must lead us to learn how to choose and to abide steadfast by our choices, as men of principle and character have always done.

came into existence, which was at once both Church and Empire, and its ideology was theocratic. This theocratic idea could be developed in two versions, different but correlated. Theocratic authority could be exercised by the Church directly, through the hierarchic ministry of the Church. Or the state could be invested with a theocratic authority, and its officers commissioned to establish and propagate the Christian order.

In both cases the unity of Christian society was strongly emphasized, and two orders were distinguished within this unique structure: an ecclesiastical in the strict sense, and a temporal (that is, the Church and the state), with the basic assumption that *imperium* was also a divine gift, in a sense coordinated with *sacerdotium,* and subordinate to the ultimate authority of the Faith. The theory seemed to be reasonable and well balanced, but in practice it led to an agelong tension and strife within the theocratic structure and ultimately to its disruption.

The modern conception of the two separated spheres, that of the Church and that of the state, lacks both theoretical and practical consistency. In fact, we are still facing the same dilemma or the same antinomy. Either Christians ought to go out of the world in which there is another Master besides Christ (whatever name this Master may bear: Caesar or Mammon or any other), and start a separate society, or they should transform the outer world and rebuild it according to the law of the Gospel. What is important, however, is that even those who go out cannot dispense with the main problem; they still have to build up a society and cannot therefore dispense with this basic element of social culture. Anarchism is in any case excluded by the Gospel. Nor does monasticism mean or imply a denunciation of culture. Monasteries were for a long time precisely the most powerful centers of cultural activity, both in the West and in the East. The practical problem is therefore reduced to the question of a sound and faithful orientation in a concrete historical situation.

Christians are not committed to the denial of culture as such. But they are to be critical of any existing cultural situation and must measure it by the measure of Christ.

III

In conclusion, we must turn to the main subject of our symposium, to the problem of Christian education. It is but fair to remind ourselves that there is no common agreement either about the nature of Christian education or about its purpose and scope. Nor is there any agreement about the nature and purpose of education at large. Is education the training of a man or of a citizen, of a white man, of a citizen of a particular country, etc.? Christians as Christians can be more frank and at the same time more emphatic at this point. They are, or they ought to be, concerned with the training of good Christians. The phrase, unfortunately, will be differently interpreted in the divided Christendom. And yet we may ignore in the present context this divergence of interpretation. What is to be commonly accepted by all faithful Christians is that Christian education should include training for the age to come. For Christians are the Sons of Eternity: prospective citizens of the Heavenly Jerusalem.

No education which is confined to the limits of this age can be genuinely Christian. But problems and needs of this age cannot be dismissed or disregarded, since Christians are called to work and service precisely in this world and in this age. Only all these needs and problems and aims must be viewed in that new and wider perspective which is disclosed by the Christian Revelation and illumined by its light. It is not enough to train men or good citizens. Christian education must aim at a higher purpose. It must train for membership in the Church, which is the Body of Christ, the Fullness of Him Who filleth all in all, the Pillar and the Foundation of Truth.

The Two Sources of Western Culture

REINHOLD NIEBUHR

I

IT MAY WELL BE that the dynamic superiority of Western culture, with its sense of the importance of history and with its conquest of natural forces, has its origin and source in the double root of our culture, the Hellenic and the Hebraic. Each supplied a necessary tool for the definition of the meaning of human existence which every culture seeks to supply. Thus the two facets of meaning were more adequately supplied than in other cultures, which were either too rational or too mystical to define the meaning of existence in terms which would do justice to the unity and the richness and variety of life.

The meaning of existence is established on the one hand by the order and coherence of our world. We establish meaning by any theoretic and practical pursuits which display the coherence, the causal sequences, and the dependabilities of our existence and our world. But pure order would destroy the meaning of human existence insofar as our existence displays the freedom of the person, his responsibility, his capacity to transcend the sequences and necessities of nature, to elaborate a realm of history which is not simply rational because it is not governed by either metaphysical or natural necessity but contains configurations in which freedom and necessity are variously compounded.

Furthermore, human life contains various corruptions of man's freedom, man's sins in short, for which either there

237

is no answer or the answer must be the divine grace of which the Bible speaks. The grace of God as a final answer to the human problem points to God's freedom, which can be comprehended as little in a rational system as the freedom, the responsibility, and the sin of man.

In short, the realm of meaning has dimensions of both order and freedom, and every culture seeks to do justice to these two dimensions. The religious element in a culture is the capstone of the realm of meaning. It furnishes the framework for the structure of meaning and states the ultimate principle and power which is presupposed in that structure.

Western culture is unique in human history in that it draws upon two different sources for its conceptions of meaning, the Hebraic and the Hellenic. Each of these sources has the capacity to do justice to one of the dimensions of meaning and is defective in comprehending the other, but the two together comprehend both natural and historical reality more adequately than any other culture. The Greeks were gifted philosophers, metaphysicians, and mathematicians who were consistently seeking for the rational coherence of things. Their metaphysical speculations laid the foundation not only for modern philosophy but for modern science insofar as science is derived from the rational analysis of causes, particularly of efficient cause. The Greeks were not predominantly naturalistic. The atomists and Epicureans were vanquished by Platonists, Aristotelians, and Stoics; and this triumph proves that they were more interested in the ultimate issues of meaning than in the analysis of efficient cause. Since then the Hellenic component of our culture has tended more and more to naturalistic metaphysics as the project of understanding nature and harnessing her resources became the preoccupation of our culture and its success in doing so gave the determinisms, which were the by-product of the understanding of nature, unusual prestige.

It would be untrue and unfair to say that we derived our